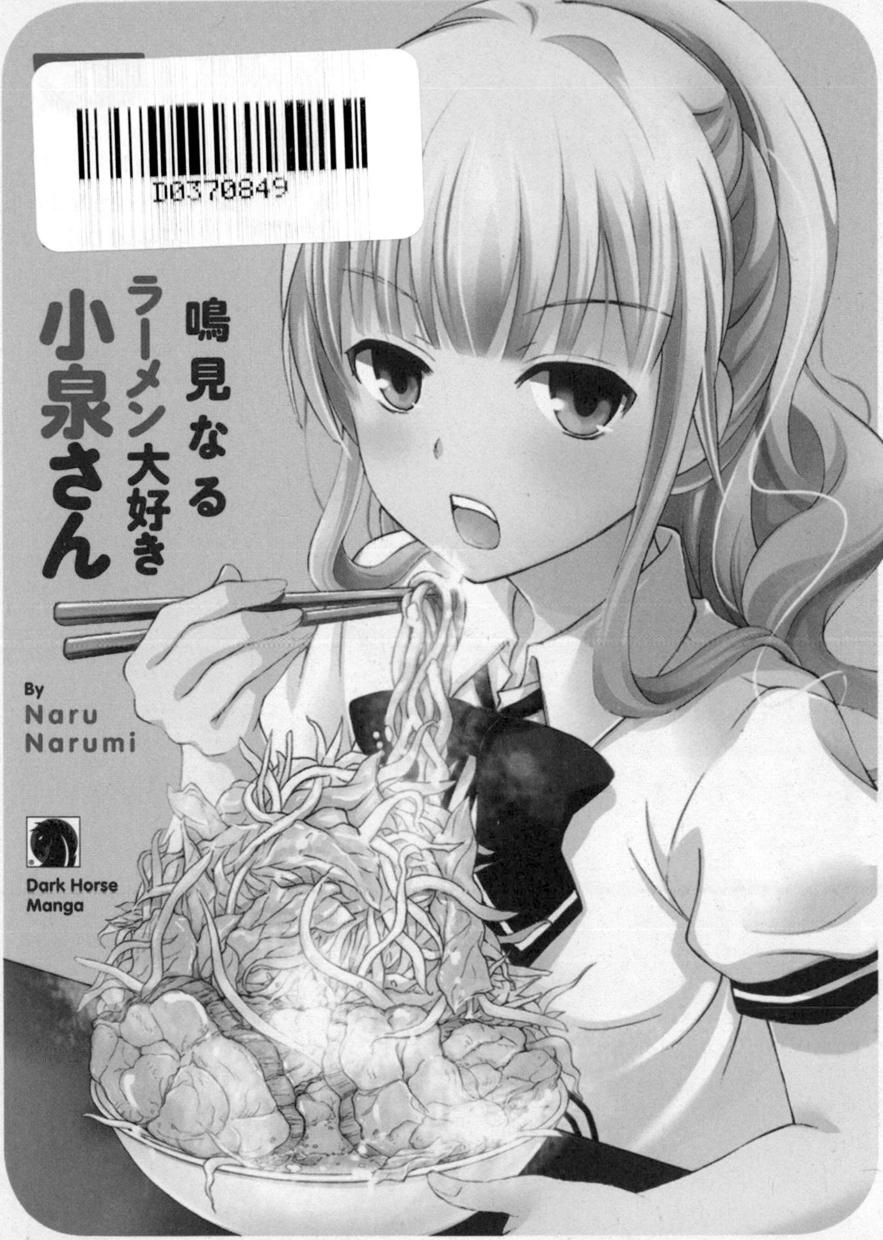
鳴見なる
ラーメン大好き
小泉さん
By
Naru
Narumi
Dark Horse
Manga

Ms. Koizumi loves
ramen noodles.

contents

9th Bowl: Instant Ramen Noodles 111

8th Bowl: The Taste-Focus Counter 99

7th Bowl: Ms. Kokokokokoizumi, Part 2 85

6th Bowl: Ms. Kokokokokoizumi, Part 1 73

5th Bowl: Hokkyoku (North Pole) 53

4th Bowl: Saimin 45

3rd Bowl: Thick and Rich 31

2nd Bowl: Maayu 21

1st Bowl: Extra Veggie Garlic Spicy Oil 3

Postscript 126

Ms. Koizumi Extra 128

From the Translator 130

Local Ramen! 131

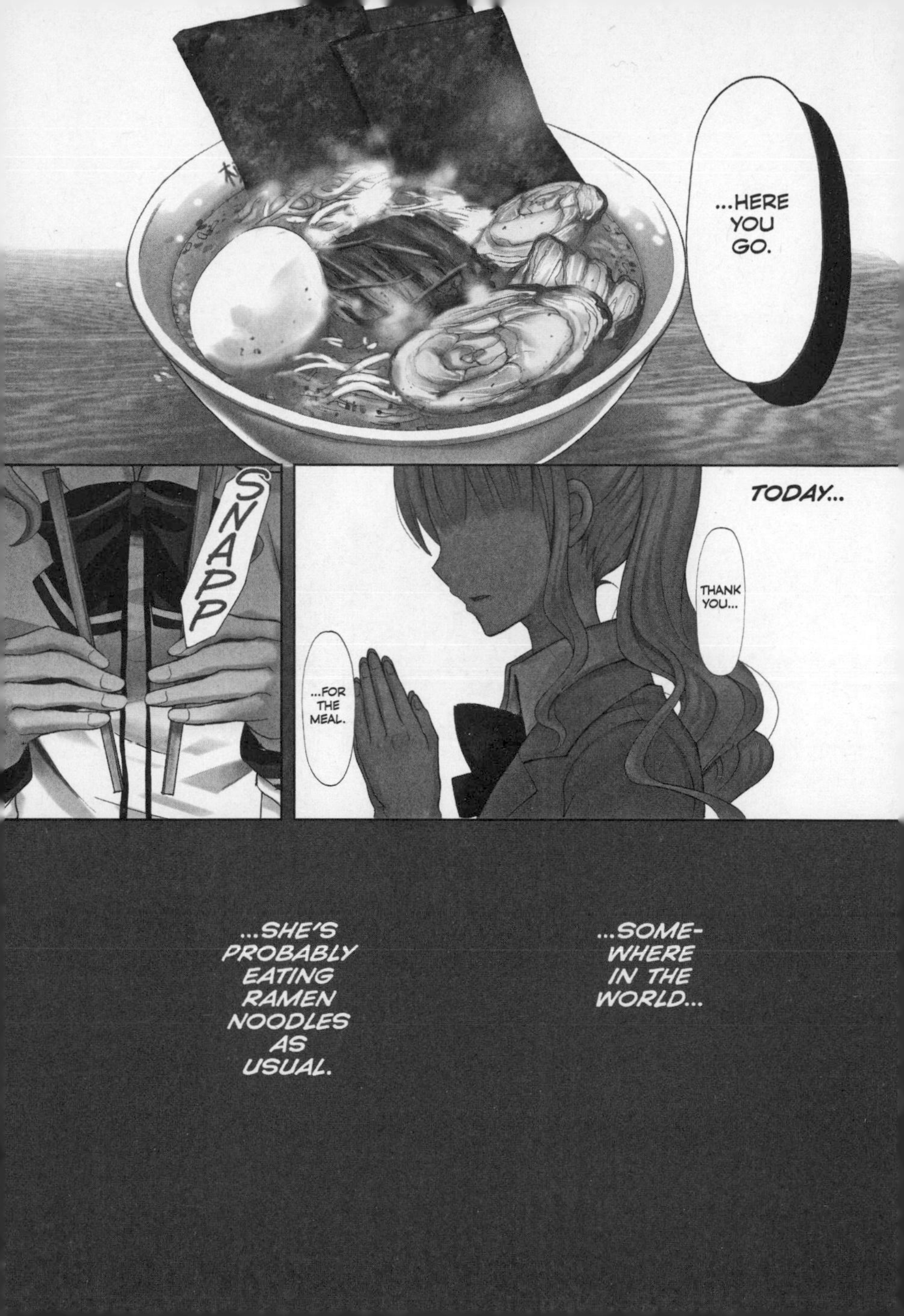
...HERE YOU GO.
TODAY...
THANK YOU...
...FOR THE MEAL.
SNAPP
...SOME-WHERE IN THE WORLD...
...SHE'S PROBABLY EATING RAMEN NOODLES AS USUAL.

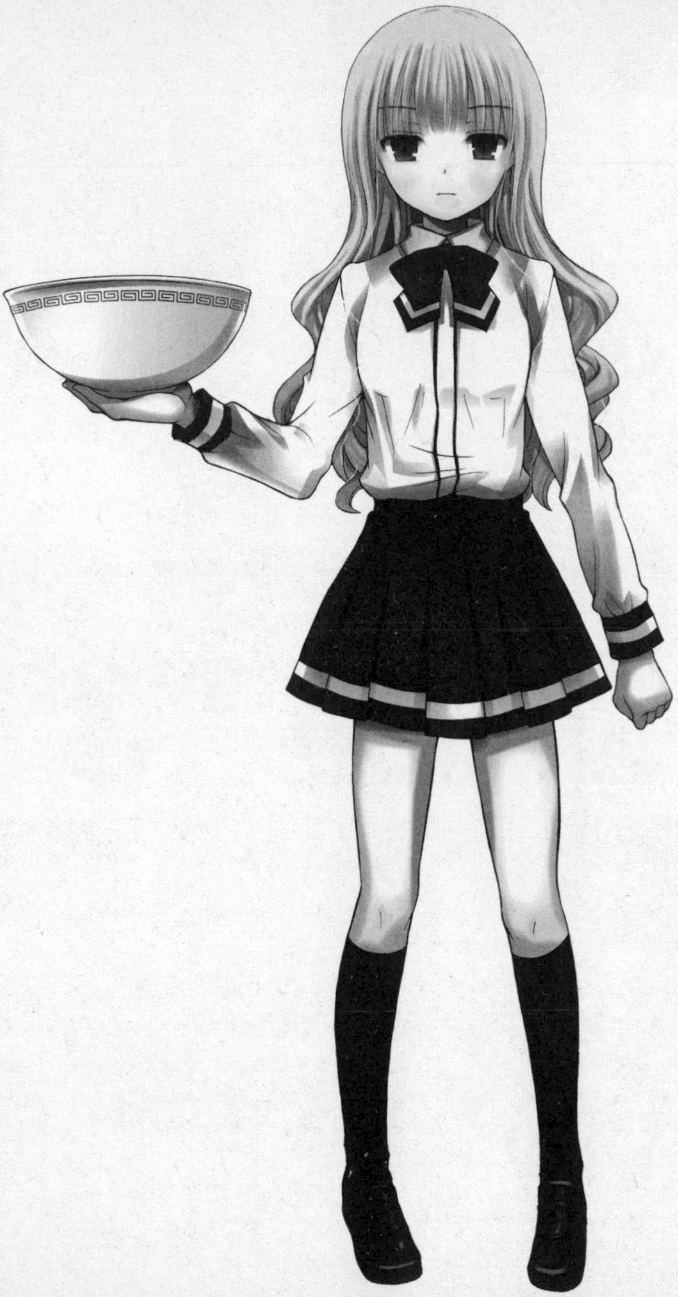

1st Bowl: Extra Veggie Garlic Spicy Oil

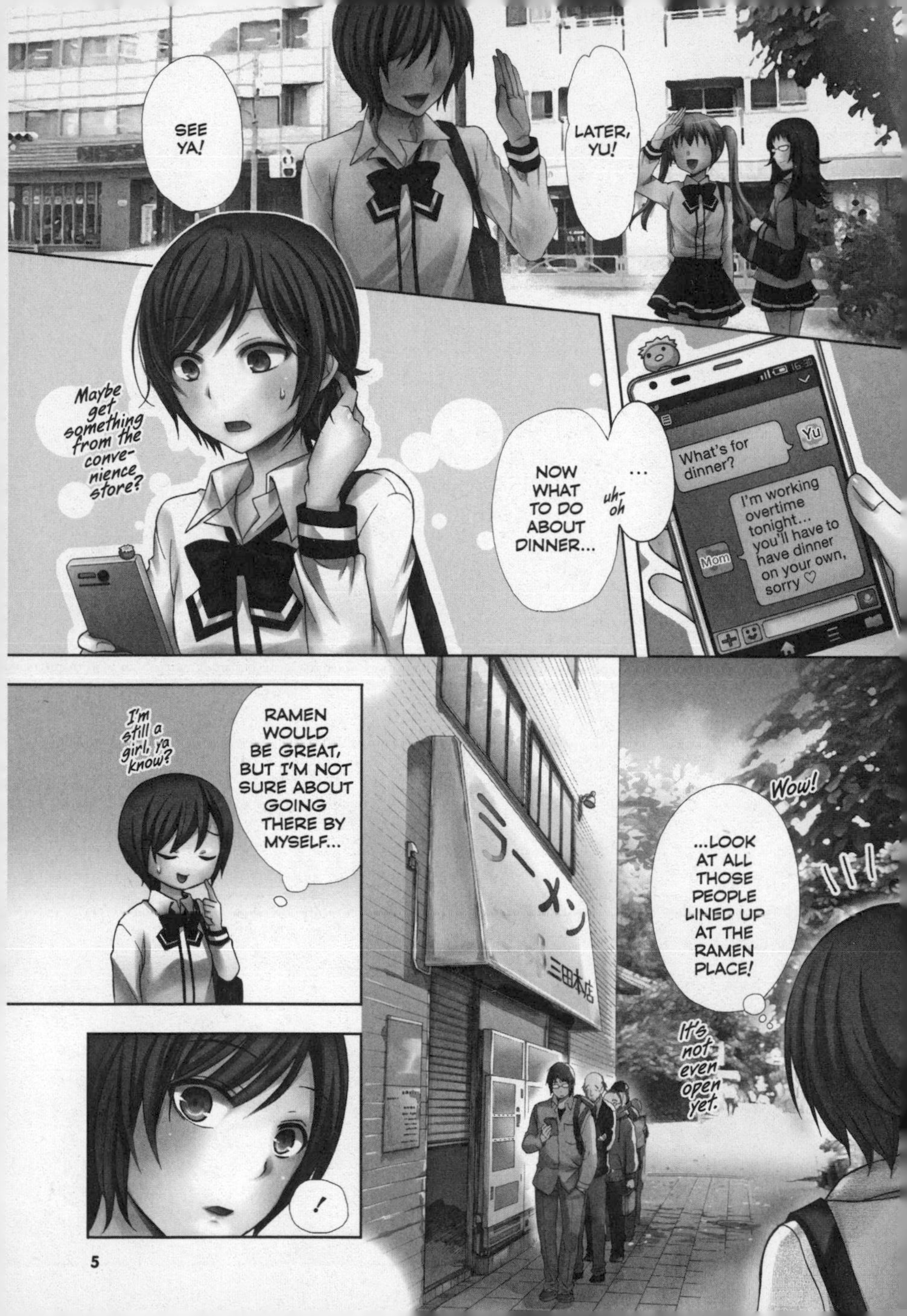
LATER, YU!
SEE YA!
Yu
What's for dinner?
Mom
I'm working overtime tonight... you'll have to have dinner on your own, sorry ♡
...
uh-oh
NOW WHAT TO DO ABOUT DINNER...
Maybe get something from the convenience store?
Wow!
...LOOK AT ALL THOSE PEOPLE LINED UP AT THE RAMEN PLACE!
It's not even open yet.
ラーメン
三田本店
RAMEN WOULD BE GREAT, BUT I'M NOT SURE ABOUT GOING THERE BY MYSELF...
I'm still a girl, ya know?
!

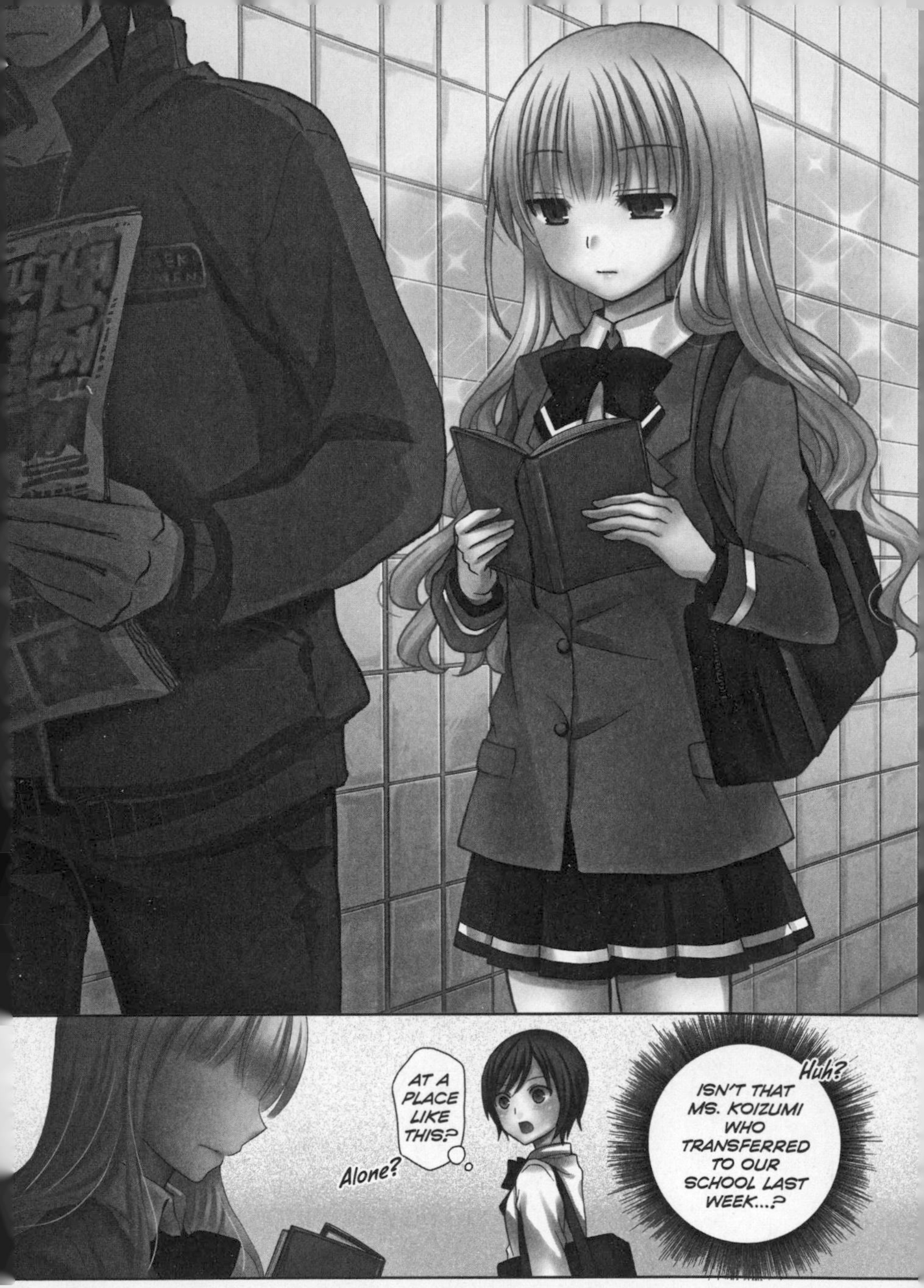
Huh?
ISN'T THAT MS. KOIZUMI WHO TRANSFERRED TO OUR SCHOOL LAST WEEK...?
AT A PLACE LIKE THIS?
Alone?

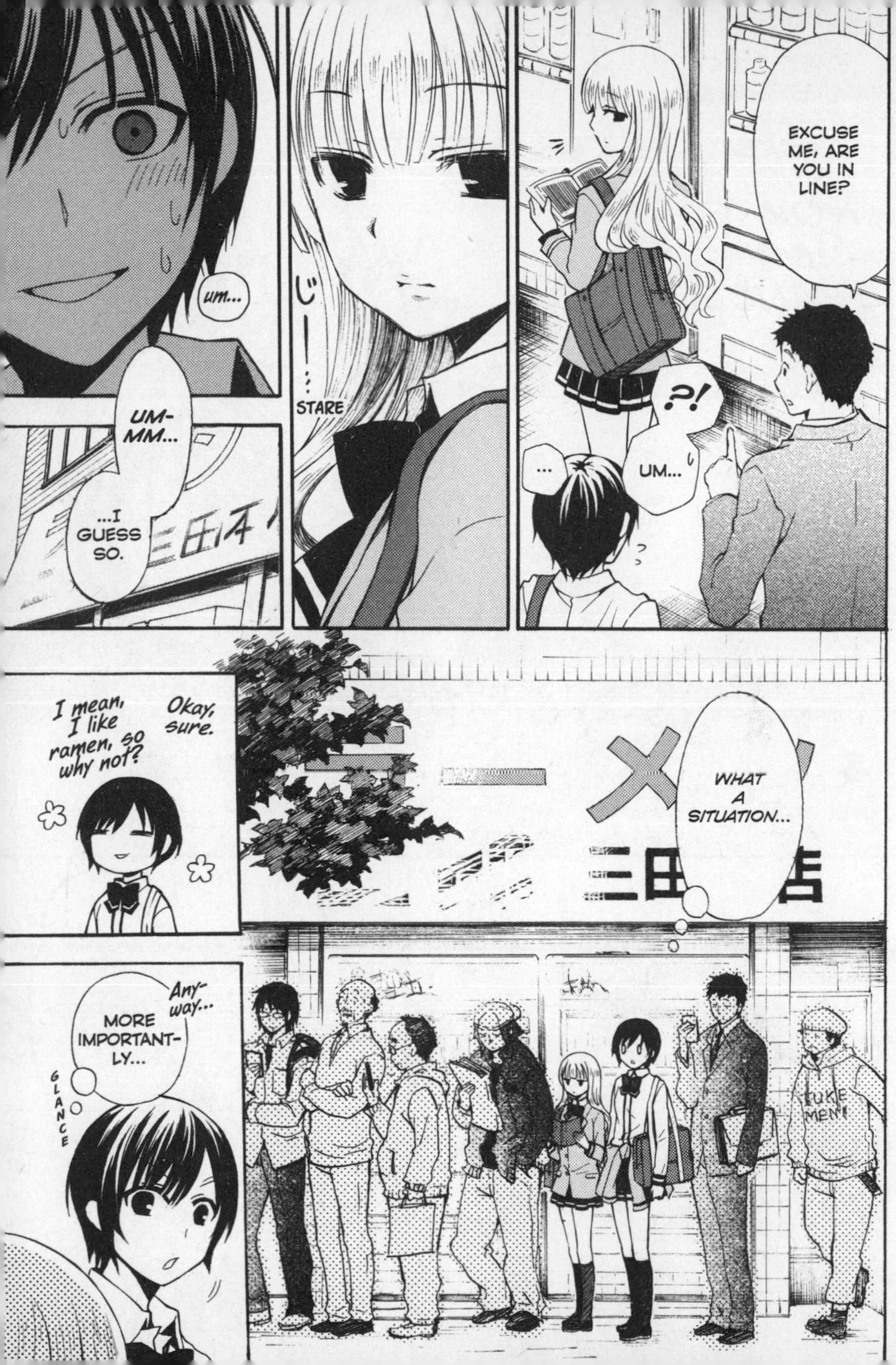
EXCUSE ME, ARE YOU IN LINE?
?!
UM...
...
じー
STARE
um...
UM-MM...
...I GUESS SO.
WHAT A SITUATION...
Okay, sure.
I mean, I like ramen, so why not?
Any-way...
MORE IMPORTANT-LY...
GLANCE

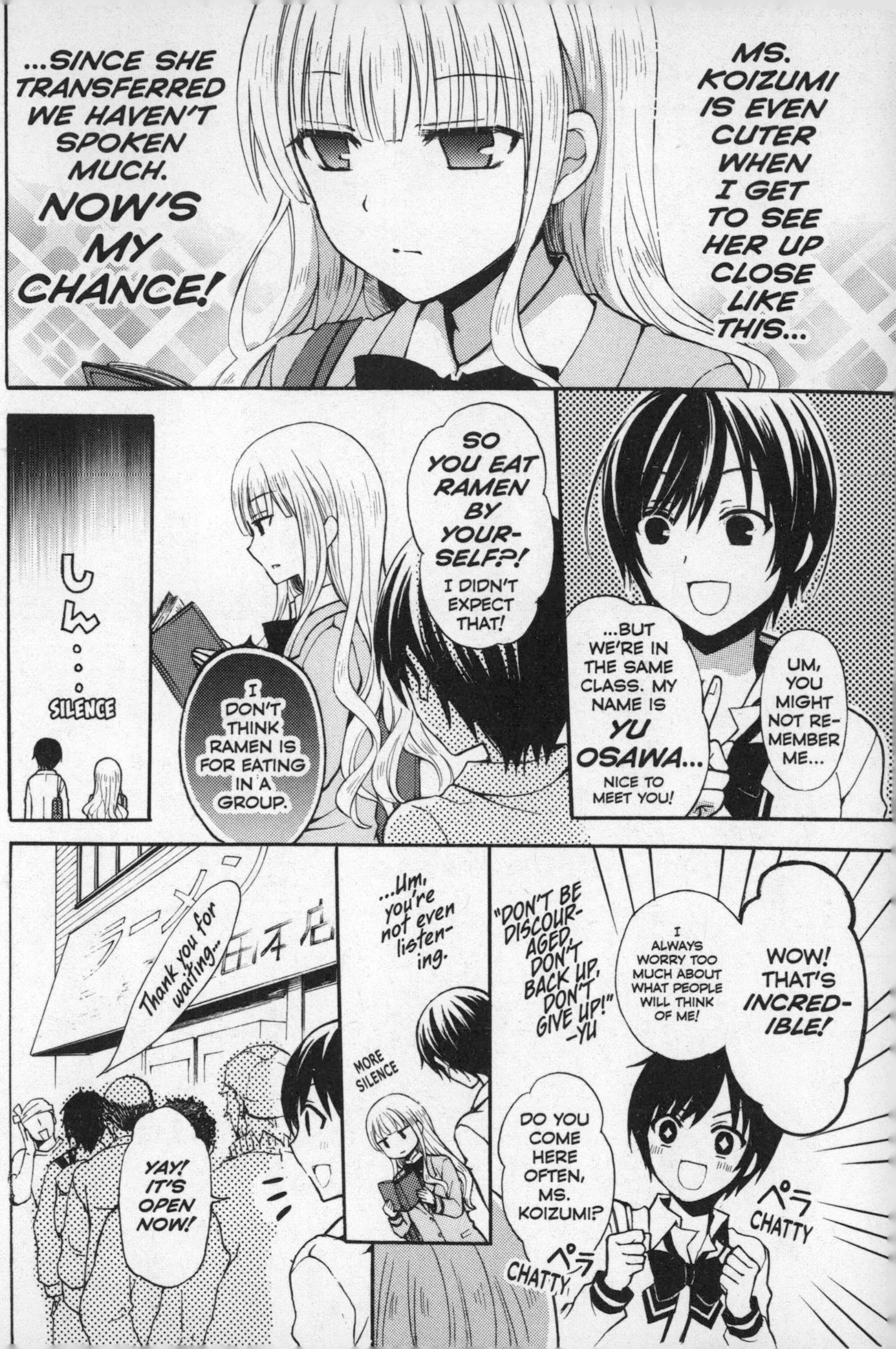
MS. KOIZUMI IS EVEN CUTER WHEN I GET TO SEE HER UP CLOSE LIKE THIS...
...SINCE SHE TRANSFERRED WE HAVEN'T SPOKEN MUCH.
NOW'S MY CHANCE!
UM, YOU MIGHT NOT RE-MEMBER ME...
...BUT WE'RE IN THE SAME CLASS. MY NAME IS YU OSAWA... NICE TO MEET YOU!
SO YOU EAT RAMEN BY YOUR-SELF?! I DIDN'T EXPECT THAT!
I DON'T THINK RAMEN IS FOR EATING IN A GROUP.
しん・・・
SILENCE
WOW! THAT'S INCRED-IBLE!
I ALWAYS WORRY TOO MUCH ABOUT WHAT PEOPLE WILL THINK OF ME!
DO YOU COME HERE OFTEN, MS. KOIZUMI?
ペラ CHATTY
ペラ CHATTY
"DON'T BE DISCOUR-AGED, DON'T BACK UP, DON'T GIVE UP!" -YU
...Um, you're not even listen-ing.
MORE SILENCE
Thank you for waiting...
YAY! IT'S OPEN NOW!

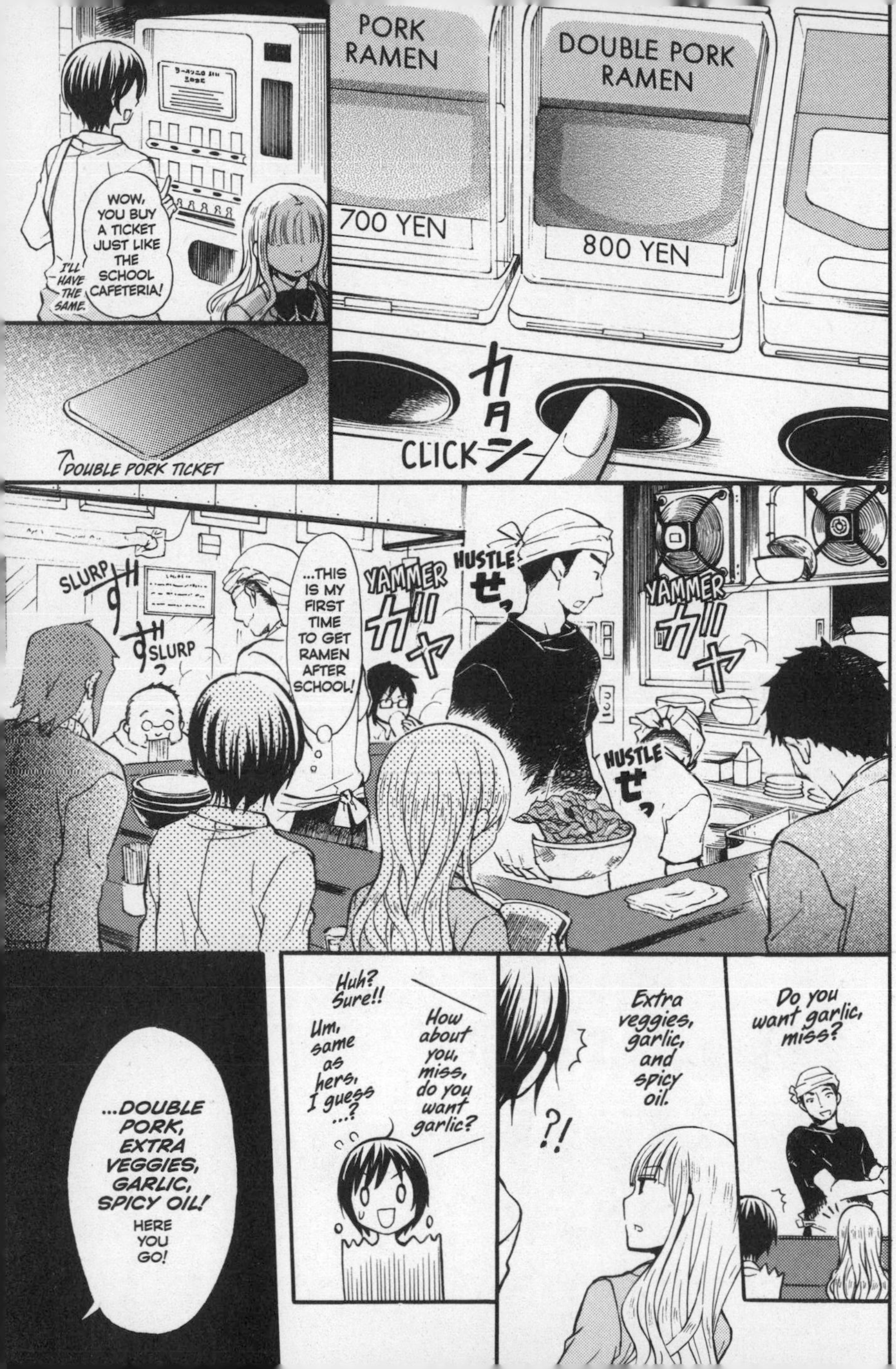
PORK RAMEN
700 YEN
DOUBLE PORK RAMEN
800 YEN
WOW, YOU BUY A TICKET JUST LIKE THE SCHOOL CAFETERIA!
I'LL HAVE THE SAME.
CLICK カタン
DOUBLE PORK TICKET
YAMMER ガヤ
HUSTLE せっ
HUSTLE せっ
YAMMER ガヤ
...THIS IS MY FIRST TIME TO GET RAMEN AFTER SCHOOL!
SLURP ず
SLURP ず
Do you want garlic, miss?
Extra veggies, garlic, and spicy oil.
?!
How about you, miss, do you want garlic?
Huh? Sure!!
Um, same as hers, I guess ...?
...DOUBLE PORK, EXTRA VEGGIES, GARLIC, SPICY OIL!
HERE YOU GO!

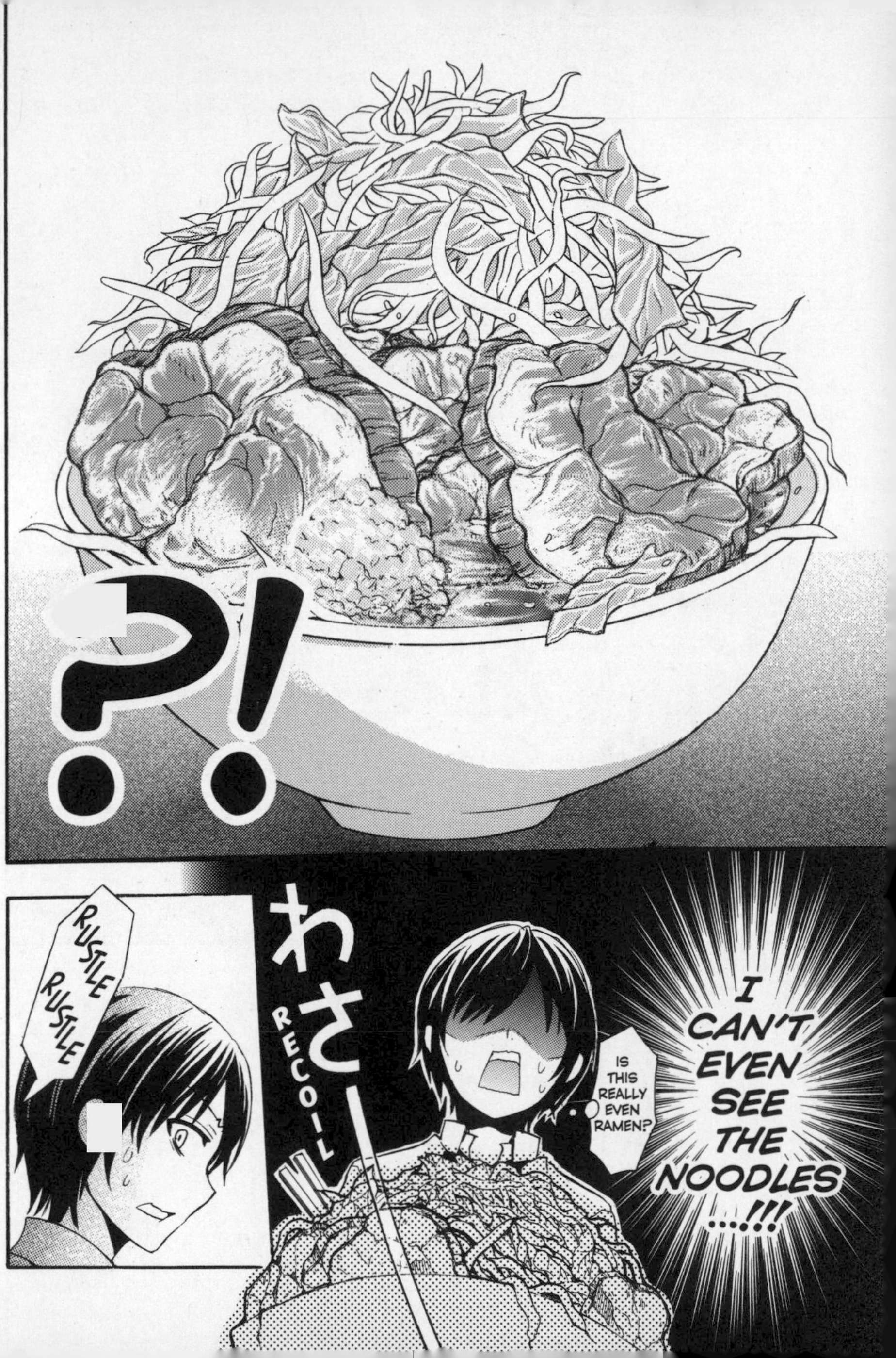
?!
I CAN'T EVEN SEE THE NOODLES ...!!!
わさ
RECOIL
IS THIS REALLY EVEN RAMEN?
RUSTLE RUSTLE

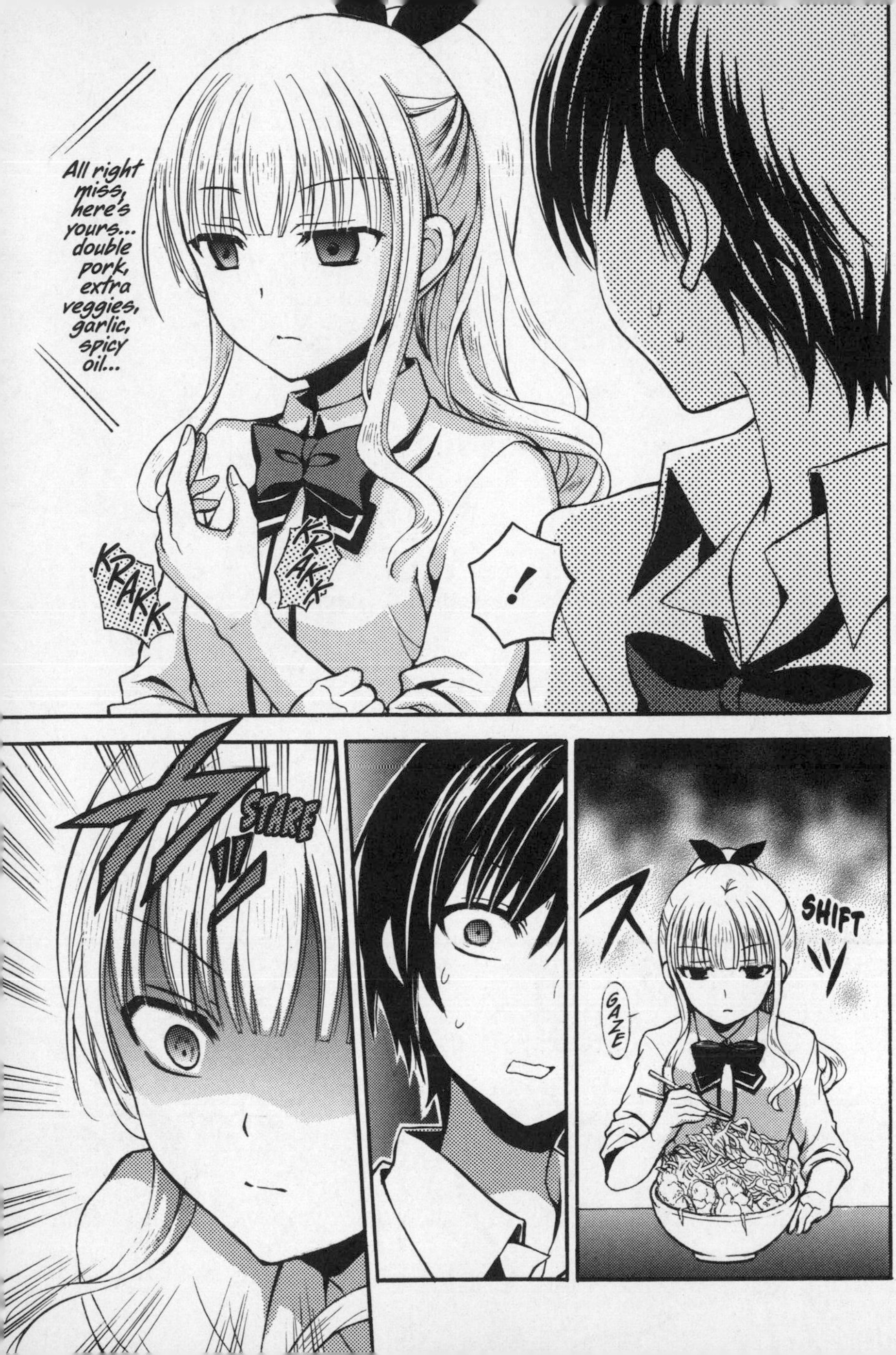
All right miss, here's yours... double pork, extra veggies, garlic, spicy oil...
KRAKK
KRAKK
!
SHIFT
GAZE
STARE

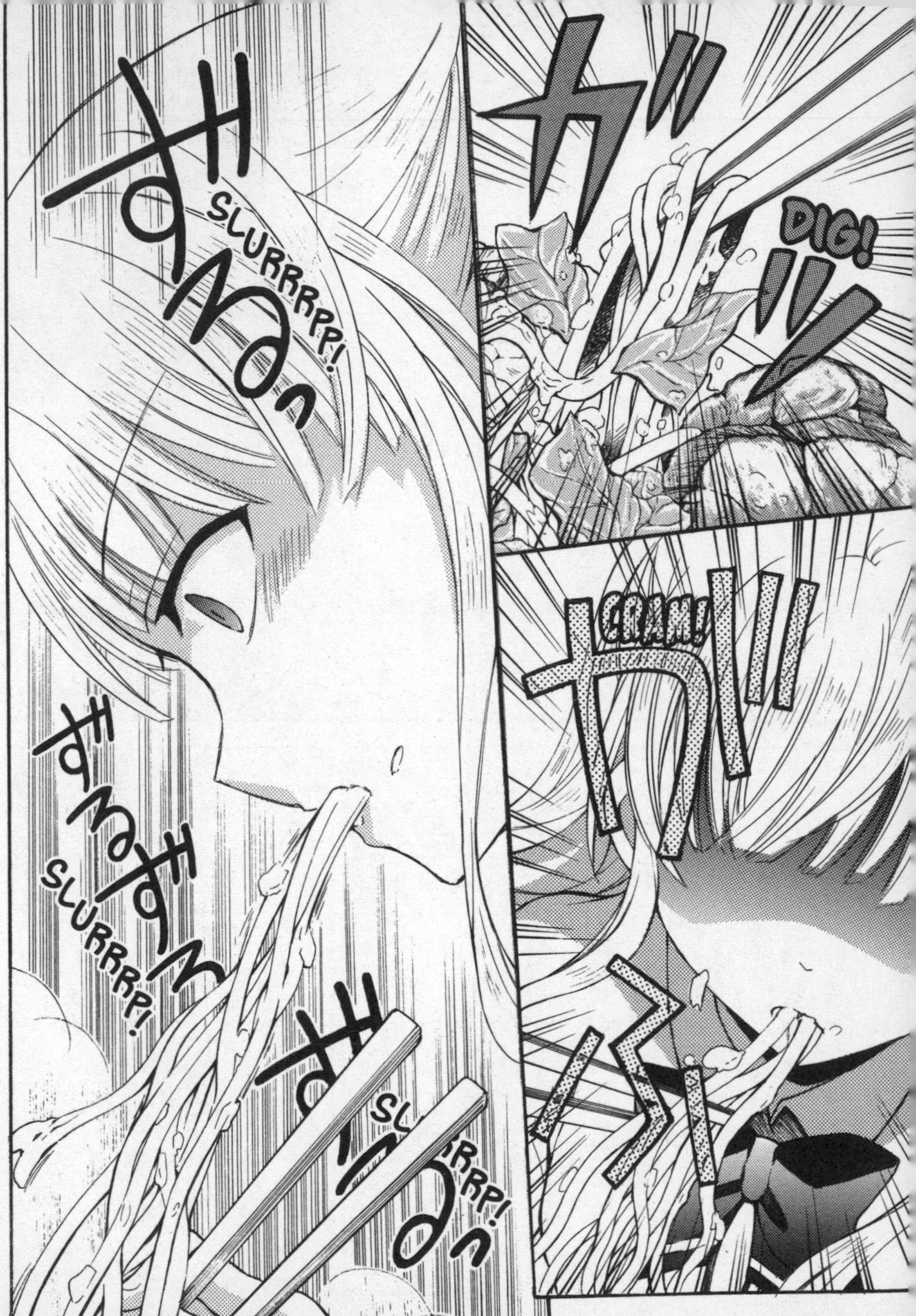
DIG!
CRAM!
SLURRRPP!
SLURRRP!
SLURRRP!

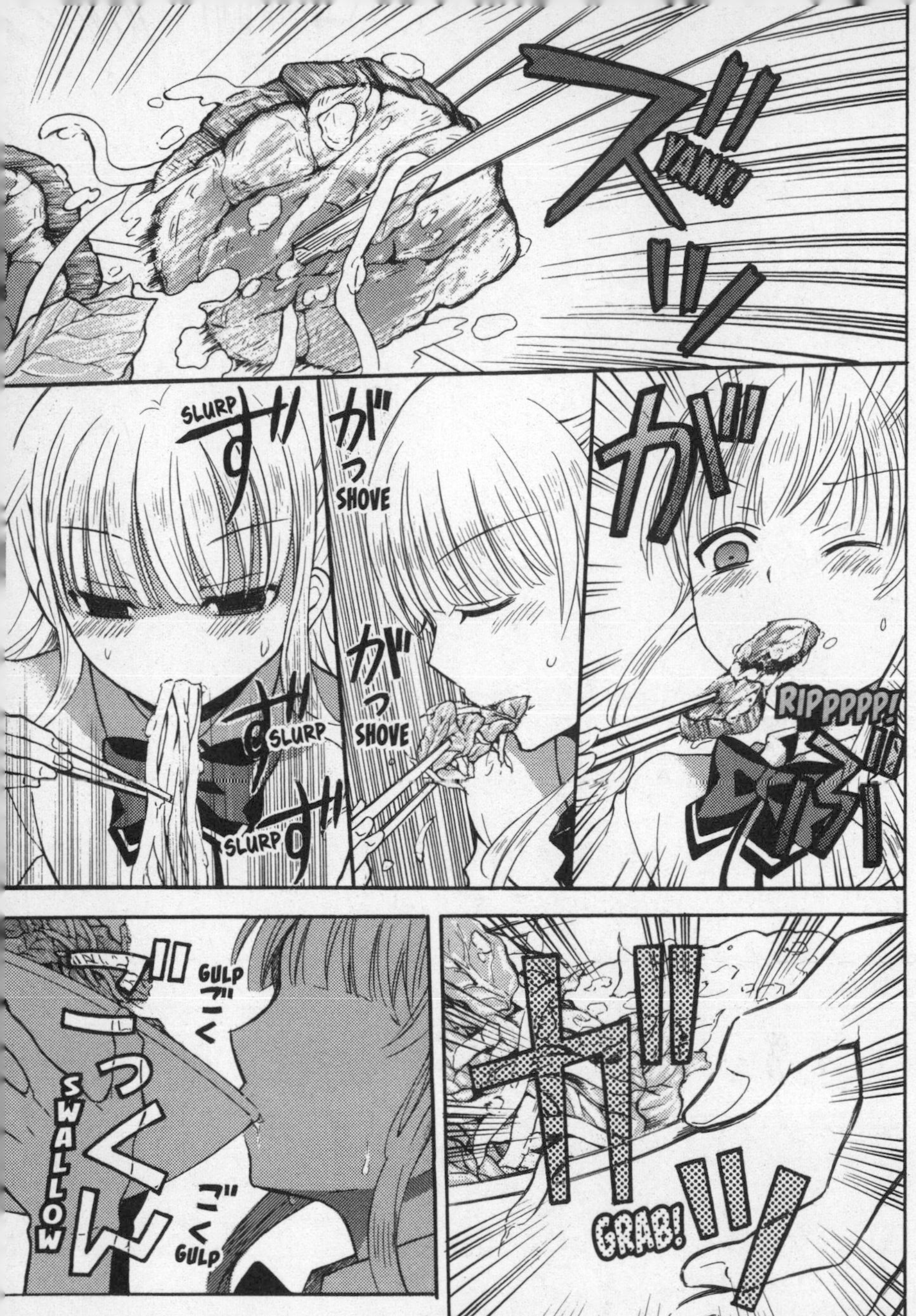
ズッ
YANK!
が
RIPPPPP!
がっ
SHOVE
がっ
SHOVE
ず
SLURP
ず
SLURP
ず
SLURP
ガッ
GRAB!
ごっくん
SWALLOW
ごく
GULP
ごく
GULP

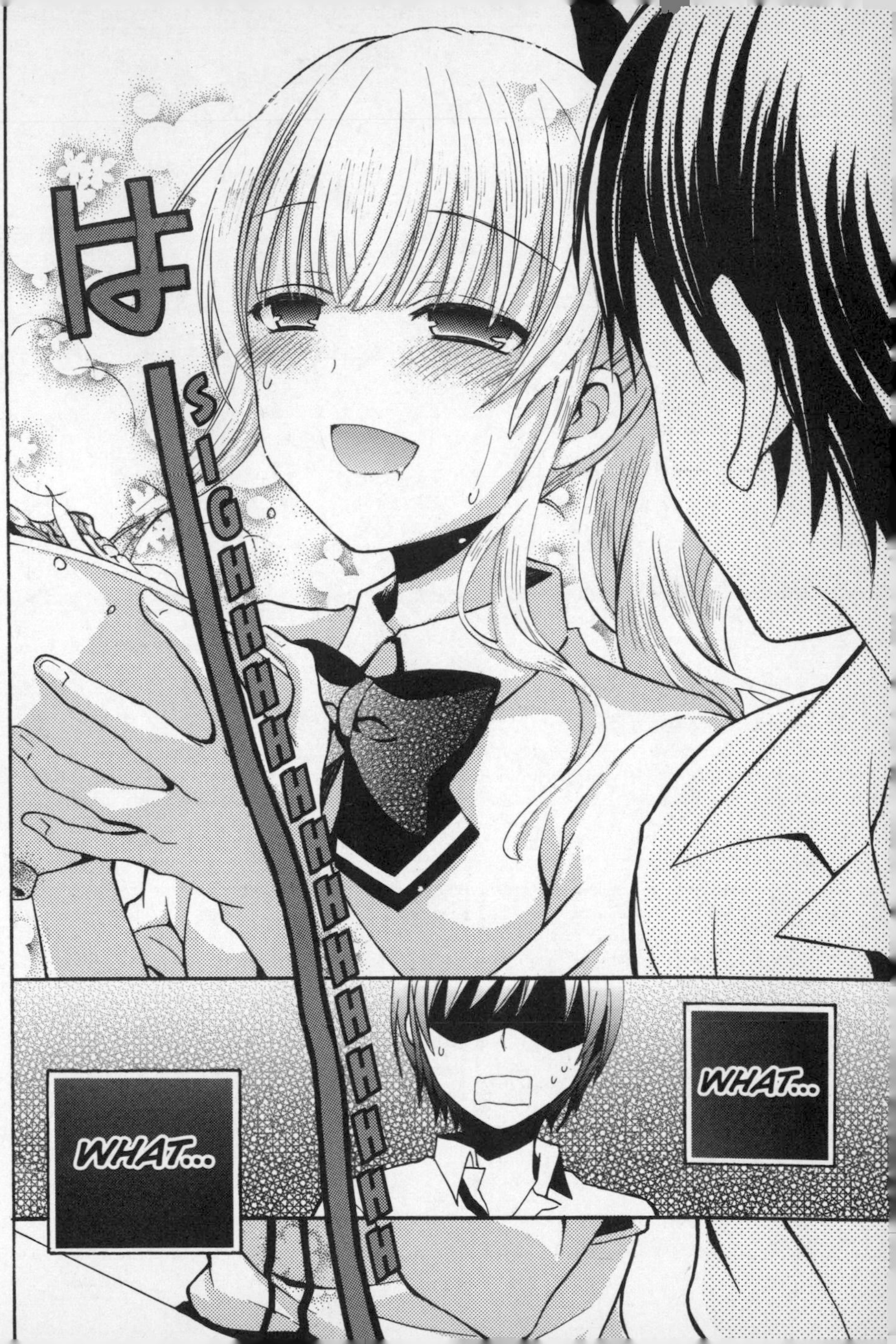
は
SIGHHHHHHHHHHHHHHH
WHAT...
WHAT...

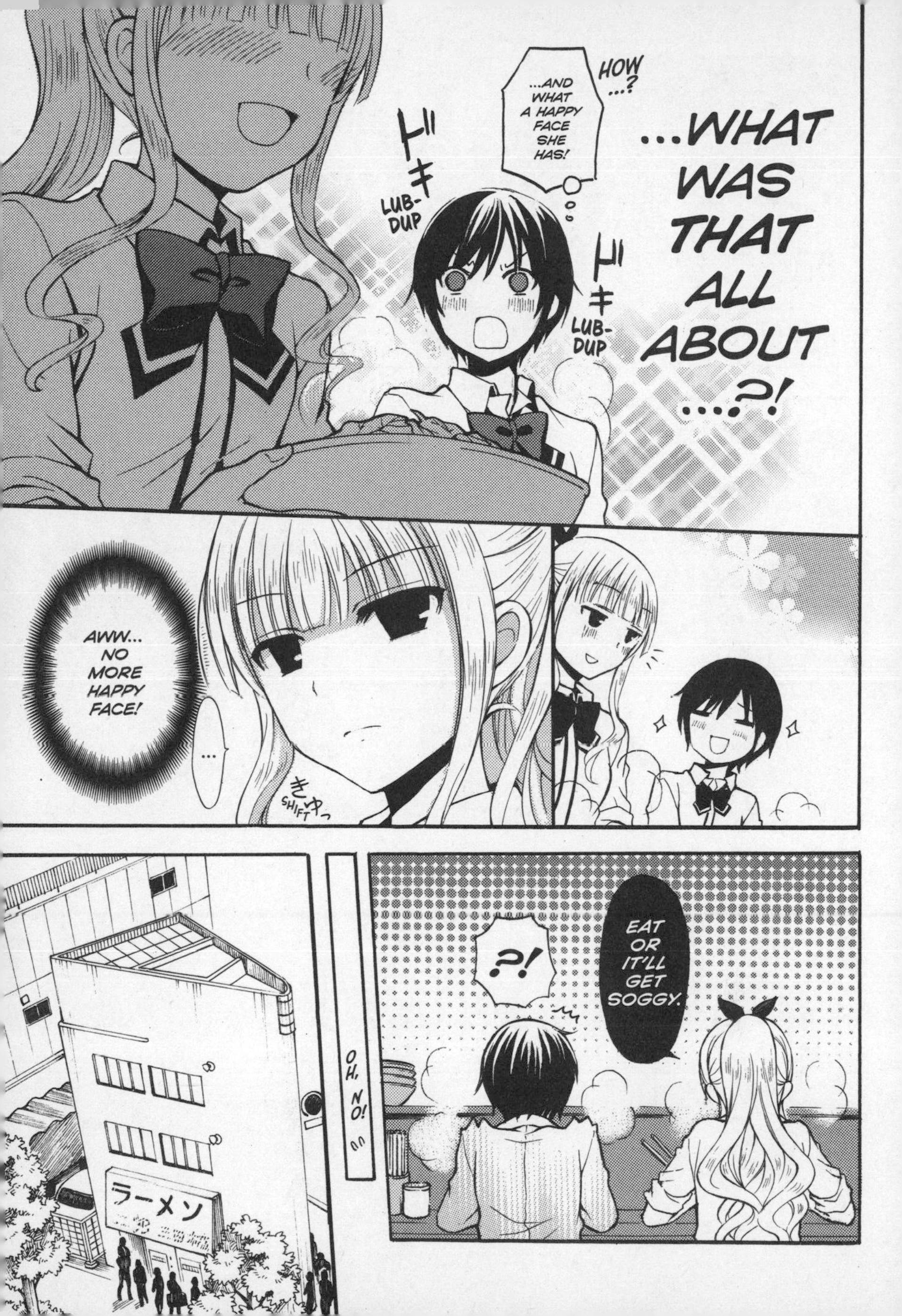

...WHAT WAS THAT ALL ABOUT ...?!
HOW ...?
...AND WHAT A HAPPY FACE SHE HAS!
ドキ LUB-DUP
ドキ LUB-DUP
...
AWW... NO MORE HAPPY FACE!
きゅっ SHIFT
EAT OR IT'LL GET SOGGY.
?!
OH, NO!
ラーメン

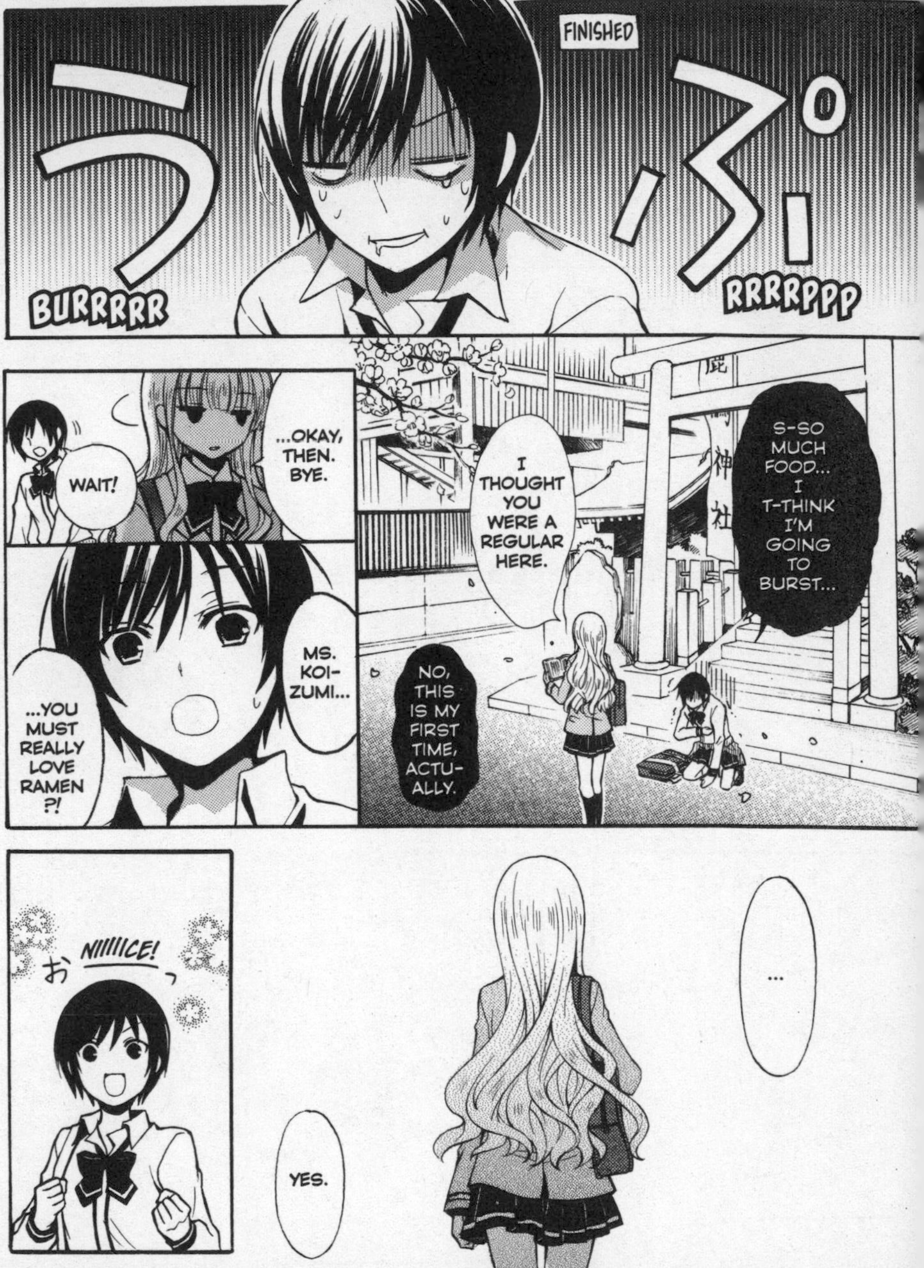
FINISHED
うっぷ
BURRRRR
RRRRPPP
S-SO MUCH FOOD... I T-THINK I'M GOING TO BURST...
I THOUGHT YOU WERE A REGULAR HERE.
NO, THIS IS MY FIRST TIME, ACTU-ALLY.
...OKAY, THEN. BYE.
WAIT!
MS. KOI-ZUMI...
...YOU MUST REALLY LOVE RAMEN ?!
...
YES.
お NIIIIICE! っ

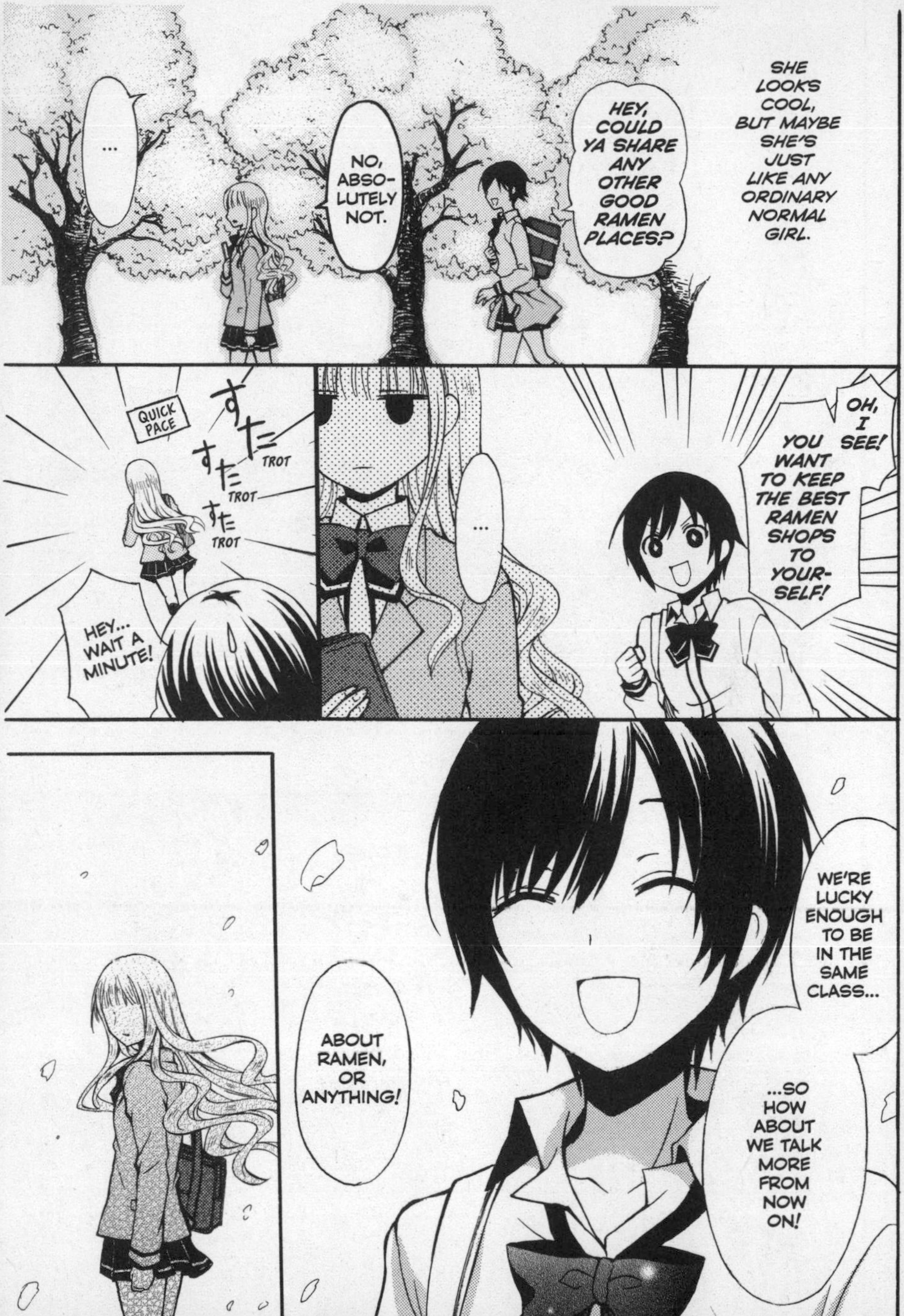
SHE LOOKS COOL, BUT MAYBE SHE'S JUST LIKE ANY ORDINARY NORMAL GIRL.
HEY, COULD YA SHARE ANY OTHER GOOD RAMEN PLACES?
NO, ABSO-LUTELY NOT.
...
OH, I SEE!
YOU WANT TO KEEP THE BEST RAMEN SHOPS TO YOUR-SELF!
...
QUICK PACE
すた TROT
すた TROT
すた TROT
HEY... WAIT A MINUTE!
WE'RE LUCKY ENOUGH TO BE IN THE SAME CLASS...
...SO HOW ABOUT WE TALK MORE FROM NOW ON!
ABOUT RAMEN, OR ANYTHING!

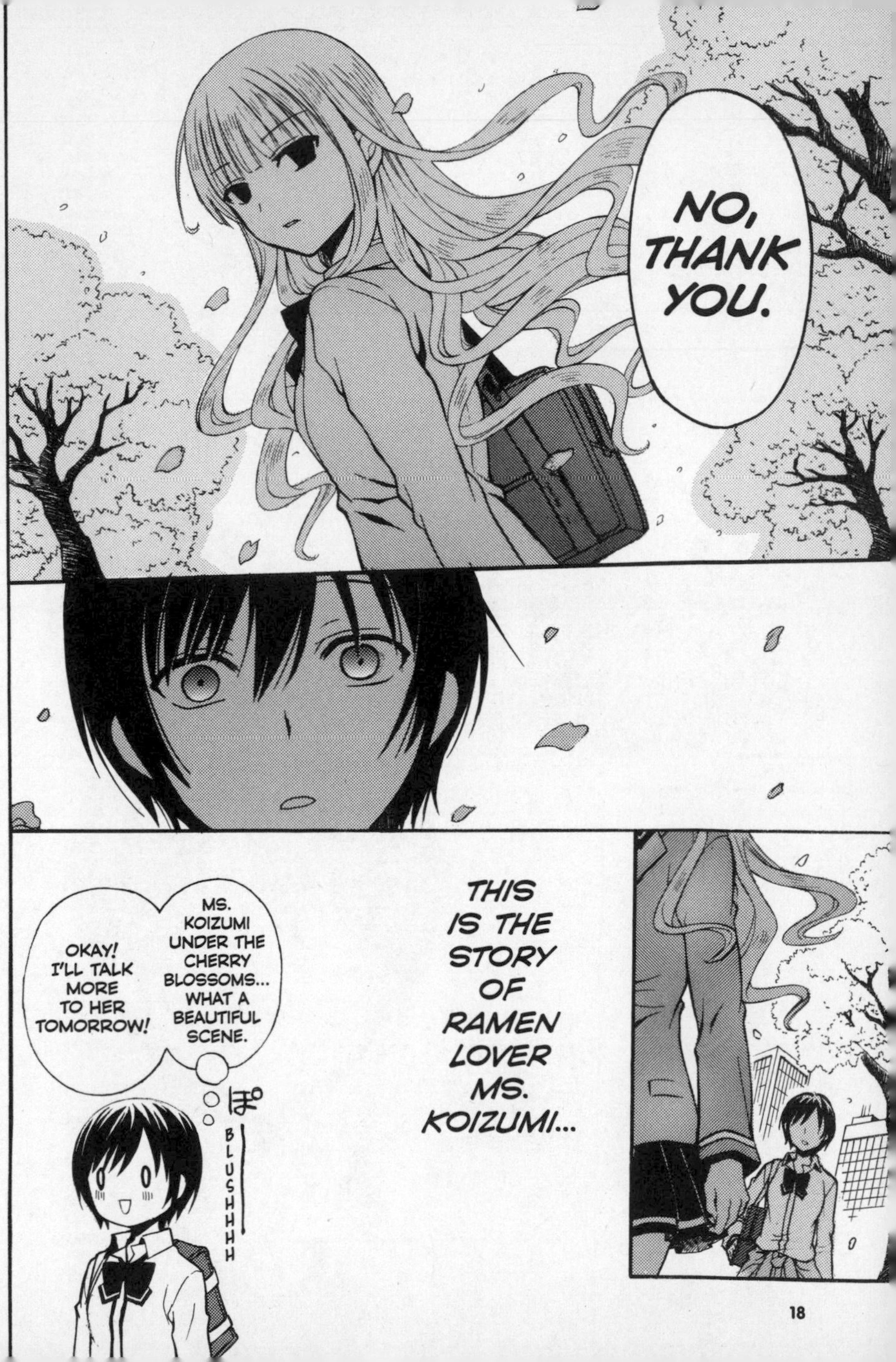
NO, THANK YOU.
THIS IS THE STORY OF RAMEN LOVER MS. KOIZUMI...
MS. KOIZUMI UNDER THE CHERRY BLOSSOMS... WHAT A BEAUTIFUL SCENE.
OKAY! I'LL TALK MORE TO HER TOMORROW!
ぽ
BLUSHHHH

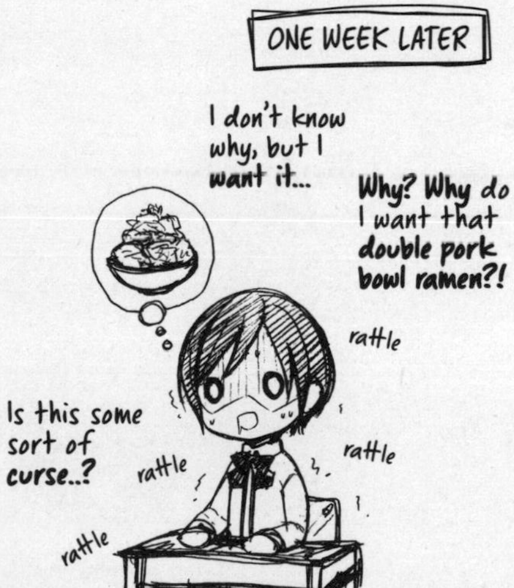
ONE WEEK LATER
I don't know why, but I want it...
Why? Why do I want that double pork bowl ramen?!
rattle
rattle
Is this some sort of curse..?
rattle
rattle

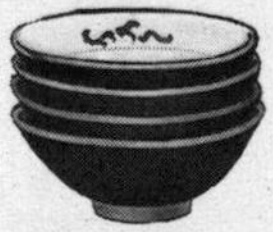

Ms. Koizumi loves ramen noodles

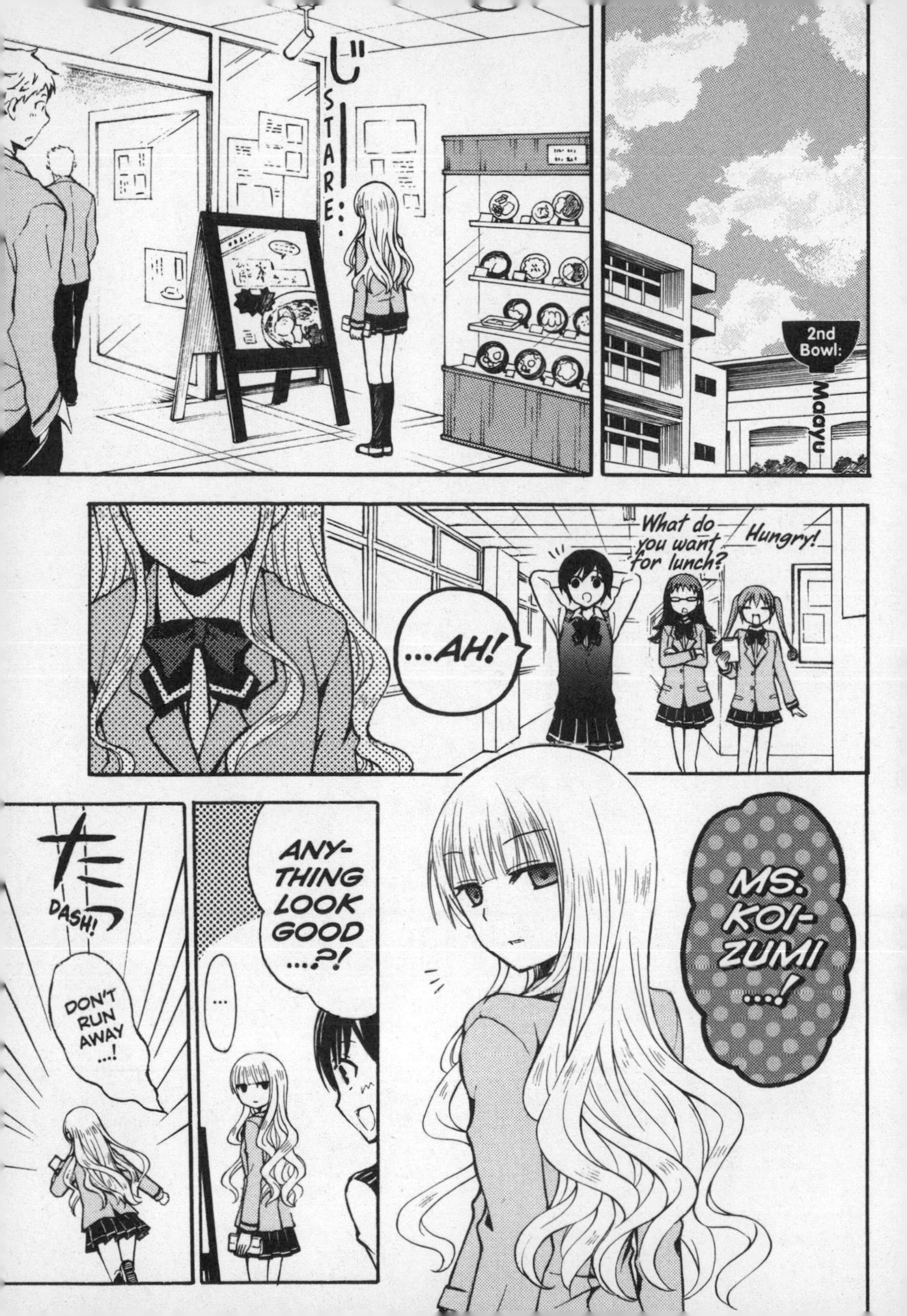
2nd Bowl: Maayu
STARE...
Hungry!
What do you want for lunch?
...AH!
MS. KOI-ZUMI...!
ANY-THING LOOK GOOD...?!
...
DASH!
DON'T RUN AWAY...!

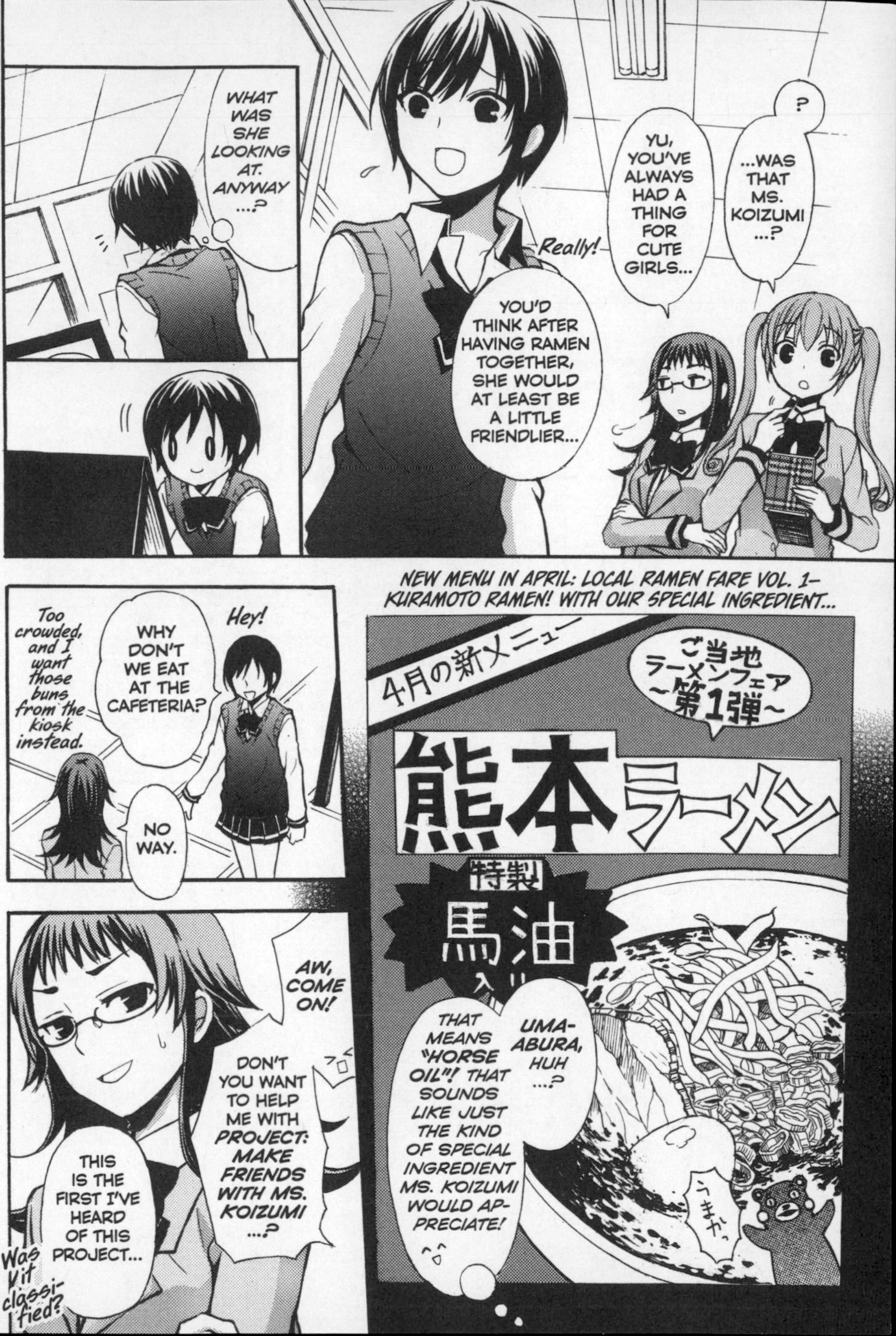
?
...WAS THAT MS. KOIZUMI ...?
YU, YOU'VE ALWAYS HAD A THING FOR CUTE GIRLS...
Really!
YOU'D THINK AFTER HAVING RAMEN TOGETHER, SHE WOULD AT LEAST BE A LITTLE FRIENDLIER...
WHAT WAS SHE LOOKING AT, ANYWAY ...?
NEW MENU IN APRIL: LOCAL RAMEN FARE VOL. 1– KURAMOTO RAMEN! WITH OUR SPECIAL INGREDIENT...
4月の新メニュー
ご当地ラーメンフェア〜第1弾〜
熊本ラーメン
特製
馬油入り
UMA-ABURA, HUH ...?
THAT MEANS "HORSE OIL"! THAT SOUNDS LIKE JUST THE KIND OF SPECIAL INGREDIENT MS. KOIZUMI WOULD AP-PRECIATE!
うまかっ
Hey!
WHY DON'T WE EAT AT THE CAFETERIA?
Too crowded, and I want those buns from the kiosk instead.
NO WAY.
AW, COME ON!
DON'T YOU WANT TO HELP ME WITH PROJECT: MAKE FRIENDS WITH MS. KOIZUMI ...?
THIS IS THE FIRST I'VE HEARD OF THIS PROJECT...
Was it classi-fied?

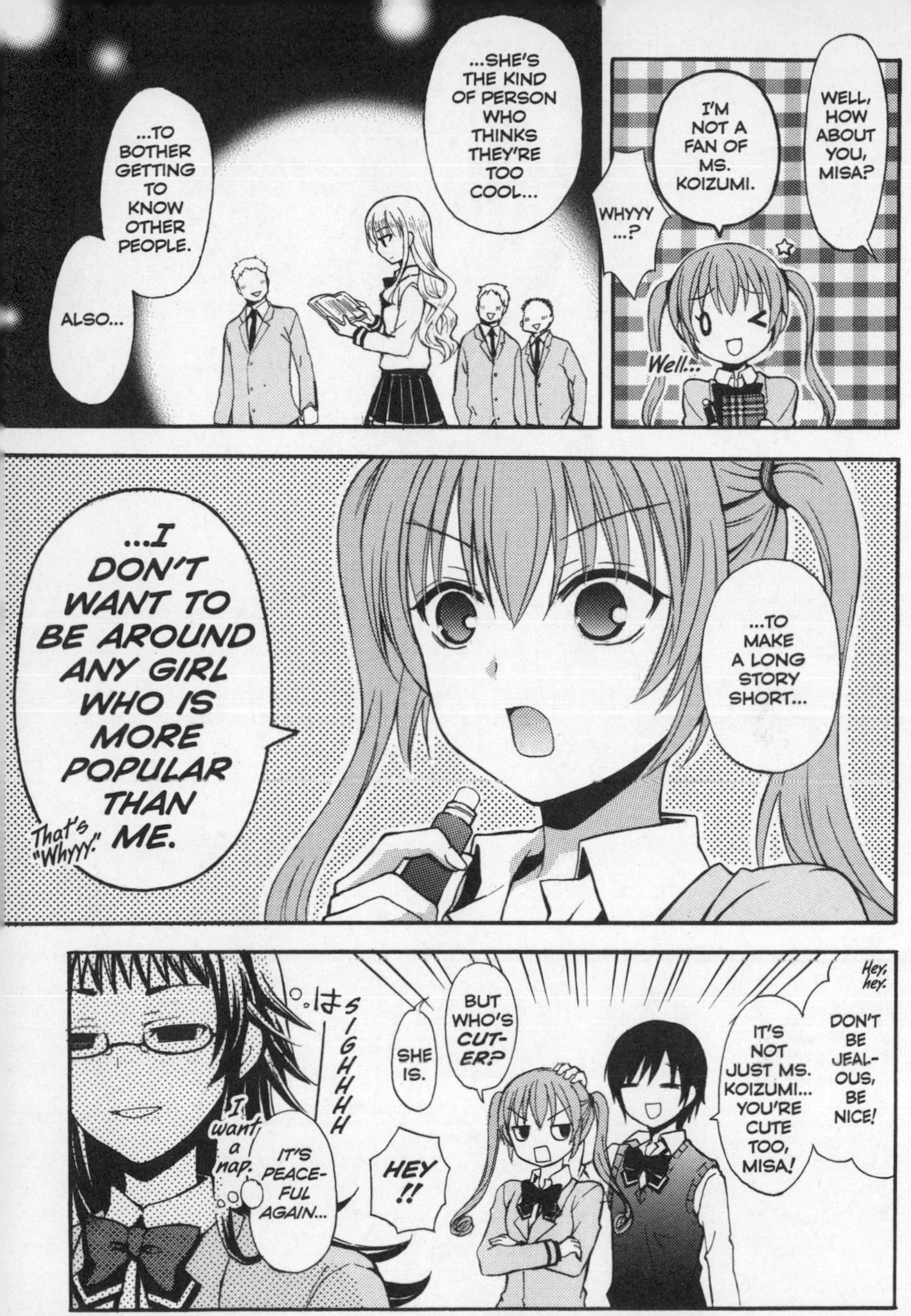
WELL, HOW ABOUT YOU, MISA?
I'M NOT A FAN OF MS. KOIZUMI.
WHYYY ...?
Well...
...SHE'S THE KIND OF PERSON WHO THINKS THEY'RE TOO COOL...
...TO BOTHER GETTING TO KNOW OTHER PEOPLE.
ALSO...
...TO MAKE A LONG STORY SHORT...
...I DON'T WANT TO BE AROUND ANY GIRL WHO IS MORE POPULAR THAN ME.
That's "Whyyy."
Hey, hey.
DON'T BE JEAL-OUS, BE NICE!
IT'S NOT JUST MS. KOIZUMI... YOU'RE CUTE TOO, MISA!
BUT WHO'S CUT-ER?
SHE IS.
HEY!!
SIGHHHH
は
IT'S PEACE-FUL AGAIN...
I want a nap.

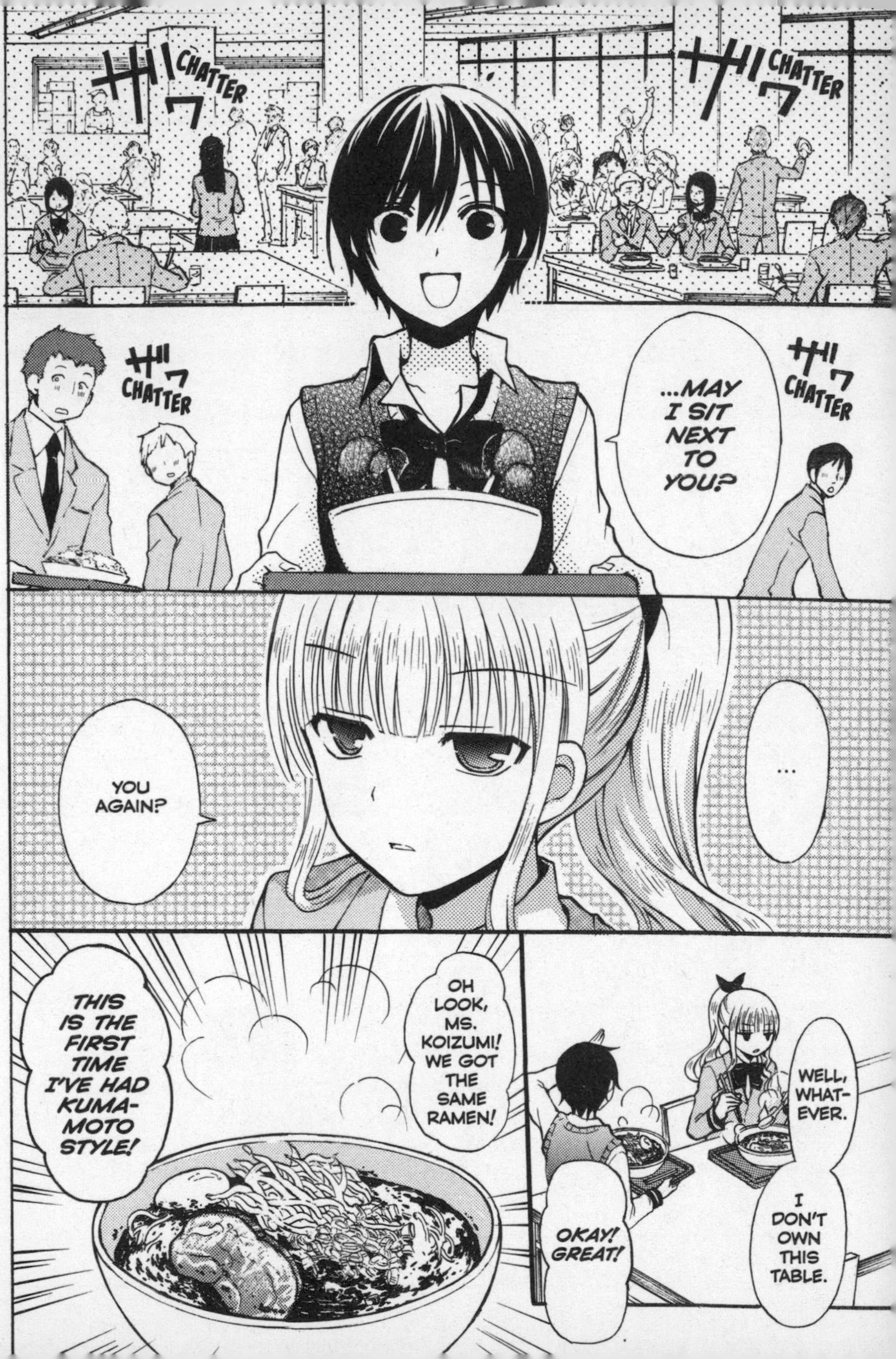
ザワ CHATTER
ザワ CHATTER
ザワ CHATTER
...MAY I SIT NEXT TO YOU?
ザワ CHATTER
...
YOU AGAIN?
WELL, WHAT-EVER.
I DON'T OWN THIS TABLE.
OKAY! GREAT!
OH LOOK, MS. KOIZUMI! WE GOT THE SAME RAMEN!
THIS IS THE FIRST TIME I'VE HAD KUMA-MOTO STYLE!

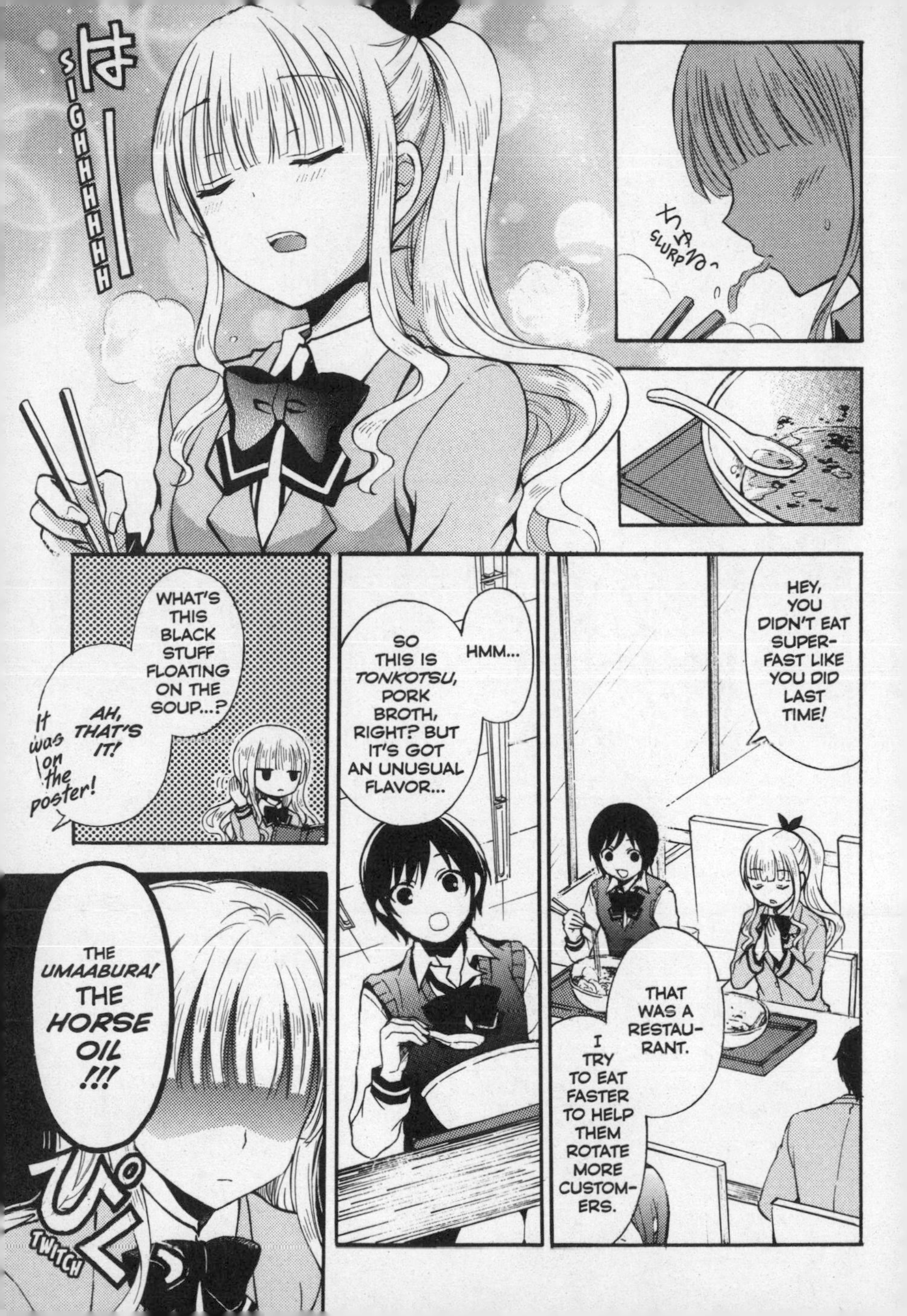

ちゅるっ
SLURP
はー
SIGHHHHHHH
HEY, YOU DIDN'T EAT SUPER-FAST LIKE YOU DID LAST TIME!
THAT WAS A RESTAURANT.
I TRY TO EAT FASTER TO HELP THEM ROTATE MORE CUSTOM-ERS.
HMM...
SO THIS IS *TONKOTSU*, PORK BROTH, RIGHT? BUT IT'S GOT AN UNUSUAL FLAVOR...
WHAT'S THIS BLACK STUFF FLOATING ON THE SOUP...?
AH, THAT'S IT!
It was on the poster!
THE *UMAABURA!* THE *HORSE OIL* !!!
ぴくっ
TWITCH

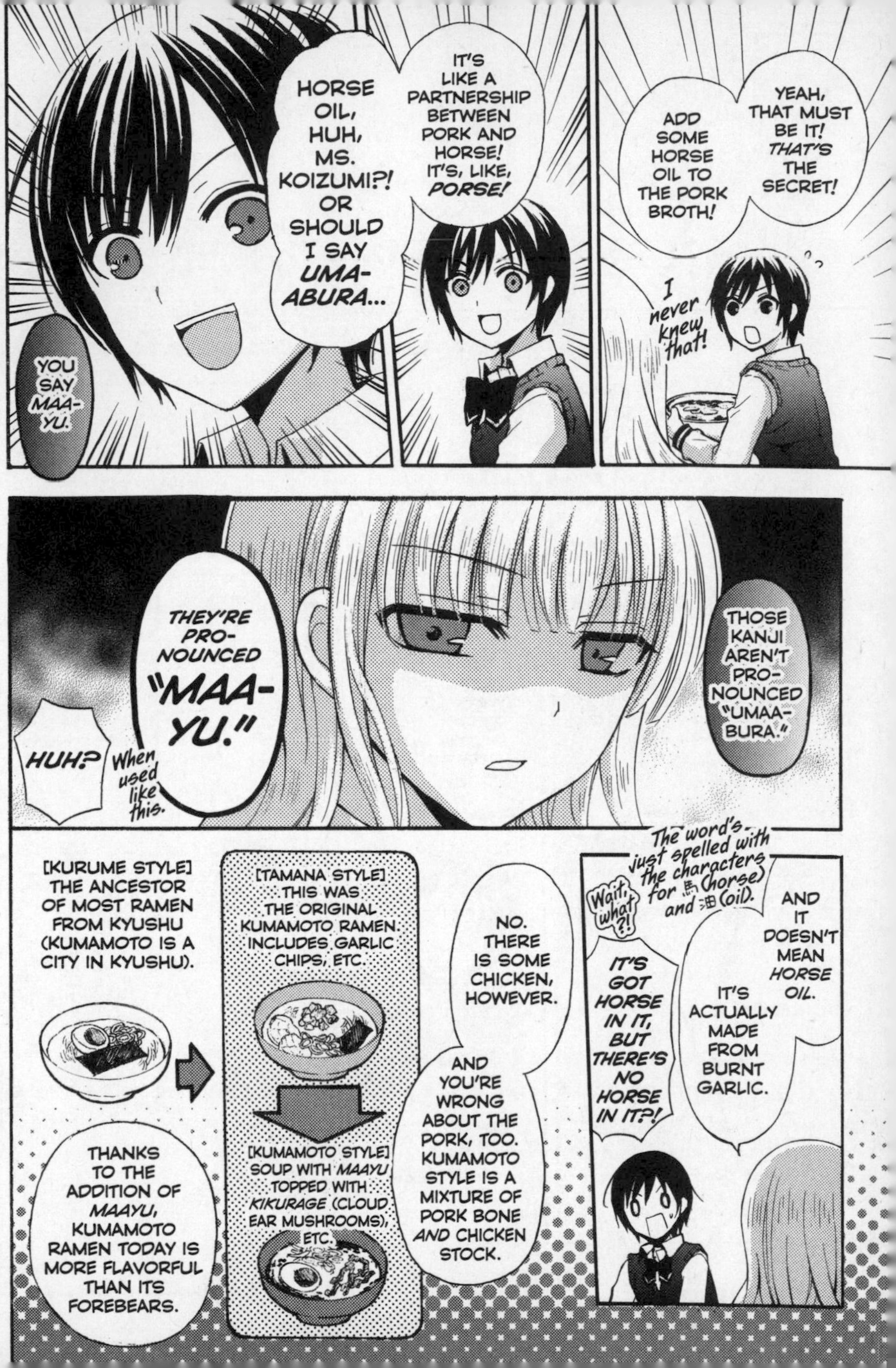
YEAH, THAT MUST BE IT! THAT'S THE SECRET!
ADD SOME HORSE OIL TO THE PORK BROTH!
I never knew that!
IT'S LIKE A PARTNERSHIP BETWEEN PORK AND HORSE! IT'S, LIKE, PORSE!
HORSE OIL, HUH, MS. KOIZUMI?! OR SHOULD I SAY UMA-ABURA...
YOU SAY MAA-YU.
THOSE KANJI AREN'T PRONOUNCED "UMAA-BURA."
THEY'RE PRONOUNCED "MAA-YU."
When used like this.
HUH?
The word's just spelled with the characters for 馬 (horse) and 油 (oil).
Wait, what?!
AND IT DOESN'T MEAN HORSE OIL.
IT'S ACTUALLY MADE FROM BURNT GARLIC.
IT'S GOT HORSE IN IT, BUT THERE'S NO HORSE IN IT?!
NO. THERE IS SOME CHICKEN, HOWEVER.
AND YOU'RE WRONG ABOUT THE PORK, TOO. KUMAMOTO STYLE IS A MIXTURE OF PORK BONE AND CHICKEN STOCK.
[KURUME STYLE] THE ANCESTOR OF MOST RAMEN FROM KYUSHU (KUMAMOTO IS A CITY IN KYUSHU).
[TAMANA STYLE] THIS WAS THE ORIGINAL KUMAMOTO RAMEN. INCLUDES GARLIC CHIPS, ETC.
[KUMAMOTO STYLE] SOUP WITH MAAYU TOPPED WITH KIKURAGE (CLOUD EAR MUSHROOMS), ETC.
THANKS TO THE ADDITION OF MAAYU, KUMAMOTO RAMEN TODAY IS MORE FLAVORFUL THAN ITS FOREBEARS.

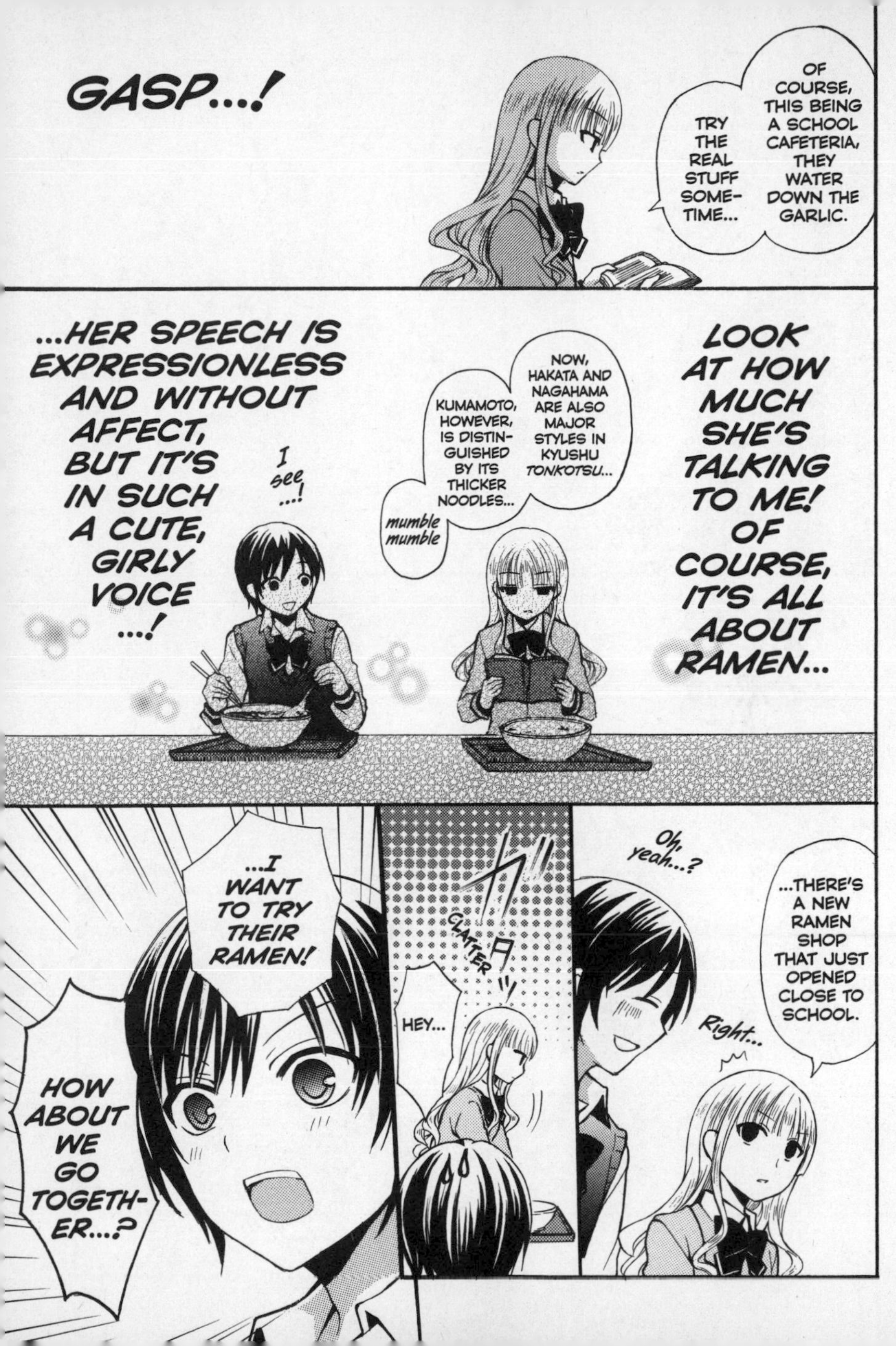

OF COURSE, THIS BEING A SCHOOL CAFETERIA, THEY WATER DOWN THE GARLIC.
TRY THE REAL STUFF SOME-TIME...
GASP...!
LOOK AT HOW MUCH SHE'S TALKING TO ME! OF COURSE, IT'S ALL ABOUT RAMEN...
NOW, HAKATA AND NAGAHAMA ARE ALSO MAJOR STYLES IN KYUSHU TONKOTSU...
KUMAMOTO, HOWEVER, IS DISTIN-GUISHED BY ITS THICKER NOODLES...
mumble mumble
I see ...!
...HER SPEECH IS EXPRESSIONLESS AND WITHOUT AFFECT, BUT IT'S IN SUCH A CUTE, GIRLY VOICE ...!
Oh, yeah...?
...THERE'S A NEW RAMEN SHOP THAT JUST OPENED CLOSE TO SCHOOL.
Right...
CLATTER
HEY...
...I WANT TO TRY THEIR RAMEN!
HOW ABOUT WE GO TOGETH-ER...?

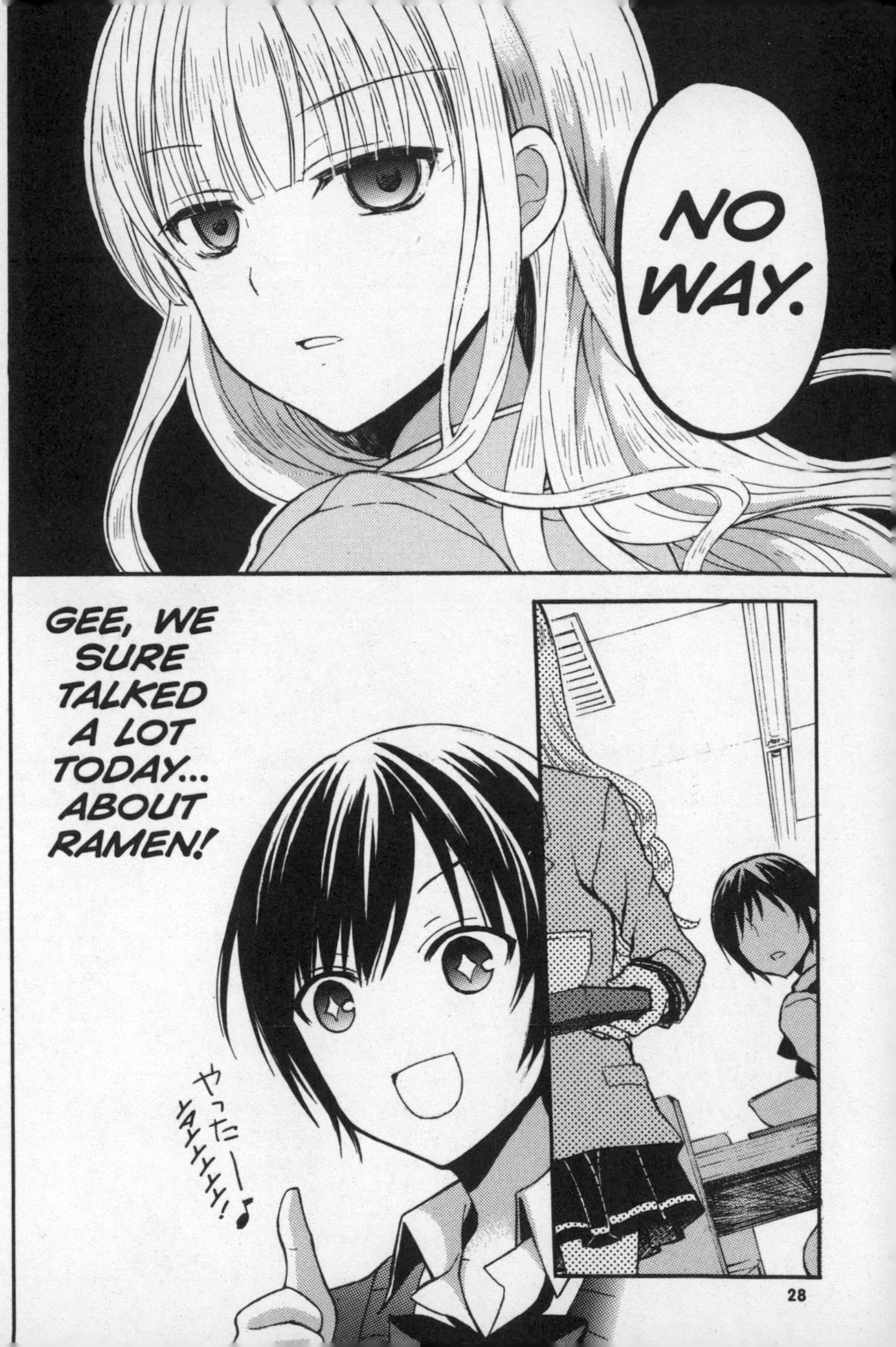
NO WAY.
GEE, WE SURE TALKED A LOT TODAY... ABOUT RAMEN!
やったーーーーーー♪

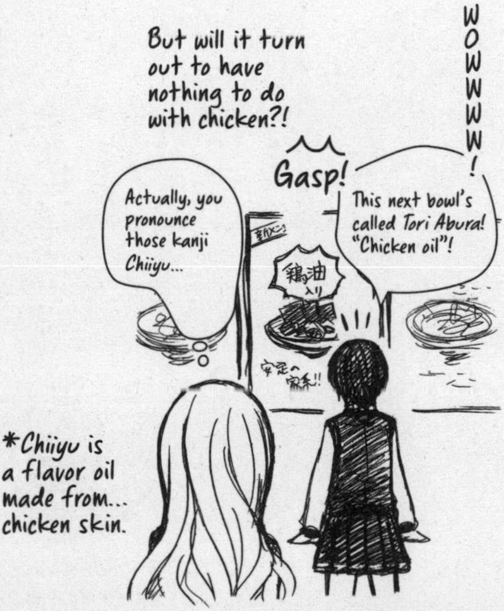
WOWWWWW!
This next bowl's called Tori Abura! "Chicken oil"!
Gasp!
Actually, you pronounce those kanji Chiiyu...
But will it turn out to have nothing to do with chicken?!
鶏油 入り
*Chiiyu is a flavor oil made from... chicken skin.

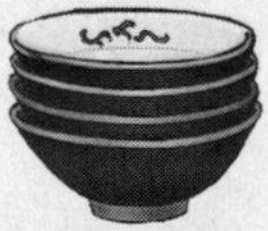

Ms. Koizumi loves
ramen noodles

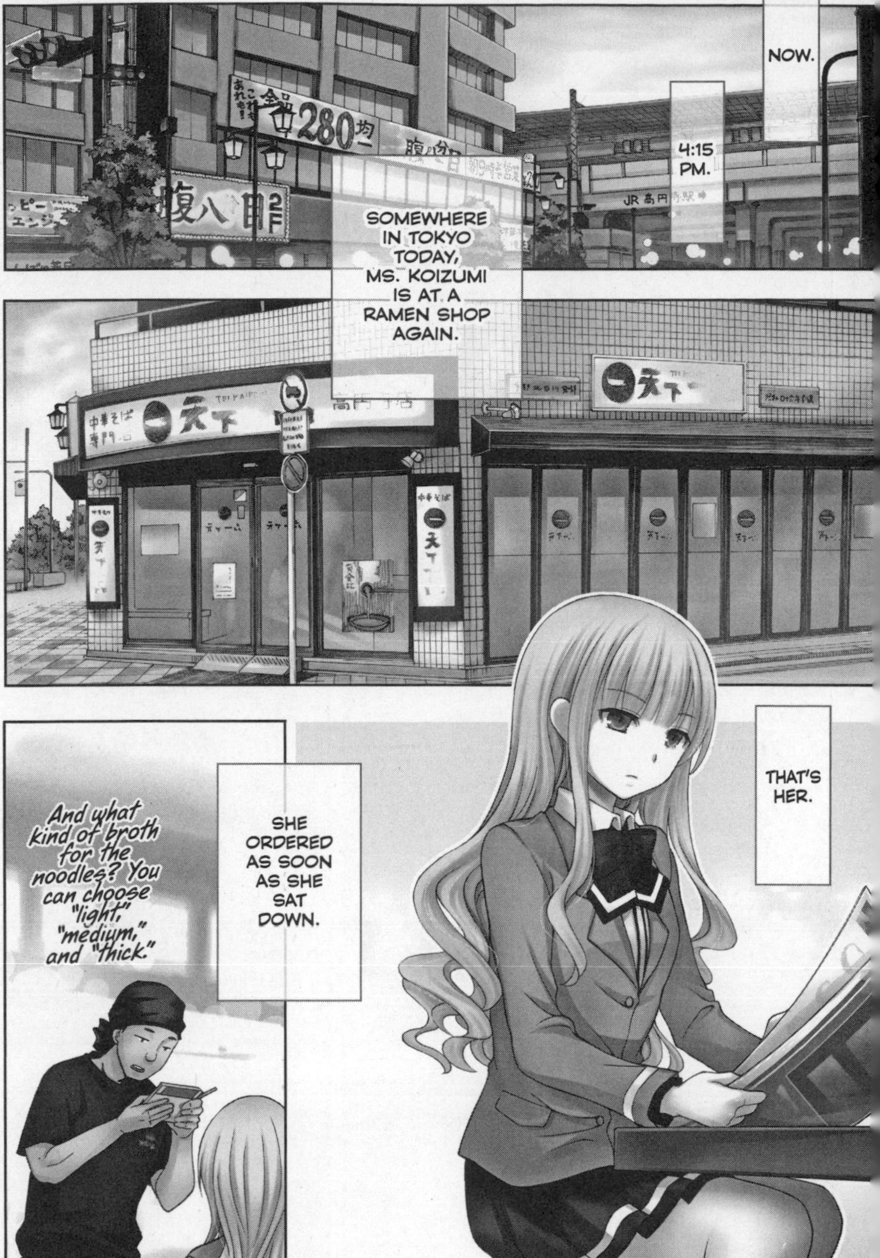
NOW.
4:15 PM.
SOMEWHERE IN TOKYO TODAY, MS. KOIZUMI IS AT A RAMEN SHOP AGAIN.
THAT'S HER.
SHE ORDERED AS SOON AS SHE SAT DOWN.
And what kind of broth for the noodles? You can choose "light," "medium," and "thick."

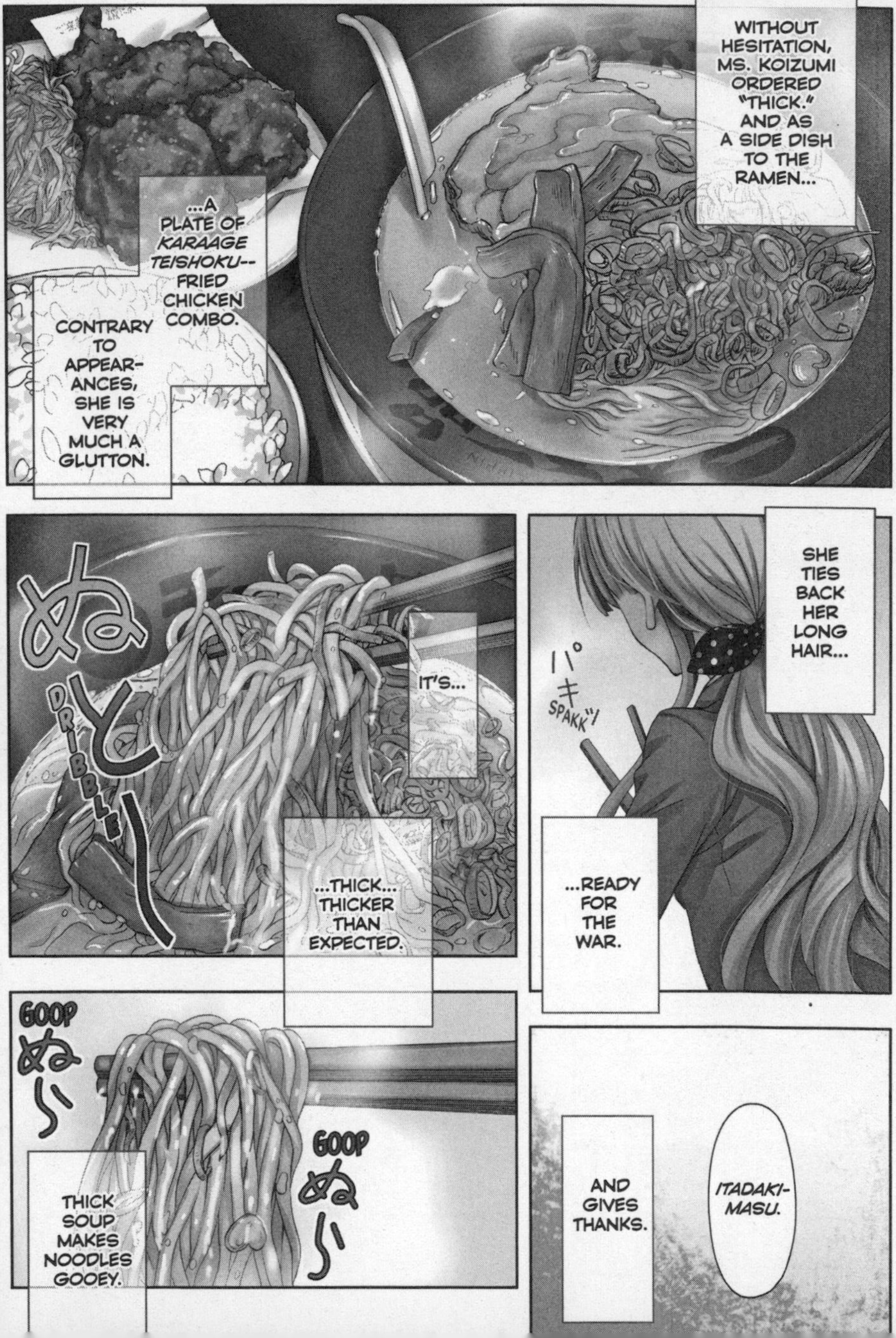
WITHOUT HESITATION, MS. KOIZUMI ORDERED "THICK." AND AS A SIDE DISH TO THE RAMEN...
...A PLATE OF *KARAAGE TEISHOKU*--FRIED CHICKEN COMBO.
CONTRARY TO APPEAR-ANCES, SHE IS VERY MUCH A GLUTTON.
SHE TIES BACK HER LONG HAIR...
パキ
SPAKK
...READY FOR THE WAR.
DRIBBLE
IT'S...
...THICK... THICKER THAN EXPECTED.
ITADAKI-MASU.
AND GIVES THANKS.
GOOP
GOOP
THICK SOUP MAKES NOODLES GOOEY.

...

SLURP
ズル
ズル
SLURP

ず
SLURP
ずる
SLURP
ずる
SLURP

ズ
ル
ル
ッ
SLURP

ズ
ル
ル
ッ
SLURRPP

SLURP
ズル
SLURP
ズルルッ

BITE

ずる
SLURP

...

ずる
SLURP
ずる
SLURP

すすすすすす
RRRRPPP

...

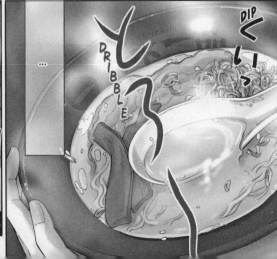

DIP
くいっ

DRIBBLE
とろ

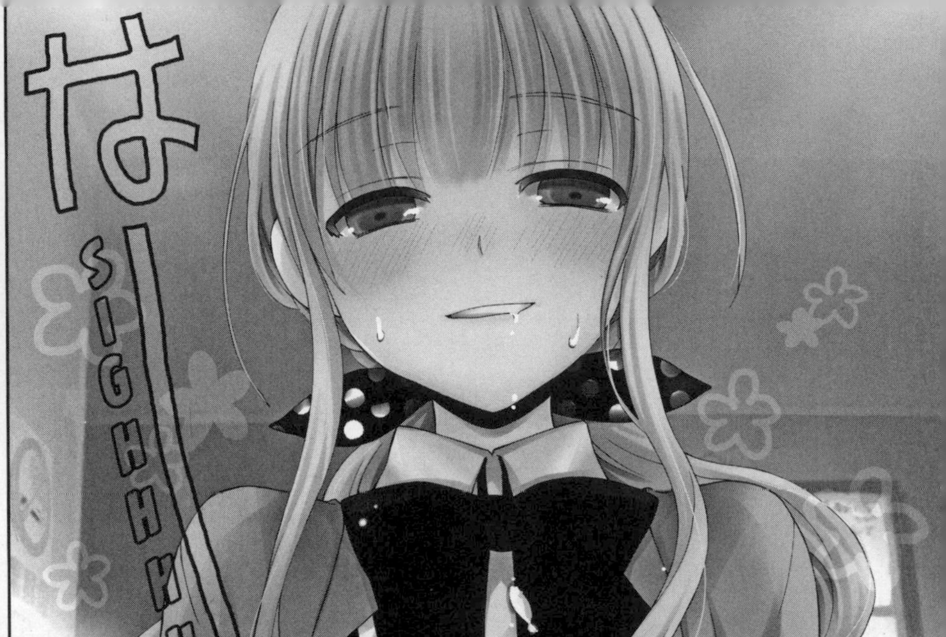
は
SIGHHHHHHHH
3rd Bowl: Thick and Rich

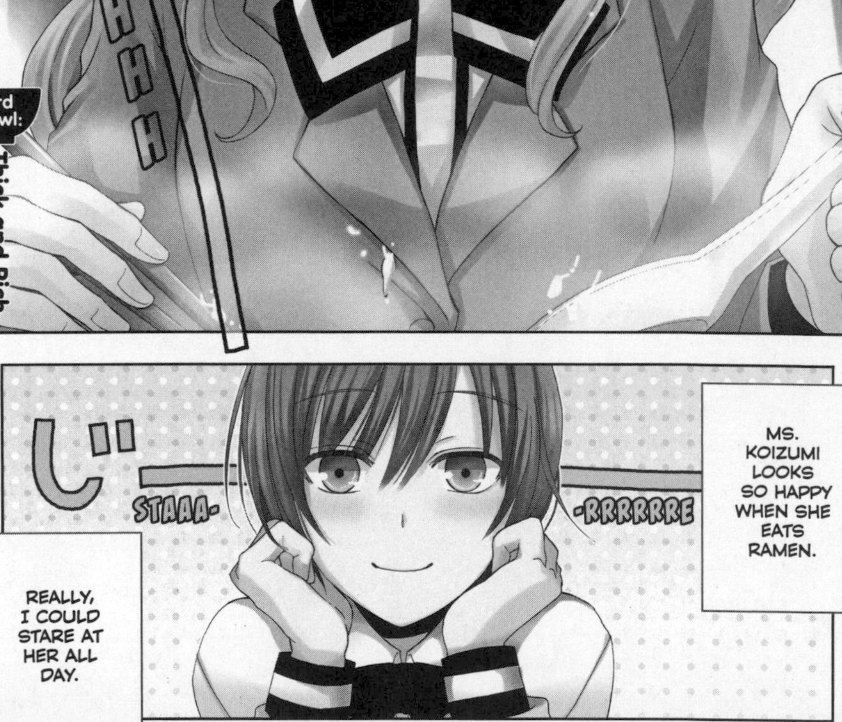
MS. KOIZUMI LOOKS SO HAPPY WHEN SHE EATS RAMEN.
じー
STAAA- -RRRRRRE
REALLY, I COULD STARE AT HER ALL DAY.

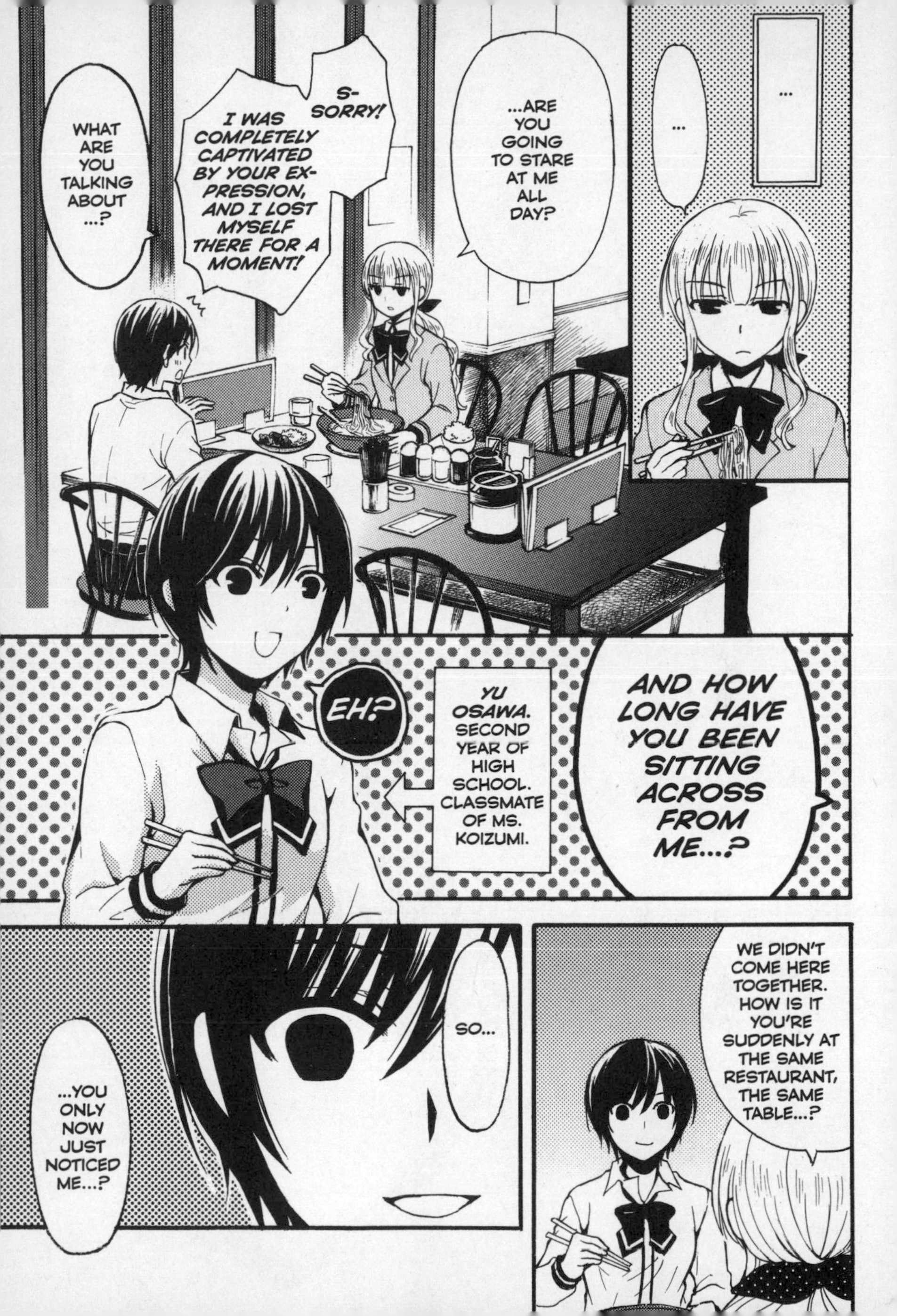
...
...
...ARE YOU GOING TO STARE AT ME ALL DAY?
S-SORRY! I WAS COMPLETELY CAPTIVATED BY YOUR EX-PRESSION, AND I LOST MYSELF THERE FOR A MOMENT!
WHAT ARE YOU TALKING ABOUT...?
AND HOW LONG HAVE YOU BEEN SITTING ACROSS FROM ME...?
YU OSAWA. SECOND YEAR OF HIGH SCHOOL. CLASSMATE OF MS. KOIZUMI.
EH?
WE DIDN'T COME HERE TOGETHER. HOW IS IT YOU'RE SUDDENLY AT THE SAME RESTAURANT, THE SAME TABLE...?
SO...
...YOU ONLY NOW JUST NOTICED ME...?

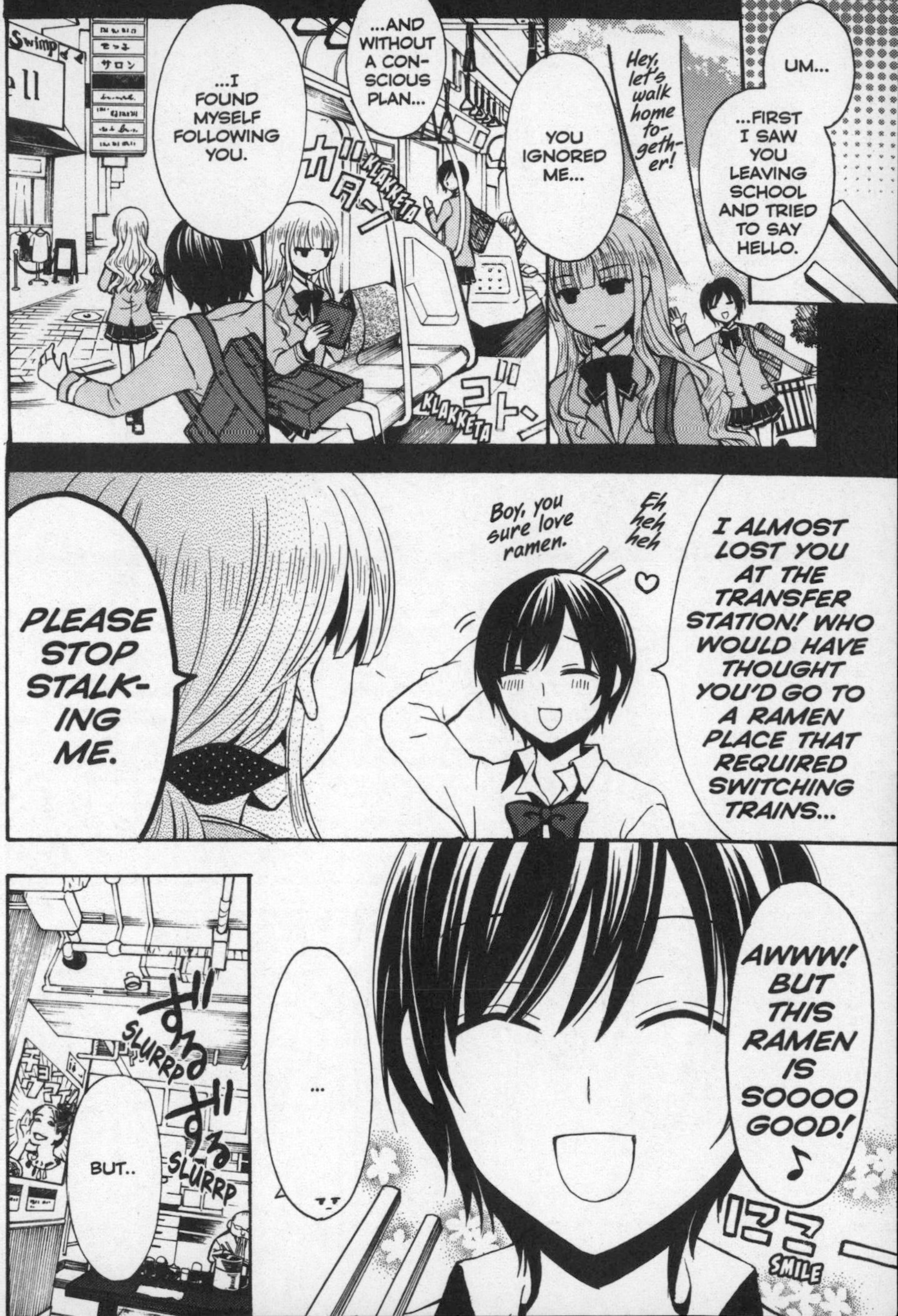
UM...
...FIRST I SAW YOU LEAVING SCHOOL AND TRIED TO SAY HELLO.
Hey, let's walk home together!
YOU IGNORED ME...
...AND WITHOUT A CONSCIOUS PLAN...
KLAKKETA
KLAKKETA
...I FOUND MYSELF FOLLOWING YOU.
I ALMOST LOST YOU AT THE TRANSFER STATION! WHO WOULD HAVE THOUGHT YOU'D GO TO A RAMEN PLACE THAT REQUIRED SWITCHING TRAINS...
Eh heh heh
Boy, you sure love ramen.
PLEASE STOP STALKING ME.
AWWW! BUT THIS RAMEN IS SOOOO GOOD!
SMILE
...
SLURRP
SLURRP
BUT..

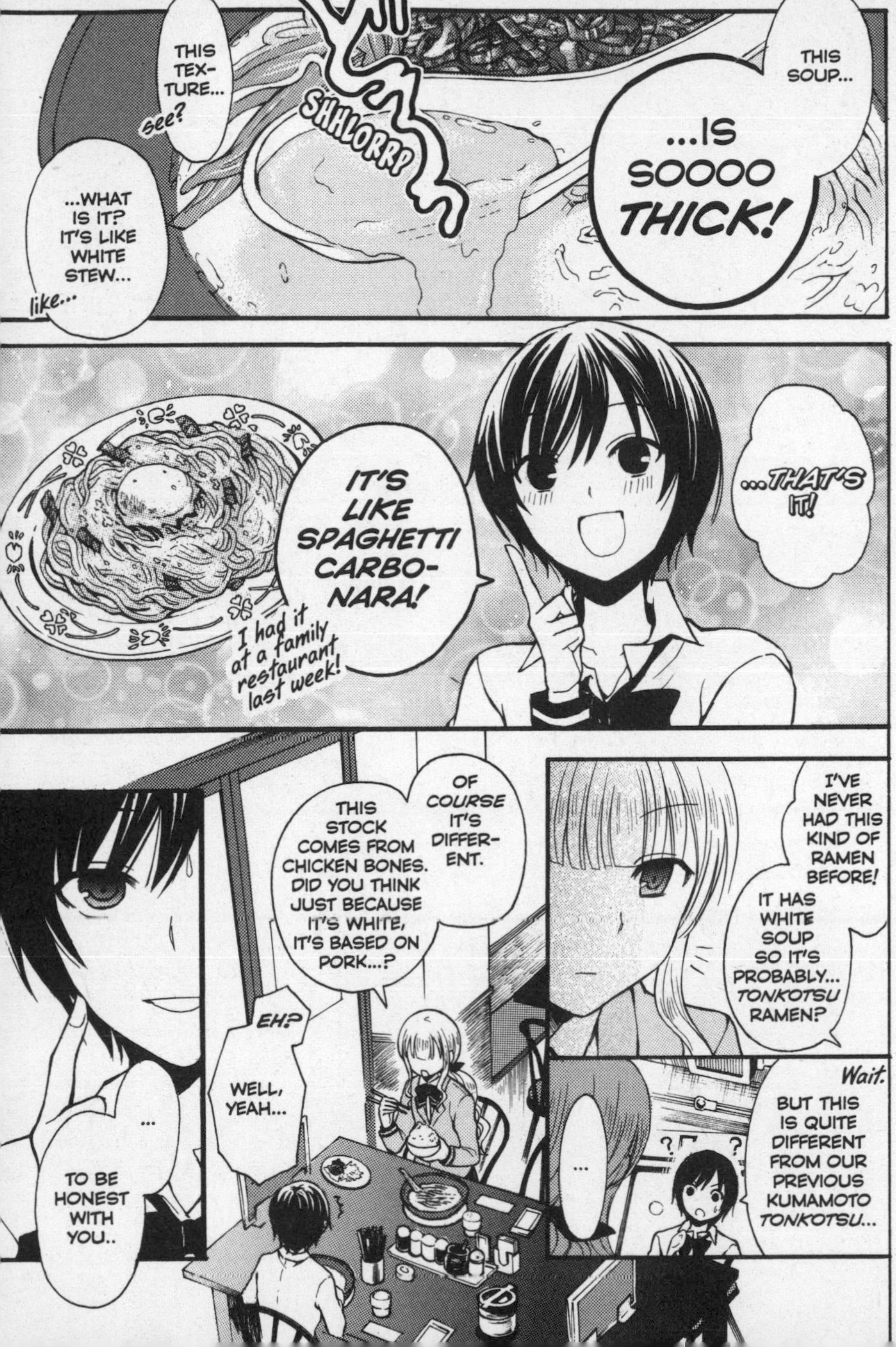
THIS SOUP...
...IS SOOOO THICK!
SHHLORRP
THIS TEX-TURE... see?
...WHAT IS IT? IT'S LIKE WHITE STEW... like...
...THAT'S IT!
IT'S LIKE SPAGHETTI CARBO-NARA!
I had it at a family restaurant last week!
I'VE NEVER HAD THIS KIND OF RAMEN BEFORE!
IT HAS WHITE SOUP SO IT'S PROBABLY... TONKOTSU RAMEN?
Wait.
BUT THIS IS QUITE DIFFERENT FROM OUR PREVIOUS KUMAMOTO TONKOTSU...
...
OF COURSE IT'S DIFFER-ENT.
THIS STOCK COMES FROM CHICKEN BONES. DID YOU THINK JUST BECAUSE IT'S WHITE, IT'S BASED ON PORK...?
EH?
WELL, YEAH...
...
TO BE HONEST WITH YOU..

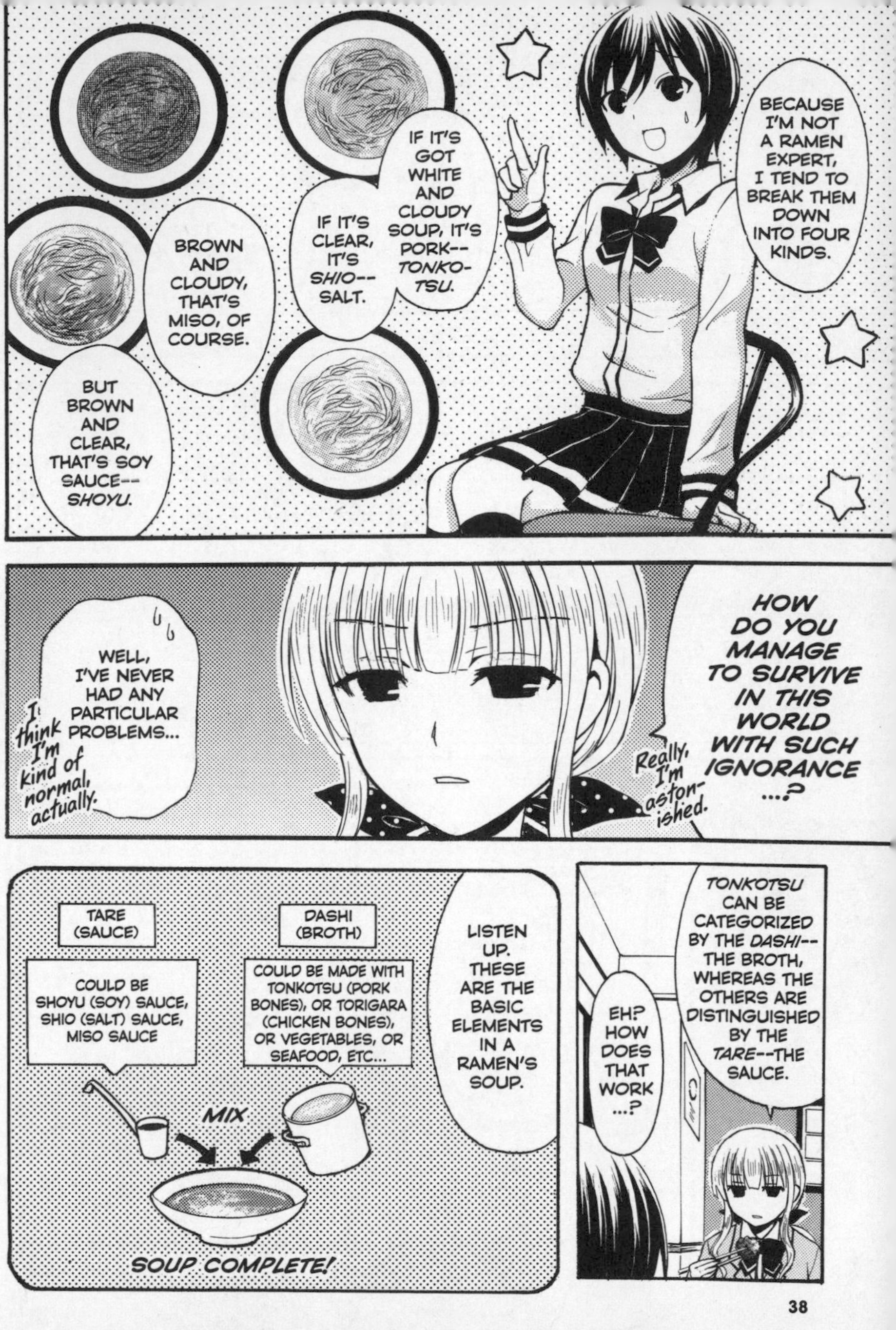
BECAUSE I'M NOT A RAMEN EXPERT, I TEND TO BREAK THEM DOWN INTO FOUR KINDS.
IF IT'S GOT WHITE AND CLOUDY SOUP, IT'S PORK--*TONKOTSU.*
IF IT'S CLEAR, IT'S *SHIO*--SALT.
BROWN AND CLOUDY, THAT'S MISO, OF COURSE.
BUT BROWN AND CLEAR, THAT'S SOY SAUCE--*SHOYU.*
HOW DO YOU MANAGE TO SURVIVE IN THIS WORLD WITH SUCH IGNORANCE ...?
Really, I'm astonished.
WELL, I'VE NEVER HAD ANY PARTICULAR PROBLEMS...
I think I'm kind of normal, actually.
TONKOTSU CAN BE CATEGORIZED BY THE *DASHI*--THE BROTH, WHEREAS THE OTHERS ARE DISTINGUISHED BY THE *TARE*--THE SAUCE.
EH? HOW DOES THAT WORK ...?
LISTEN UP. THESE ARE THE BASIC ELEMENTS IN A RAMEN'S SOUP.
DASHI (BROTH)
COULD BE MADE WITH TONKOTSU (PORK BONES), OR TORIGARA (CHICKEN BONES), OR VEGETABLES, OR SEAFOOD, ETC...
TARE (SAUCE)
COULD BE SHOYU (SOY) SAUCE, SHIO (SALT) SAUCE, MISO SAUCE
MIX
SOUP COMPLETE!

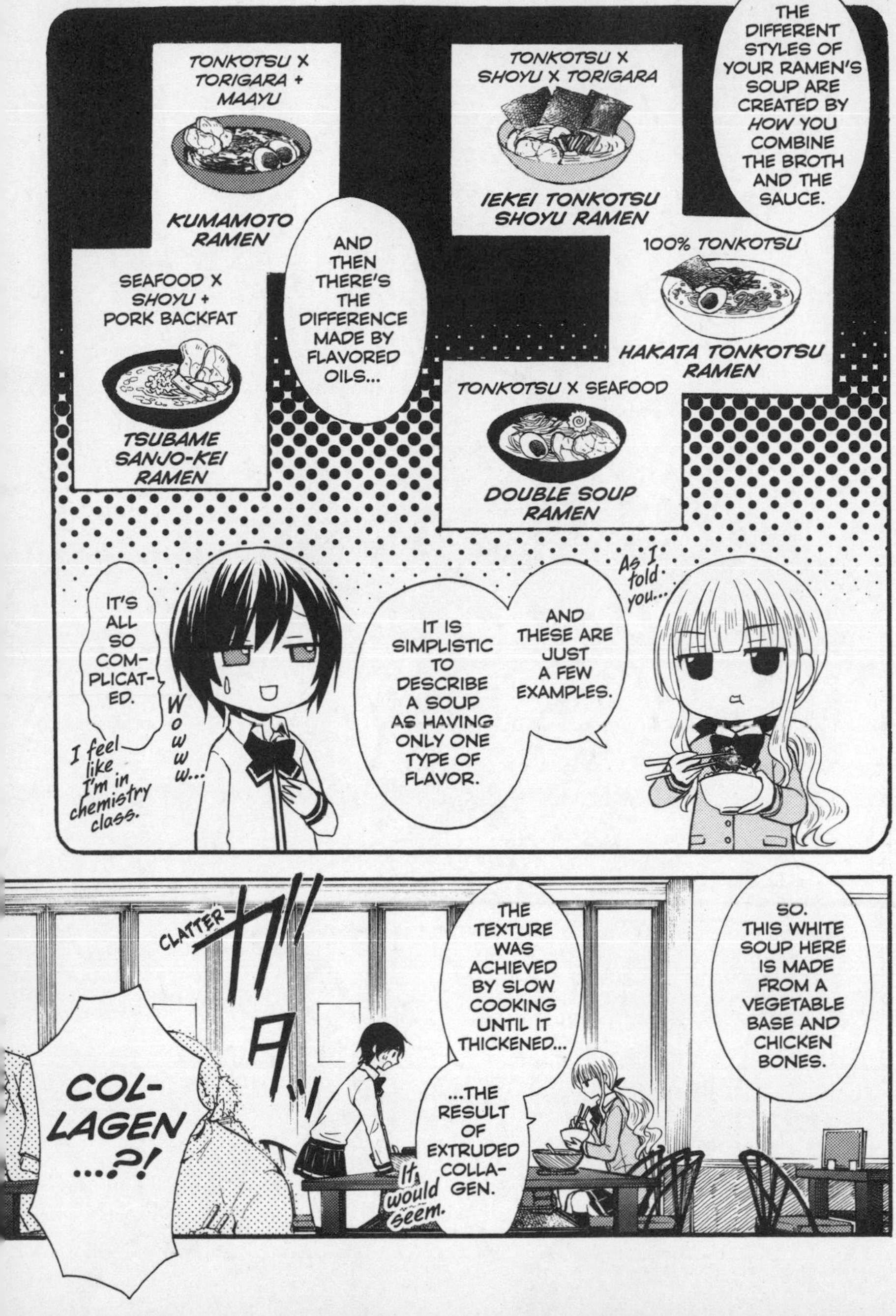
THE DIFFERENT STYLES OF YOUR RAMEN'S SOUP ARE CREATED BY *HOW* YOU COMBINE THE BROTH AND THE SAUCE.
TONKOTSU X SHOYU X TORIGARA
IEKEI TONKOTSU SHOYU RAMEN
TONKOTSU X TORIGARA + MAAYU
KUMAMOTO RAMEN
100% TONKOTSU
HAKATA TONKOTSU RAMEN
TONKOTSU X SEAFOOD
DOUBLE SOUP RAMEN
AND THEN THERE'S THE DIFFERENCE MADE BY FLAVORED OILS...
SEAFOOD X SHOYU + PORK BACKFAT
TSUBAME SANJO-KEI RAMEN
As I told you...
AND THESE ARE JUST A FEW EXAMPLES.
IT IS SIMPLISTIC TO DESCRIBE A SOUP AS HAVING ONLY ONE TYPE OF FLAVOR.
IT'S ALL SO COMPLICATED.
Wowwww...
I feel like I'm in chemistry class.
SO. THIS WHITE SOUP HERE IS MADE FROM A VEGETABLE BASE AND CHICKEN BONES.
THE TEXTURE WAS ACHIEVED BY SLOW COOKING UNTIL IT THICKENED...
...THE RESULT OF EXTRUDED COLLAGEN.
It would seem.
CLATTER
COLLAGEN...?!

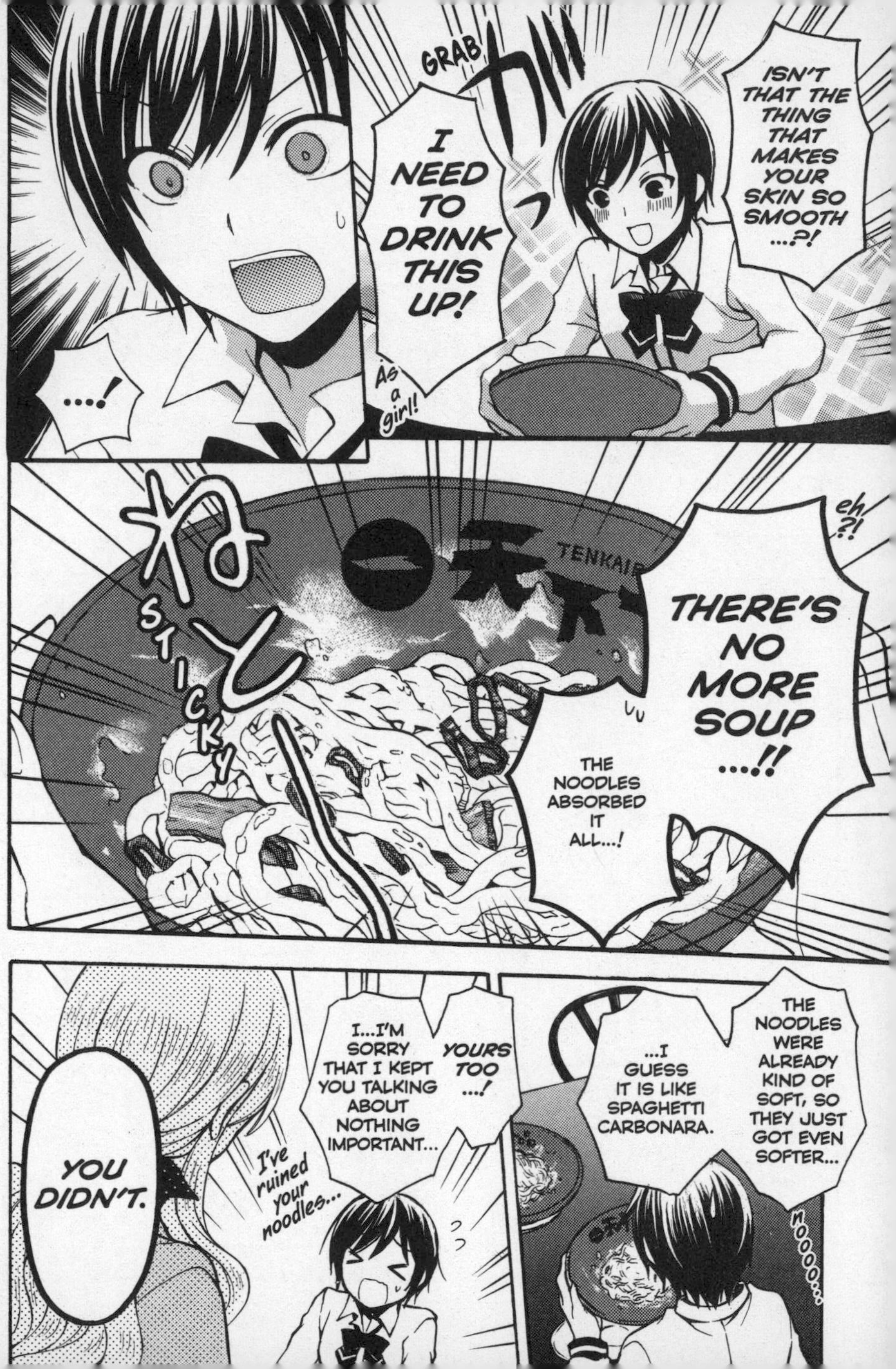
ISN'T THAT THE THING THAT MAKES YOUR SKIN SO SMOOTH ...?!
GRAB
I NEED TO DRINK THIS UP!
As a girl!!
...!
eh ?!
THERE'S NO MORE SOUP ...!!
THE NOODLES ABSORBED IT ALL...!
STICKY
THE NOODLES WERE ALREADY KIND OF SOFT, SO THEY JUST GOT EVEN SOFTER...
...I GUESS IT IS LIKE SPAGHETTI CARBONARA.
nooooo...
YOURS TOO ...!
I...I'M SORRY THAT I KEPT YOU TALKING ABOUT NOTHING IMPORTANT...
I've ruined your noodles...
YOU DIDN'T.

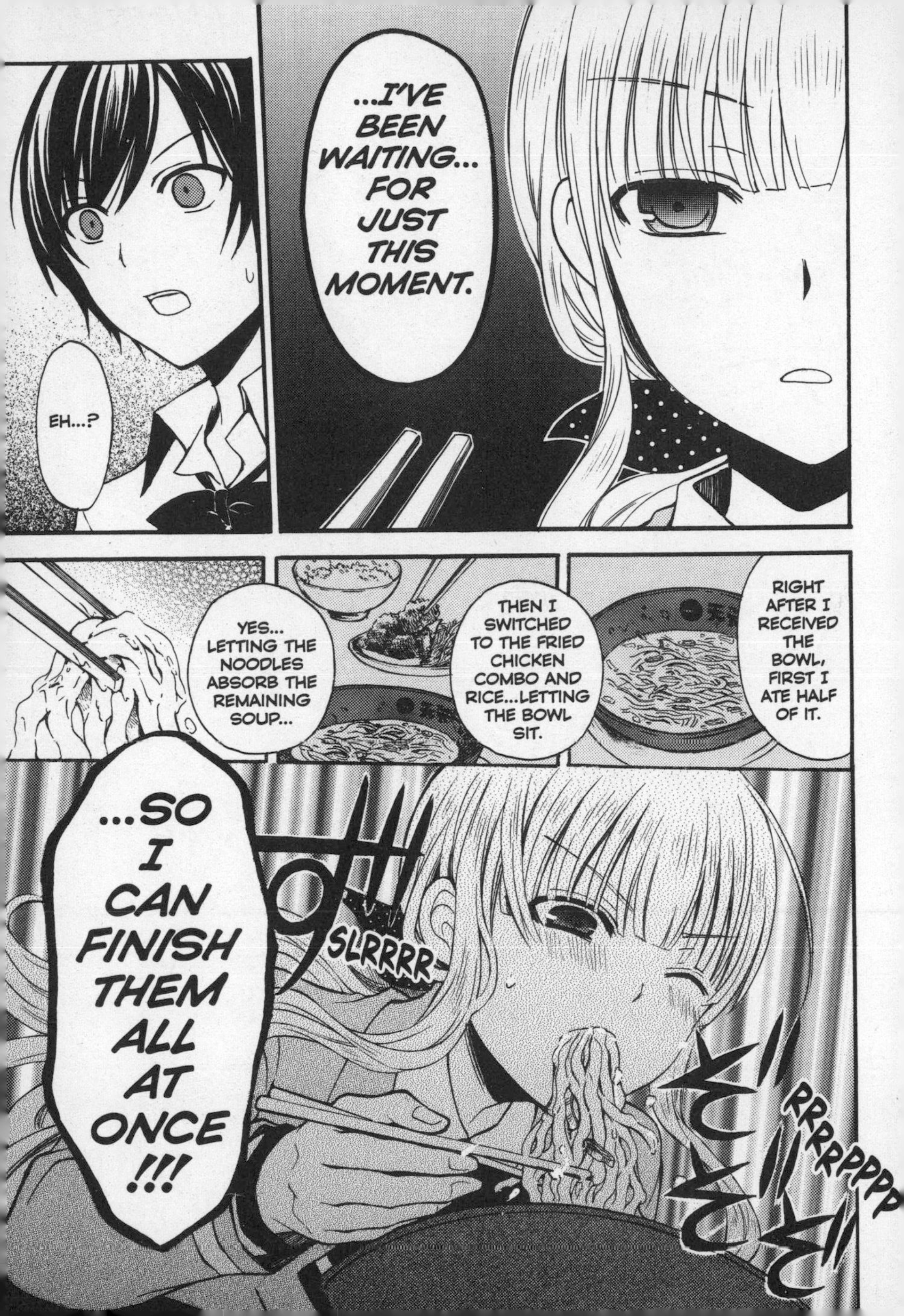
...I'VE BEEN WAITING... FOR JUST THIS MOMENT.
EH...?
RIGHT AFTER I RECEIVED THE BOWL, FIRST I ATE HALF OF IT.
THEN I SWITCHED TO THE FRIED CHICKEN COMBO AND RICE...LETTING THE BOWL SIT.
YES... LETTING THE NOODLES ABSORB THE REMAINING SOUP...
SLRRRR-
RRRRPPPP
...SO I CAN FINISH THEM ALL AT ONCE!!!

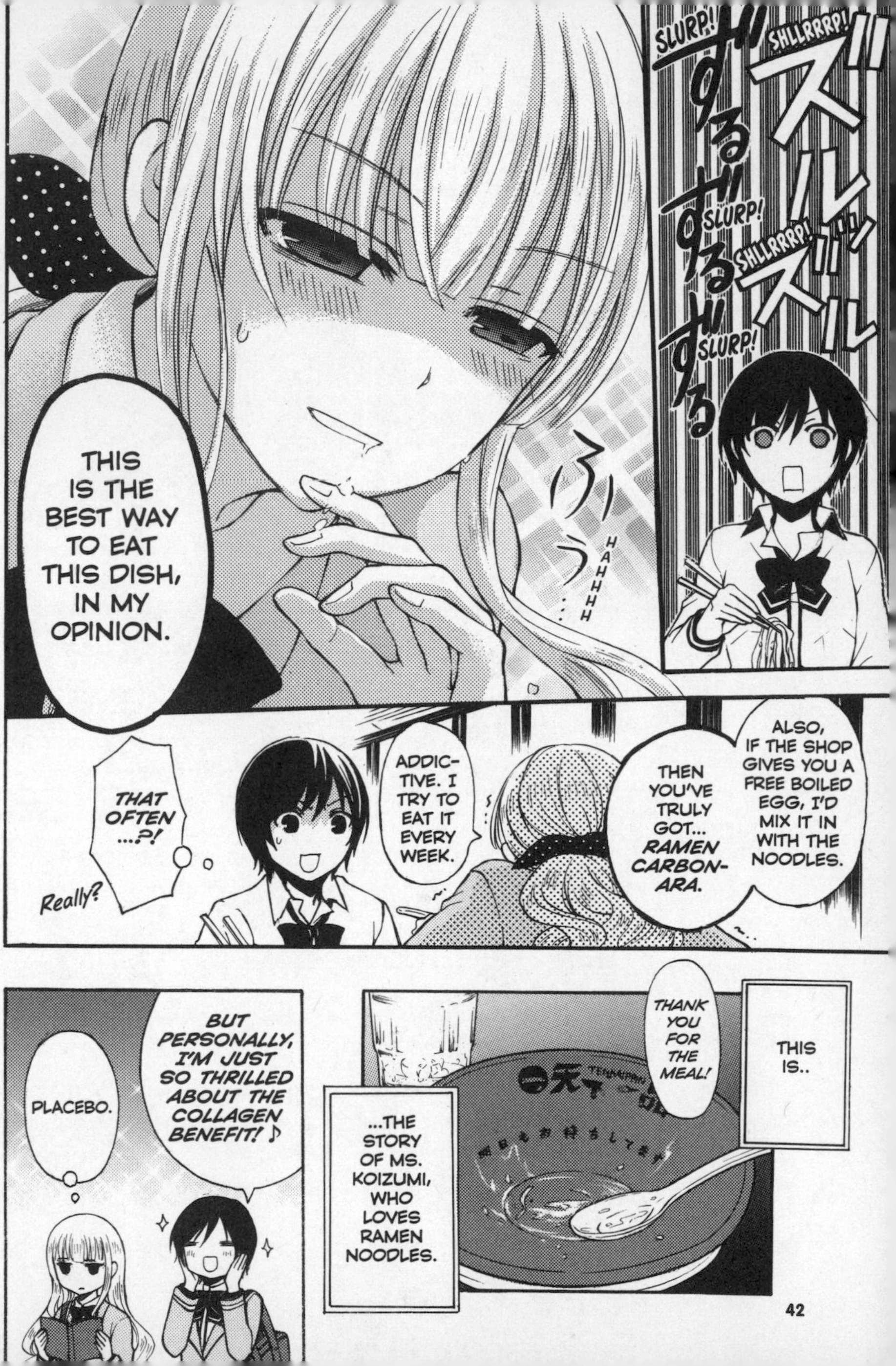
ズルッズルズル
SHLLRRRP!
SHLLRRRP!
ずるずるずるずる
SLURP!
SLURP!
SLURP!
THIS IS THE BEST WAY TO EAT THIS DISH, IN MY OPINION.
ふぅ…
HAHHHH
ALSO, IF THE SHOP GIVES YOU A FREE BOILED EGG, I'D MIX IT IN WITH THE NOODLES.
THEN YOU'VE TRULY GOT... *RAMEN CARBONARA.*
ADDICTIVE. I TRY TO EAT IT EVERY WEEK.
THAT OFTEN ...?!
Really?
THIS IS..
THANK YOU FOR THE MEAL!
...THE STORY OF MS. KOIZUMI, WHO LOVES RAMEN NOODLES.
BUT PERSONALLY, I'M JUST SO THRILLED ABOUT THE COLLAGEN BENEFIT! ♪
PLACEBO.

mutter

Kossari...*

*Ramen slang from the 1990s. *Kossari* describes a type of ramen broth that as you eat it at first tastes thick, then over time changes to tasting light.

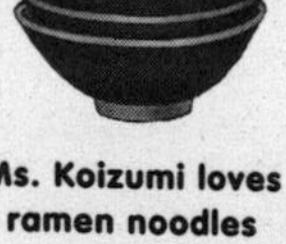

Ms. Koizumi loves
ramen noodles

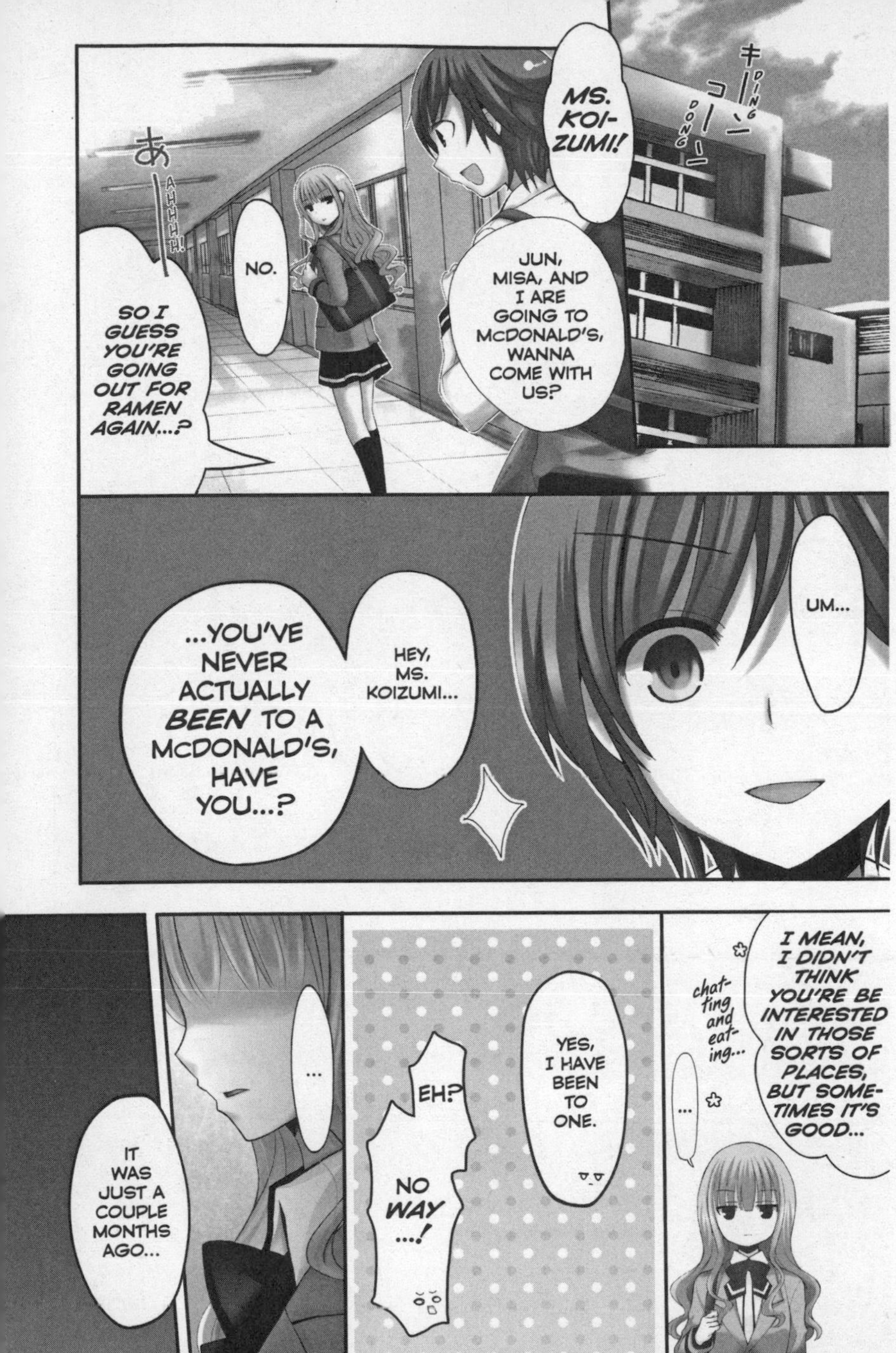
キーンコーン
DING DONG
MS. KOI-ZUMI!
JUN, MISA, AND I ARE GOING TO McDONALD'S, WANNA COME WITH US?
NO.
あー
AHHHHH!
SO I GUESS YOU'RE GOING OUT FOR RAMEN AGAIN...?
UM...
HEY, MS. KOIZUMI...
...YOU'VE NEVER ACTUALLY BEEN TO A McDONALD'S, HAVE YOU...?
I MEAN, I DIDN'T THINK YOU'RE BE INTERESTED IN THOSE SORTS OF PLACES, BUT SOMETIMES IT'S GOOD...
chat-ting and eat-ing...
...
YES, I HAVE BEEN TO ONE.
EH?
NO WAY...!
...
IT WAS JUST A COUPLE MONTHS AGO...

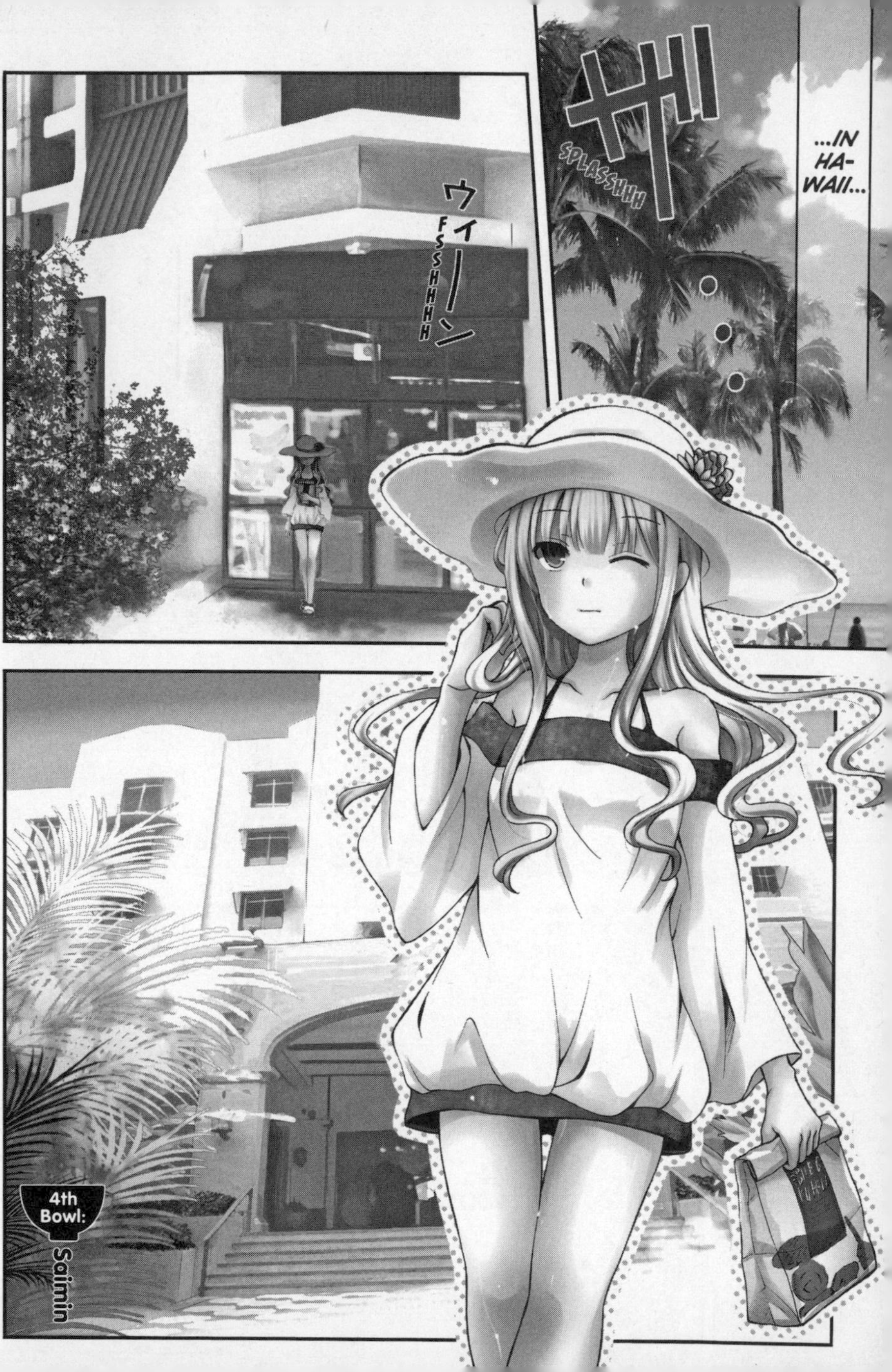
SPLASSHHH
...IN HA-WAII...
ウィーーン
FSSHHHH
4th Bowl:
Saimin

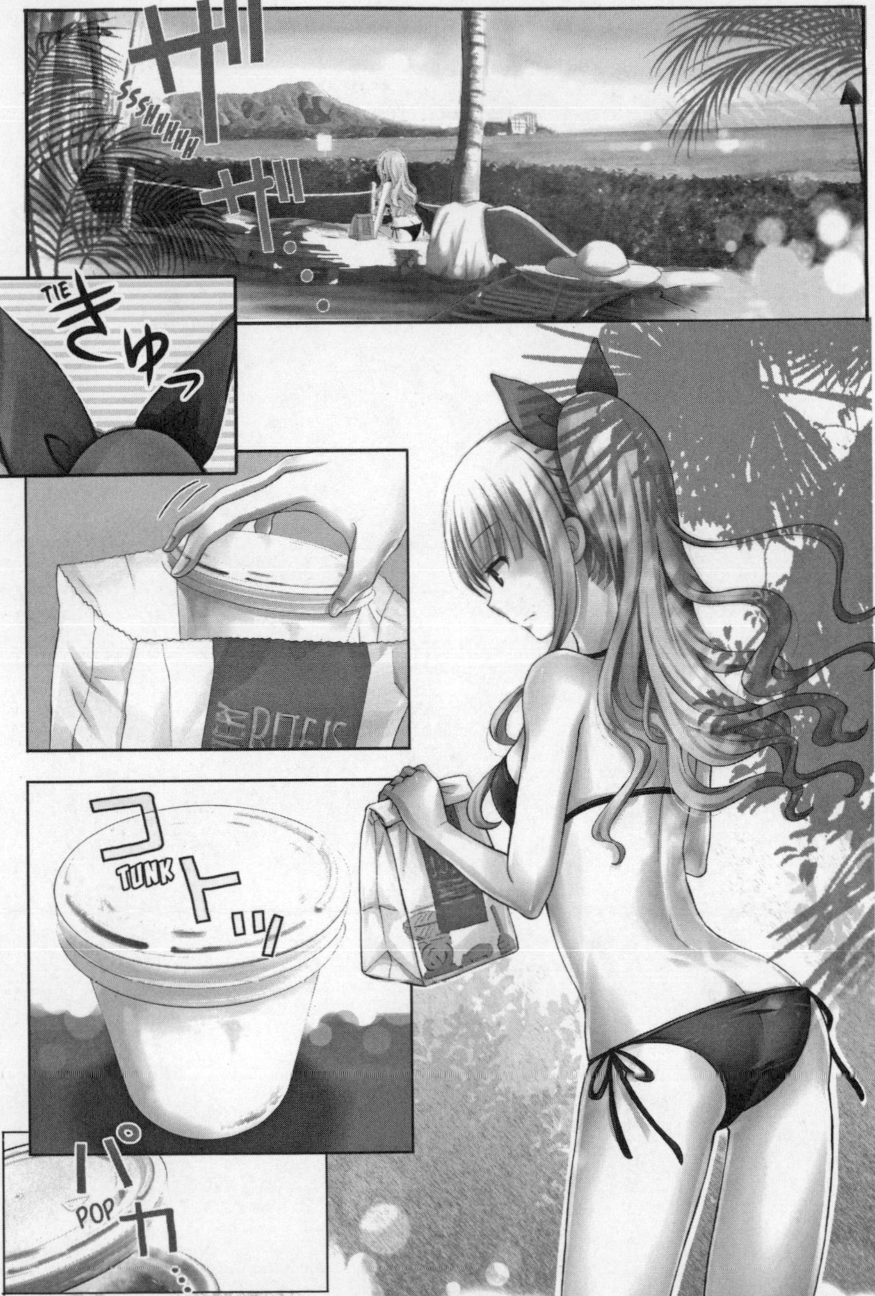

ザ
SSSHHHHH
ザ
きゅっ
TIE
コトッ
TUNK
パカ
POP

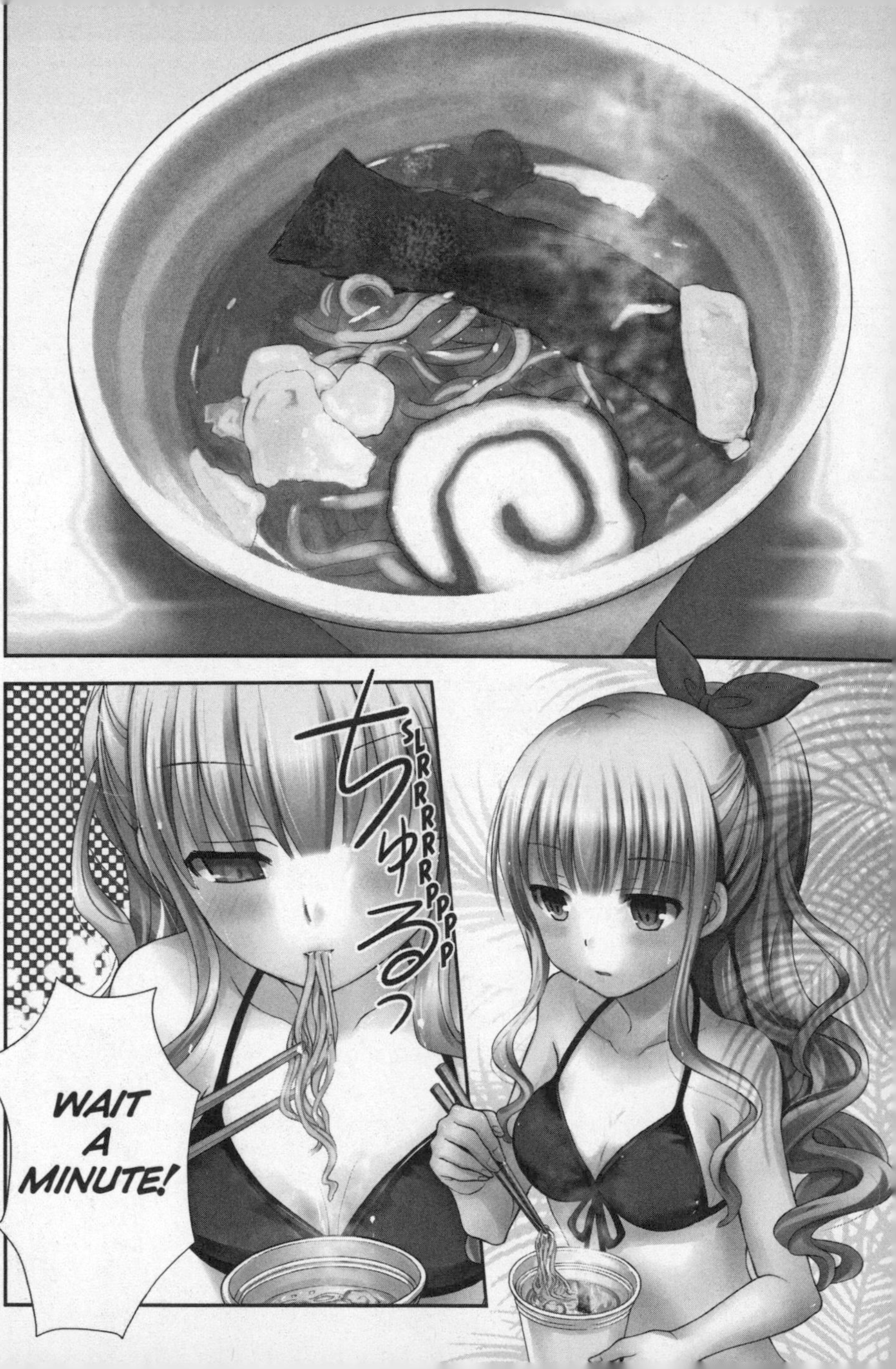
ちゅるっ
SLRRRRRPPPP
WAIT A MINUTE!

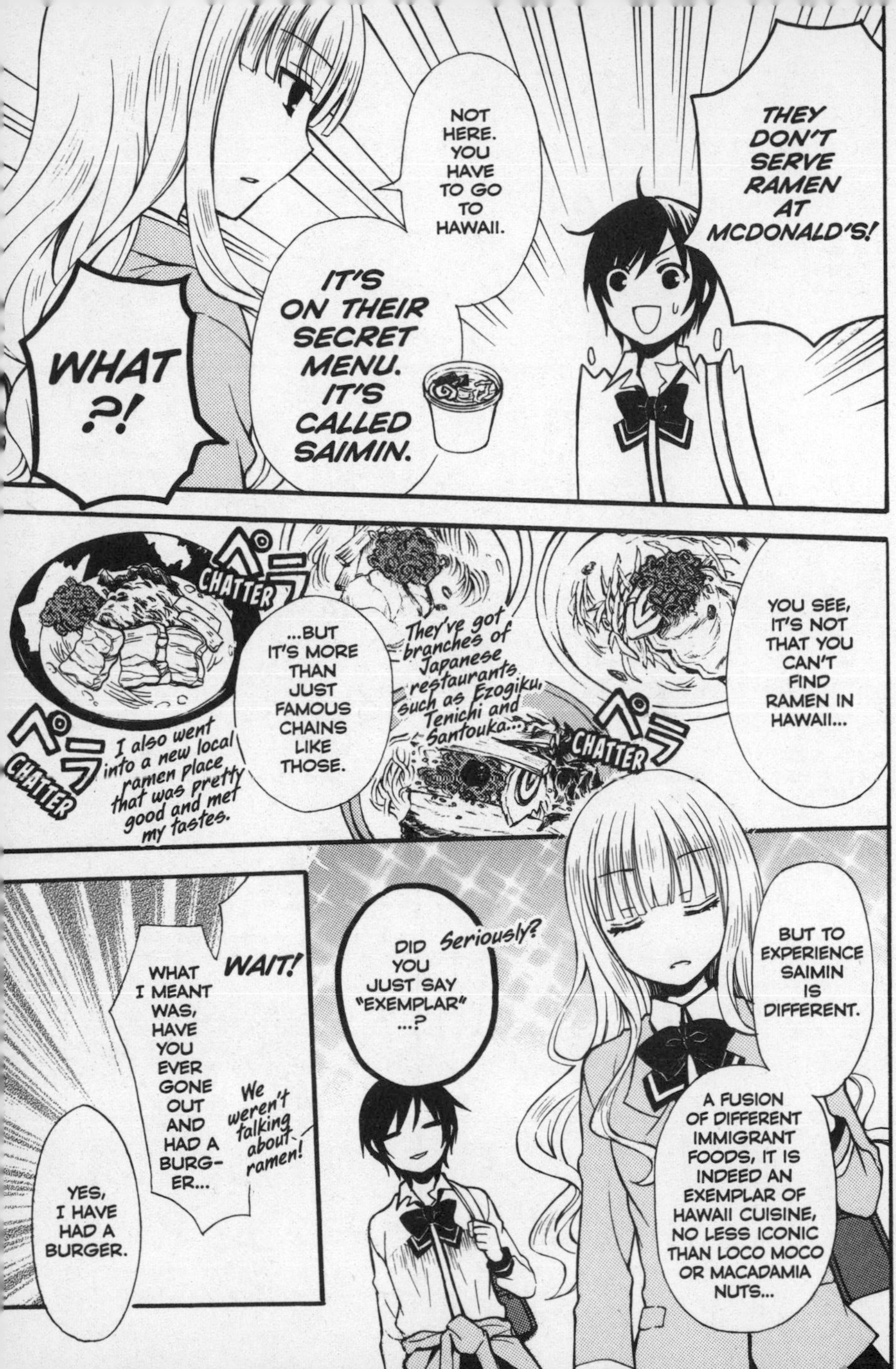
THEY DON'T SERVE RAMEN AT MCDONALD'S!
NOT HERE. YOU HAVE TO GO TO HAWAII.
IT'S ON THEIR SECRET MENU. IT'S CALLED SAIMIN.
WHAT?!
YOU SEE, IT'S NOT THAT YOU CAN'T FIND RAMEN IN HAWAII...
CHATTER
They've got branches of Japanese restaurants such as Ezogiku, Tenichi and Santouka...
CHATTER
...BUT IT'S MORE THAN JUST FAMOUS CHAINS LIKE THOSE.
I also went into a new local ramen place that was pretty good and met my tastes.
CHATTER
BUT TO EXPERIENCE SAIMIN IS DIFFERENT.
A FUSION OF DIFFERENT IMMIGRANT FOODS, IT IS INDEED AN EXEMPLAR OF HAWAII CUISINE, NO LESS ICONIC THAN LOCO MOCO OR MACADAMIA NUTS...
DID YOU JUST SAY "EXEMPLAR" ...?
Seriously?
WAIT!
WHAT I MEANT WAS, HAVE YOU EVER GONE OUT AND HAD A BURGER-ER...
We weren't talking about ramen!
YES, I HAVE HAD A BURGER.

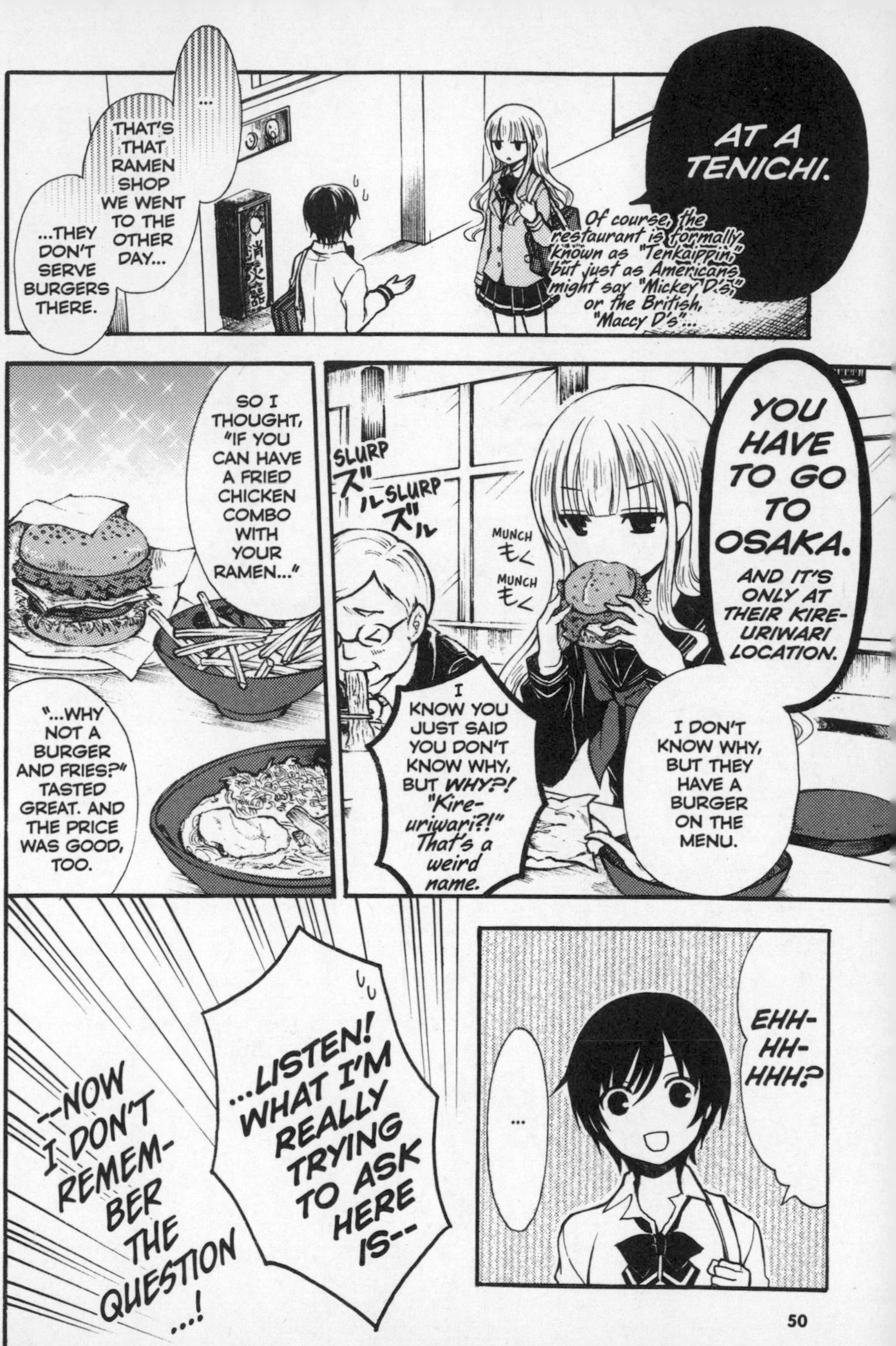
AT A TENICHI.
Of course, the restaurant is formally known as "Tenkaippin," but just as Americans might say "Mickey D's," or the British, "Maccy D's"...
...
THAT'S THAT RAMEN SHOP WE WENT TO THE OTHER DAY...
...THEY DON'T SERVE BURGERS THERE.
YOU HAVE TO GO TO OSAKA.
AND IT'S ONLY AT THEIR KIRE-URIWARI LOCATION.
MUNCH もく
MUNCH もく
I DON'T KNOW WHY, BUT THEY HAVE A BURGER ON THE MENU.
SLURP ズル
SLURP ズル
I KNOW YOU JUST SAID YOU DON'T KNOW WHY, BUT WHY?! "Kire-uriwari?!" That's a weird name.
SO I THOUGHT, "IF YOU CAN HAVE A FRIED CHICKEN COMBO WITH YOUR RAMEN..."
"...WHY NOT A BURGER AND FRIES?" TASTED GREAT. AND THE PRICE WAS GOOD, TOO.
EHH-HH-HHH?
...
...LISTEN! WHAT I'M REALLY TRYING TO ASK HERE IS--
--NOW I DON'T REMEMBER THE QUESTION...!

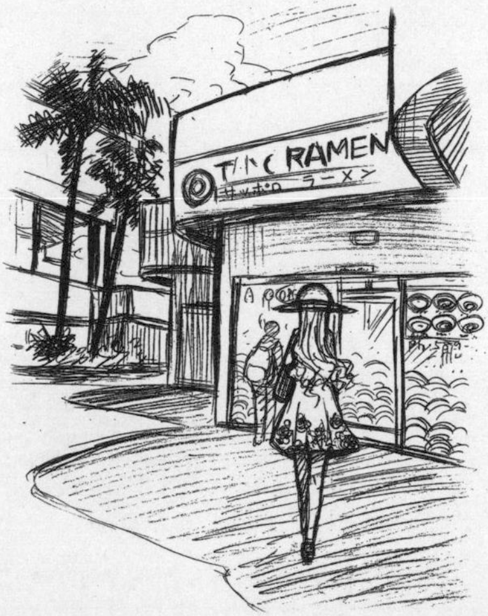
RAMEN
ラーメン

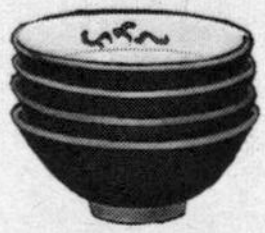
らーめん

Ms. Koizumi loves
ramen noodles

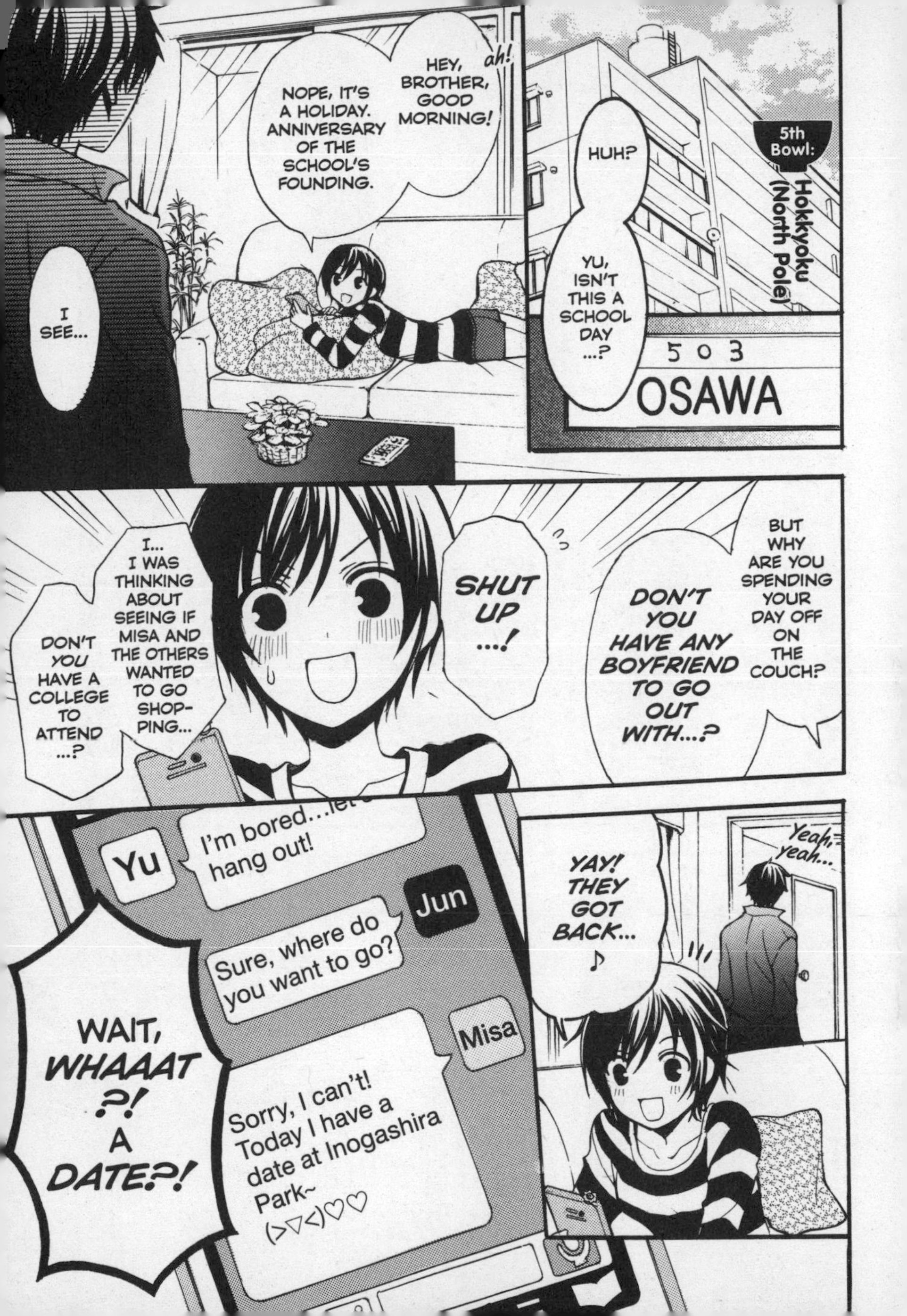
5th Bowl:
Hokkyoku (North Pole)
HUH?
YU, ISN'T THIS A SCHOOL DAY ...?
503
OSAWA
ah!
HEY, BROTHER, GOOD MORNING!
NOPE, IT'S A HOLIDAY. ANNIVERSARY OF THE SCHOOL'S FOUNDING.
I SEE...
BUT WHY ARE YOU SPENDING YOUR DAY OFF ON THE COUCH?
DON'T YOU HAVE ANY BOYFRIEND TO GO OUT WITH...?
SHUT UP ...!
I... I WAS THINKING ABOUT SEEING IF MISA AND THE OTHERS WANTED TO GO SHOP-PING...
DON'T YOU HAVE A COLLEGE TO ATTEND ...?
Yeah, yeah...
YAY! THEY GOT BACK... ♪
Yu
I'm bored...let's hang out!
Jun
Sure, where do you want to go?
Misa
Sorry, I can't! Today I have a date at Inogashira Park~ (>▽<)♡♡
WAIT, WHAAAT?! A DATE?!

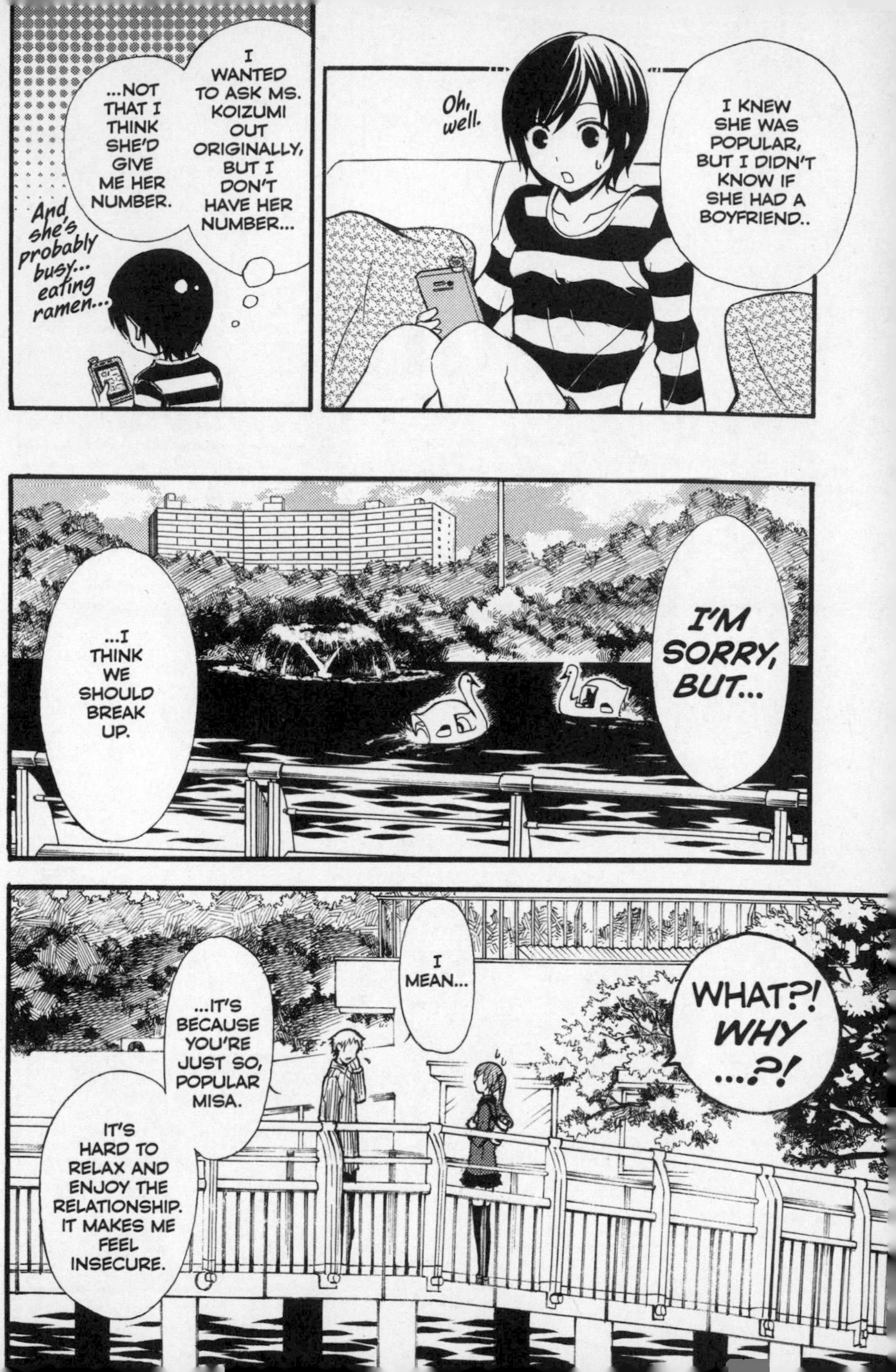
I KNEW SHE WAS POPULAR, BUT I DIDN'T KNOW IF SHE HAD A BOYFRIEND..
Oh, well.
I WANTED TO ASK MS. KOIZUMI OUT ORIGINALLY, BUT I DON'T HAVE HER NUMBER...
...NOT THAT I THINK SHE'D GIVE ME HER NUMBER.
And she's probably busy... eating ramen...
I'M SORRY, BUT...
...I THINK WE SHOULD BREAK UP.
WHAT?! WHY ...?!
I MEAN...
...IT'S BECAUSE YOU'RE JUST SO, POPULAR MISA.
IT'S HARD TO RELAX AND ENJOY THE RELATIONSHIP. IT MAKES ME FEEL INSECURE.

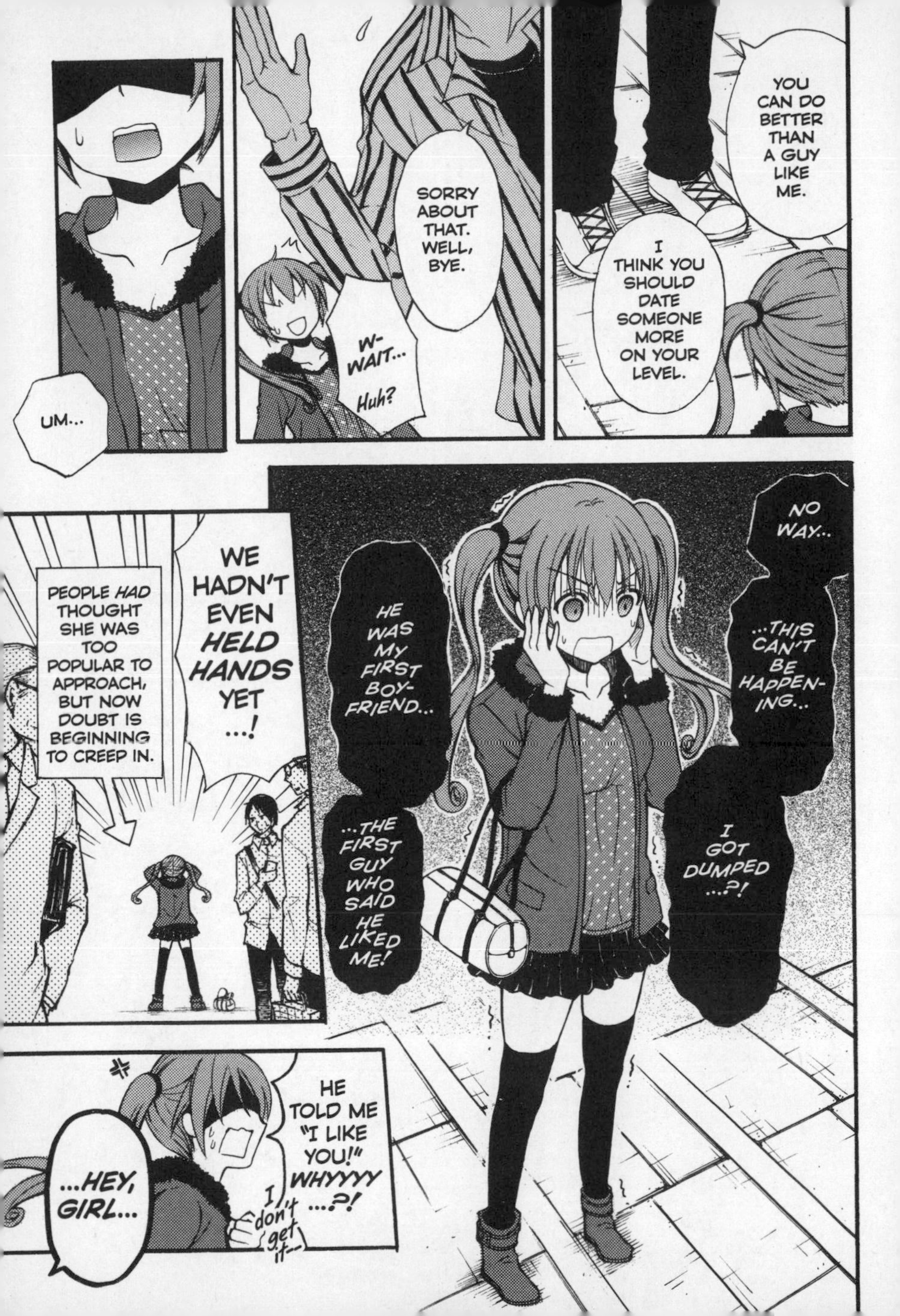
YOU CAN DO BETTER THAN A GUY LIKE ME.
I THINK YOU SHOULD DATE SOMEONE MORE ON YOUR LEVEL.
SORRY ABOUT THAT. WELL, BYE.
W-WAIT...
Huh?
UM...
NO WAY...
...THIS CAN'T BE HAPPENING...
I GOT DUMPED...?!
HE WAS MY FIRST BOY-FRIEND...
...THE FIRST GUY WHO SAID HE LIKED ME!
WE HADN'T EVEN HELD HANDS YET...!
PEOPLE HAD THOUGHT SHE WAS TOO POPULAR TO APPROACH, BUT NOW DOUBT IS BEGINNING TO CREEP IN.
HE TOLD ME "I LIKE YOU!" WHYYYY...?!
I don't get it--
...HEY, GIRL...

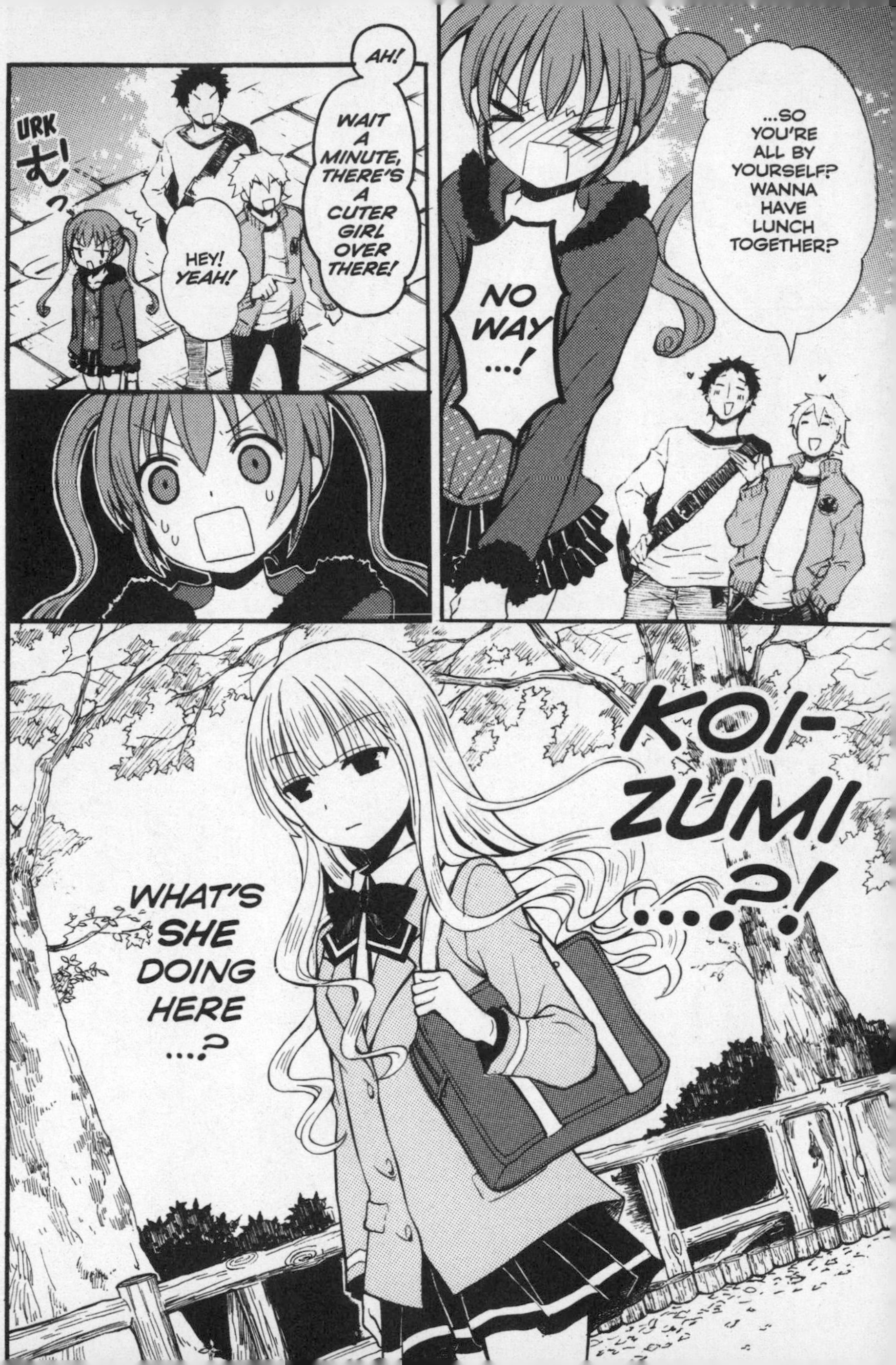
...SO YOU'RE ALL BY YOURSELF? WANNA HAVE LUNCH TOGETHER?
NO WAY ...!
AH!
WAIT A MINUTE, THERE'S A CUTER GIRL OVER THERE!
HEY! YEAH!
URK
むっ
KOI-ZUMI ...?!
WHAT'S SHE DOING HERE ...?

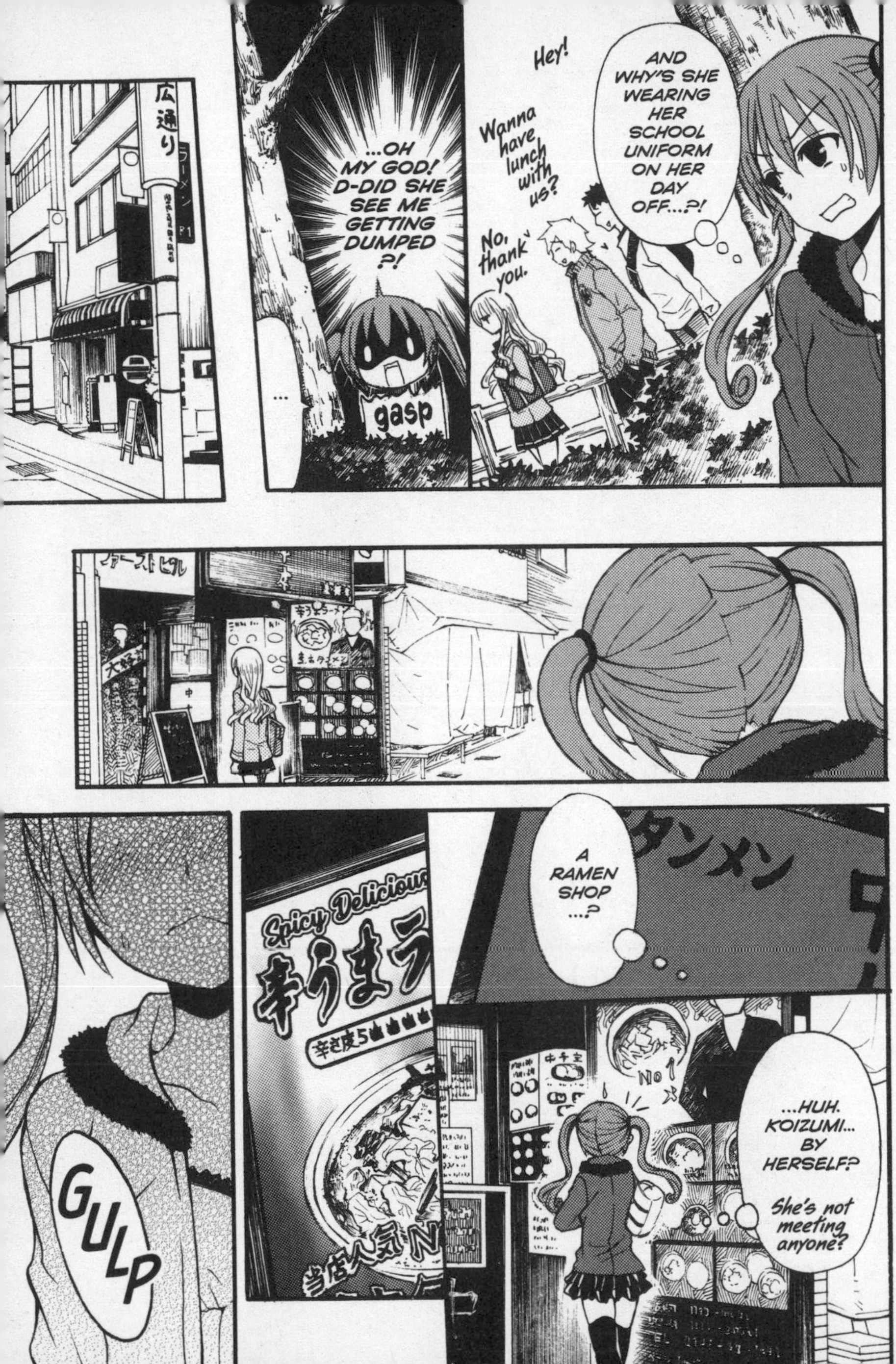
AND WHY'S SHE WEARING HER SCHOOL UNIFORM ON HER DAY OFF...?!
Hey!
Wanna have lunch with us?
No, thank you.
...OH MY GOD! D-DID SHE SEE ME GETTING DUMPED ?!
gasp
...
広通り
ラーメン
ファーストビル
A RAMEN SHOP ...?
タンメン
...HUH. KOIZUMI... BY HERSELF?
She's not meeting anyone?
No 1
Spicy Delicious
幸うまラ
辛さ度5
当店人気N
GULP

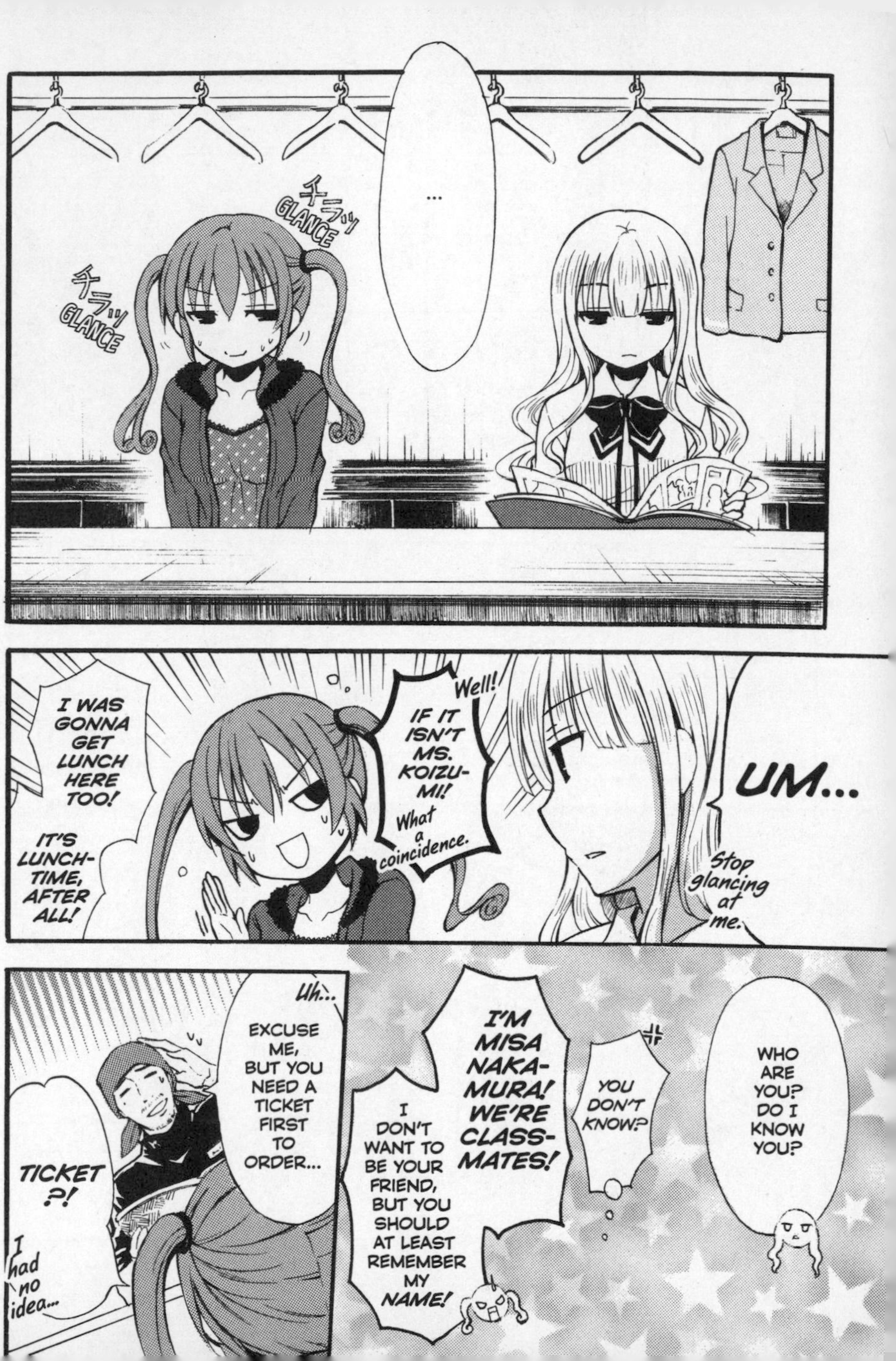
...
チラッ GLANCE
チラッ GLANCE
UM...
Stop glancing at me.
Well! IF IT ISN'T MS. KOIZUMI! What a coincidence.
I WAS GONNA GET LUNCH HERE TOO!
IT'S LUNCH-TIME, AFTER ALL!
WHO ARE YOU? DO I KNOW YOU?
YOU DON'T KNOW?
I'M MISA NAKA-MURA! WE'RE CLASS-MATES!
I DON'T WANT TO BE YOUR FRIEND, BUT YOU SHOULD AT LEAST REMEMBER MY NAME!
Uh...
EXCUSE ME, BUT YOU NEED A TICKET FIRST TO ORDER...
TICKET ?!
I had no idea...

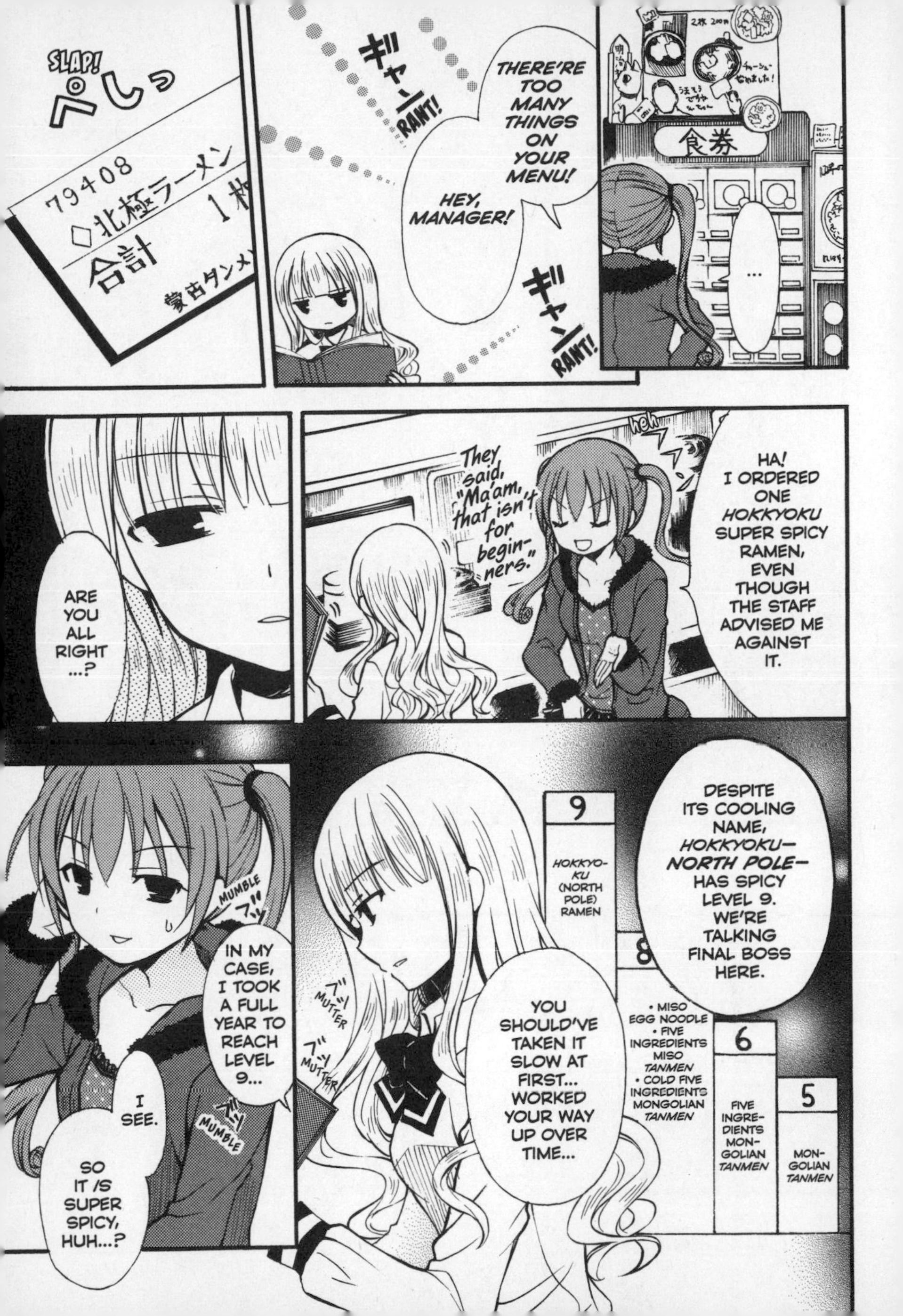
食券
...
THERE'RE TOO MANY THINGS ON YOUR MENU!
ギャン RANT!
HEY, MANAGER!
ギャン RANT!
SLAP! ぺしっ
79408
◇北極ラーメン 1枚
合計
蒙古タンメン
HA! I ORDERED ONE HOKKYOKU SUPER SPICY RAMEN, EVEN THOUGH THE STAFF ADVISED ME AGAINST IT.
heh
They said, "Ma'am, that isn't for beginners."
ARE YOU ALL RIGHT ...?
DESPITE ITS COOLING NAME, HOKKYOKU-NORTH POLE-HAS SPICY LEVEL 9. WE'RE TALKING FINAL BOSS HERE.
9
HOKKYOKU (NORTH POLE) RAMEN
8
• MISO EGG NOODLE • FIVE INGREDIENTS MISO TANMEN • COLD FIVE INGREDIENTS MONGOLIAN TANMEN
6
FIVE INGREDIENTS MONGOLIAN TANMEN
5
MONGOLIAN TANMEN
YOU SHOULD'VE TAKEN IT SLOW AT FIRST... WORKED YOUR WAY UP OVER TIME...
ブツ MUTTER
ブツ MUTTER
MUMBLE ブツ
IN MY CASE, I TOOK A FULL YEAR TO REACH LEVEL 9...
I SEE.
ブツ MUMBLE
SO IT IS SUPER SPICY, HUH...?

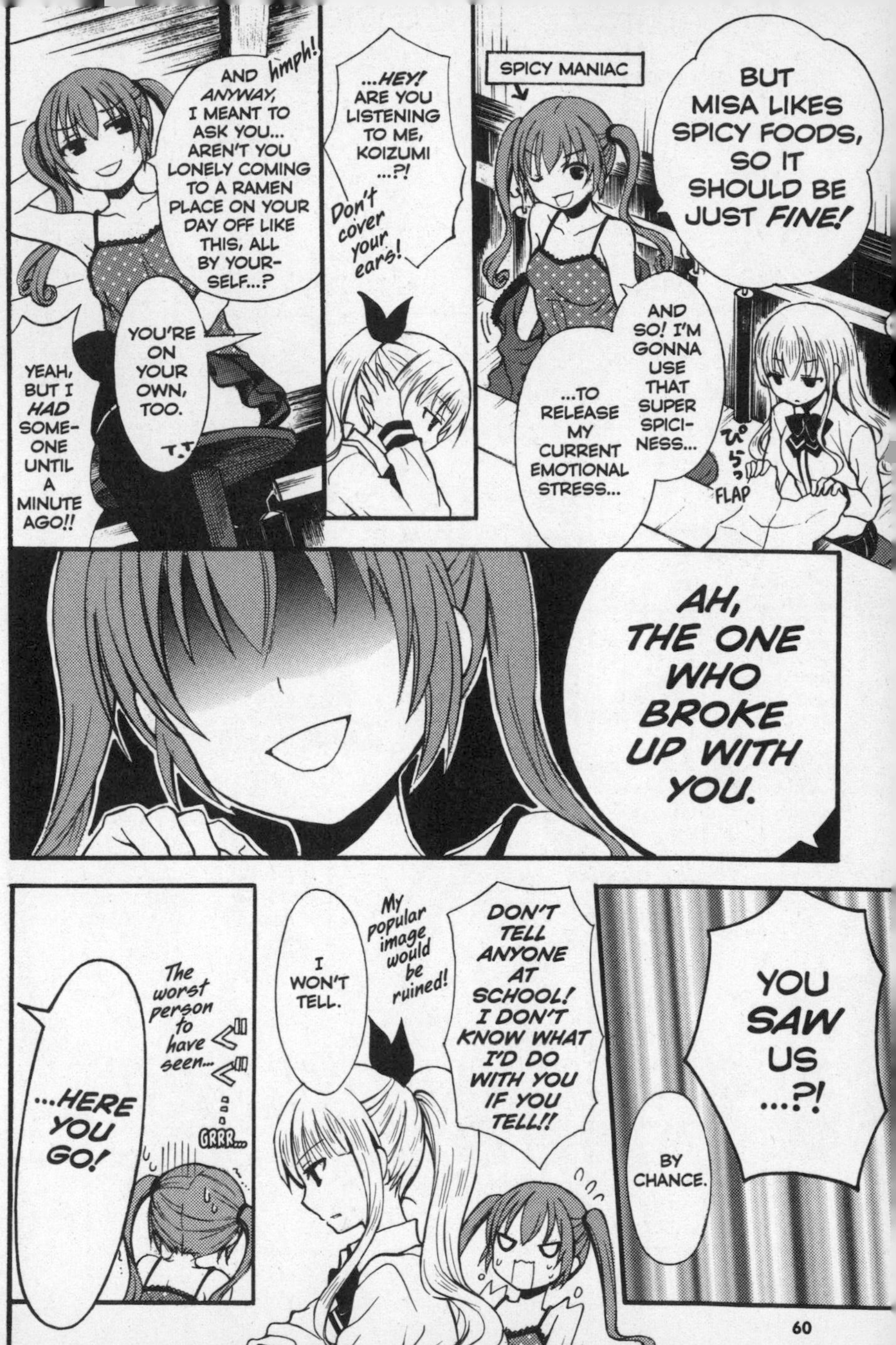
SPICY MANIAC
BUT MISA LIKES SPICY FOODS, SO IT SHOULD BE JUST FINE!
AND SO! I'M GONNA USE THAT SUPER SPICINESS...
...TO RELEASE MY CURRENT EMOTIONAL STRESS...
ぴらっ
FLAP
...HEY! ARE YOU LISTENING TO ME, KOIZUMI ...?!
Don't cover your ears!
hmph!
AND ANYWAY, I MEANT TO ASK YOU... AREN'T YOU LONELY COMING TO A RAMEN PLACE ON YOUR DAY OFF LIKE THIS, ALL BY YOURSELF...?
YOU'RE ON YOUR OWN, TOO.
YEAH, BUT I HAD SOMEONE UNTIL A MINUTE AGO!!
AH, THE ONE WHO BROKE UP WITH YOU.
YOU SAW US ...?!
BY CHANCE.
DON'T TELL ANYONE AT SCHOOL! I DON'T KNOW WHAT I'D DO WITH YOU IF YOU TELL!!
My popular image would be ruined!
I WON'T TELL.
The worst person to have seen...
GRRR...
...HERE YOU GO!

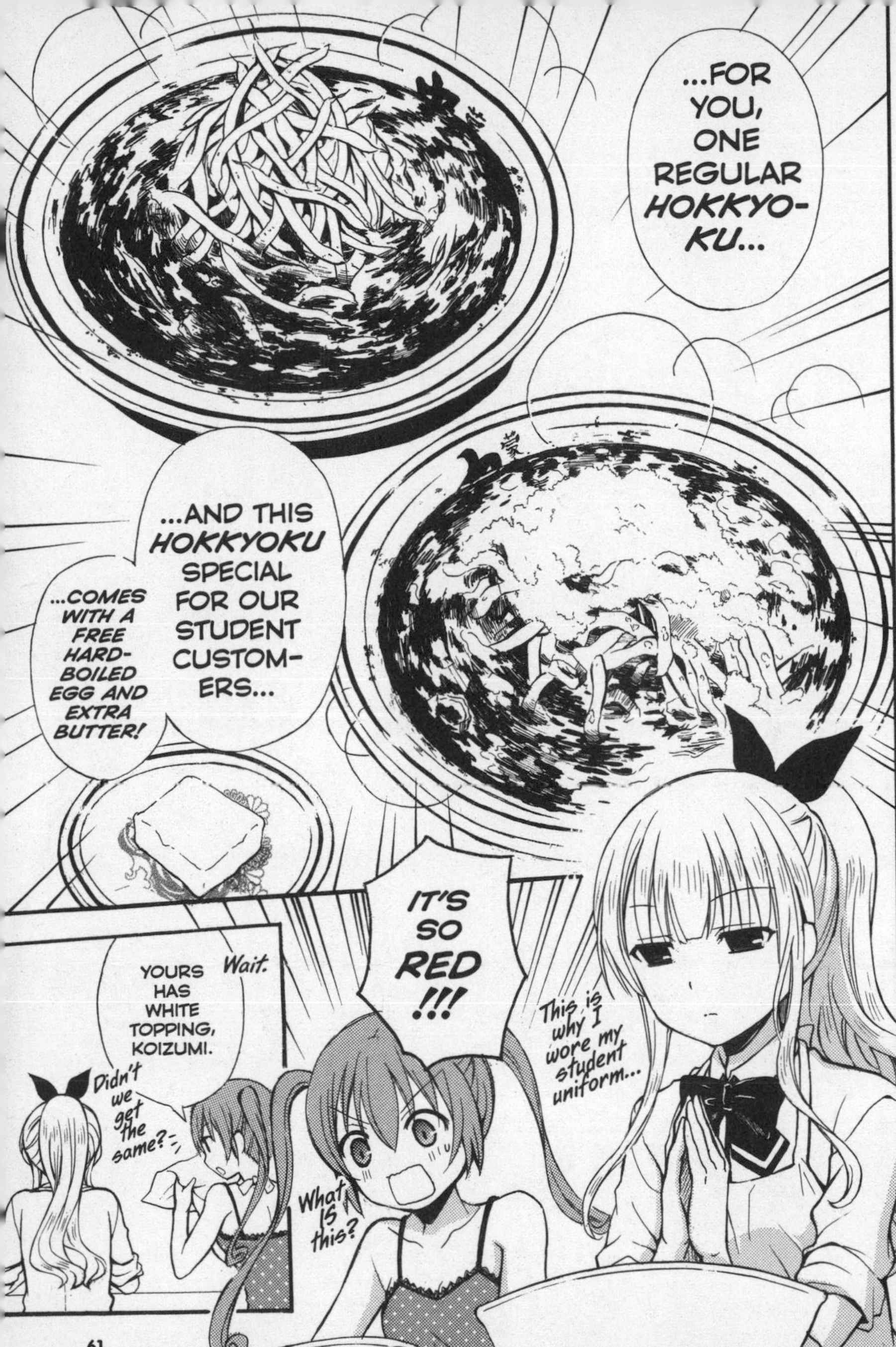
...FOR YOU, ONE REGULAR *HOKKYOKU*...
...AND THIS *HOKKYOKU* SPECIAL FOR OUR STUDENT CUSTOMERS...
...COMES WITH A FREE HARD-BOILED EGG AND EXTRA BUTTER!
IT'S SO RED!!!
This is why I wore my student uniform...
What is this?
Wait.
YOURS HAS WHITE TOPPING, KOIZUMI.
Didn't we get the same?

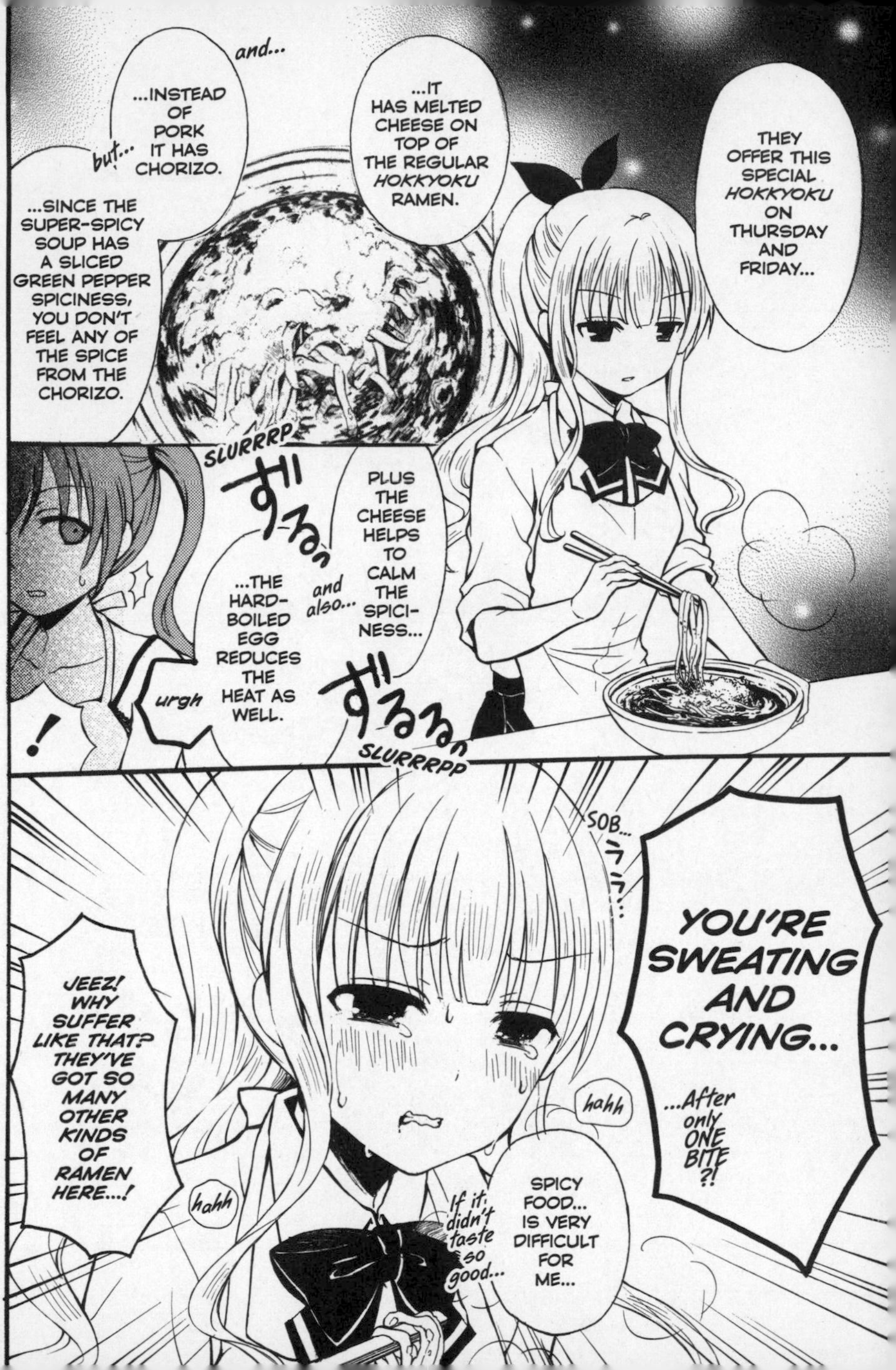
THEY OFFER THIS SPECIAL *HOKKYOKU* ON THURSDAY AND FRIDAY...
...IT HAS MELTED CHEESE ON TOP OF THE REGULAR *HOKKYOKU* RAMEN.
and...
but...
...INSTEAD OF PORK IT HAS CHORIZO.
...SINCE THE SUPER-SPICY SOUP HAS A SLICED GREEN PEPPER SPICINESS, YOU DON'T FEEL ANY OF THE SPICE FROM THE CHORIZO.
SLURRRP
ずるっ
PLUS THE CHEESE HELPS TO CALM THE SPICI-NESS...
and also...
...THE HARD-BOILED EGG REDUCES THE HEAT AS WELL.
ずるるっ
SLURRRPP
urgh
!
YOU'RE SWEATING AND CRYING...
SOB...
...After only ONE BITE?!
hahh
SPICY FOOD... IS VERY DIFFICULT FOR ME...
If it didn't taste so good...
hahh
JEEZ! WHY SUFFER LIKE THAT? THEY'VE GOT SO MANY OTHER KINDS OF RAMEN HERE...!

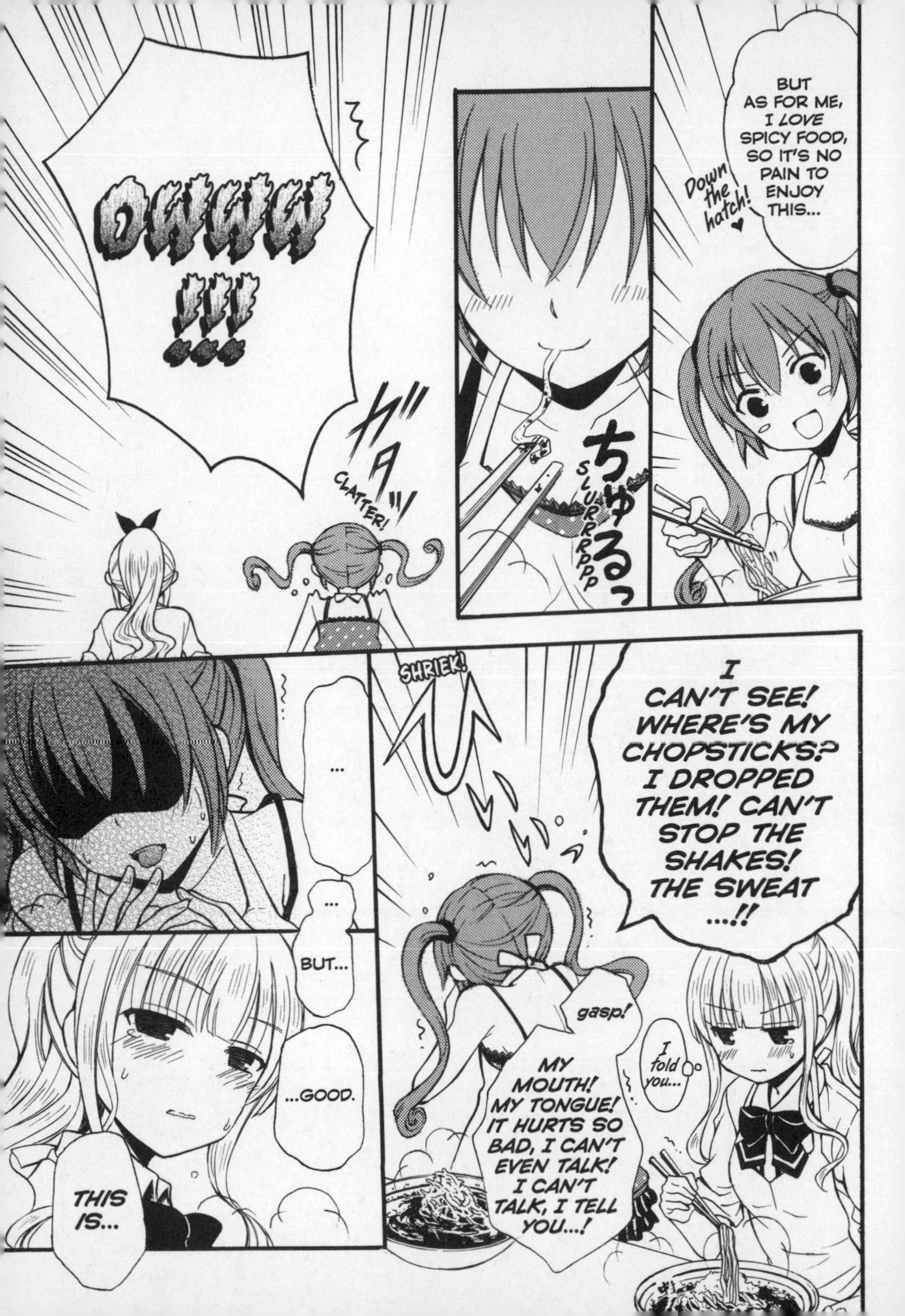
BUT AS FOR ME, I LOVE SPICY FOOD, SO IT'S NO PAIN TO ENJOY THIS...
Down the hatch! ♥
ちゅるっ
SLURRRPPP
OWWW !!!
ガタッ
CLATTER!
SHRIEK!
I CAN'T SEE! WHERE'S MY CHOPSTICKS? I DROPPED THEM! CAN'T STOP THE SHAKES! THE SWEAT ...!!
gasp!
MY MOUTH! MY TONGUE! IT HURTS SO BAD, I CAN'T EVEN TALK! I CAN'T TALK, I TELL YOU...!
I told you...
...
...
BUT...
...GOOD.
THIS IS...

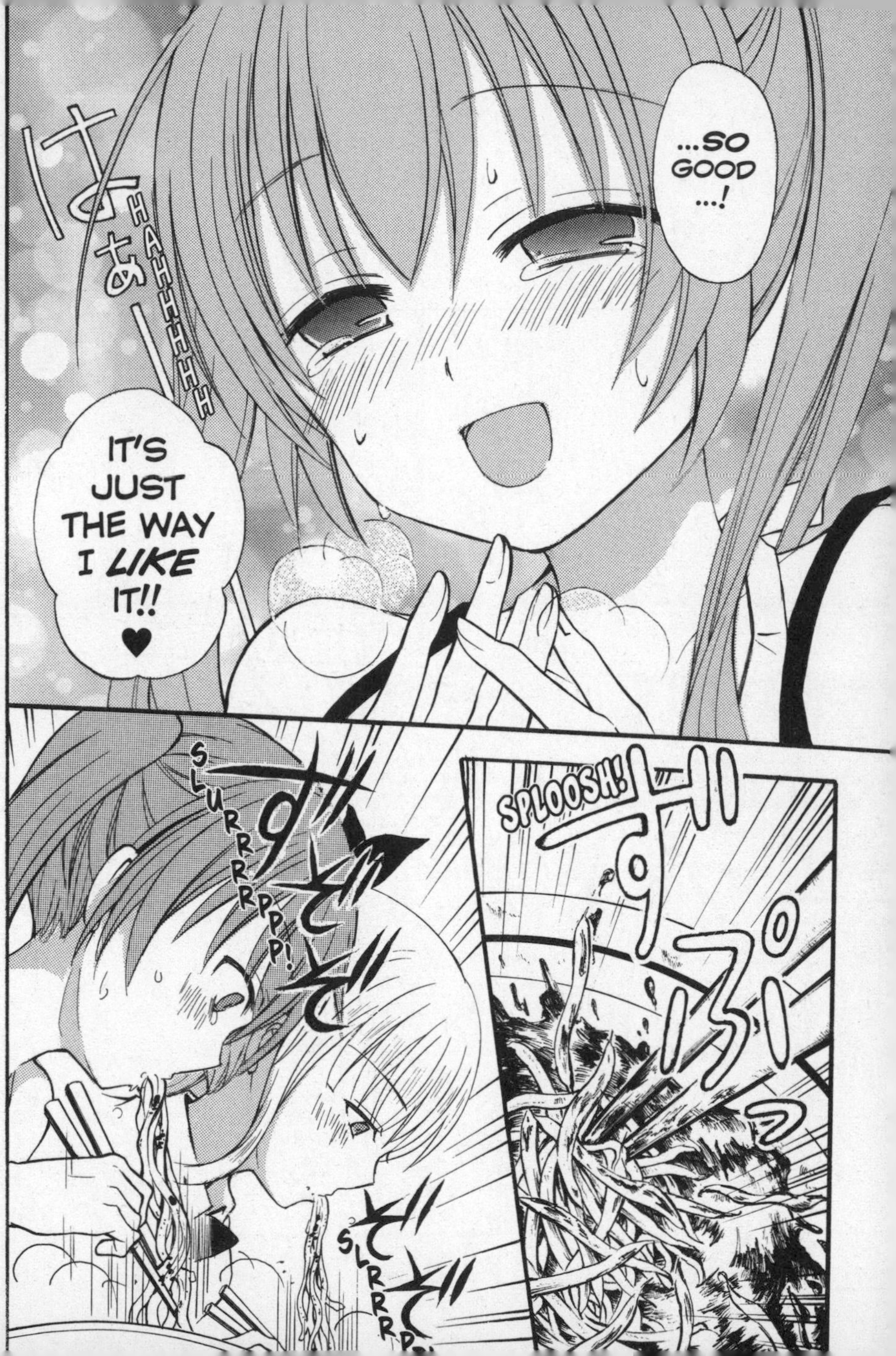
...SO GOOD ...!
はぁー
HAHHHHHHH
IT'S JUST THE WAY I LIKE IT!! ♥
SPLOOSH!
SLURRRRRPPP!
SLRRRR

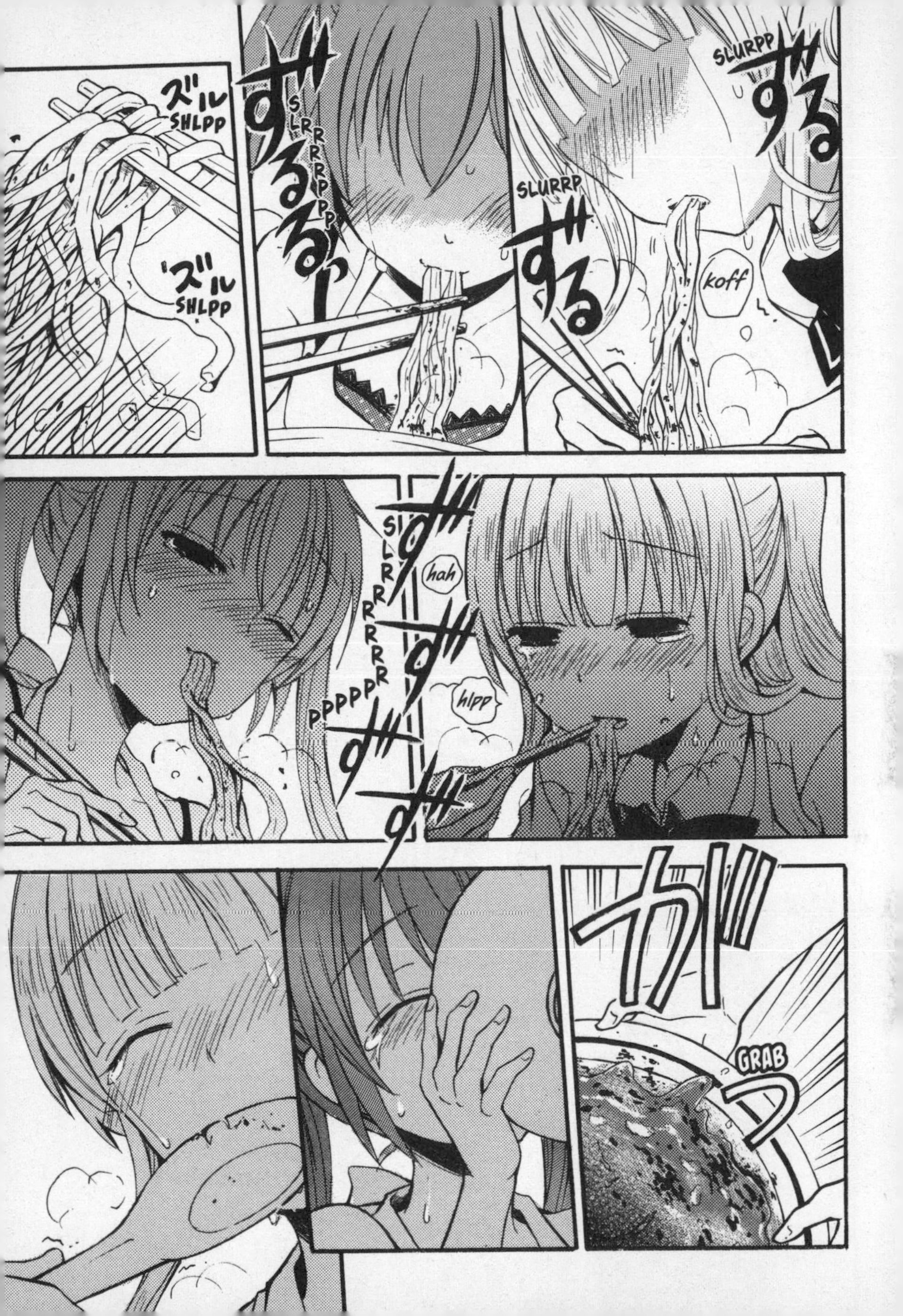
SLURRP
ずる
SLURRP
ずる
koff
ずるるっ
SLRRRRPPP
ズル
SHLPP
ズル
SHLPP
hah
hlpp
ずずず
SLRRRRRRRPPPPP
GRAB
つ

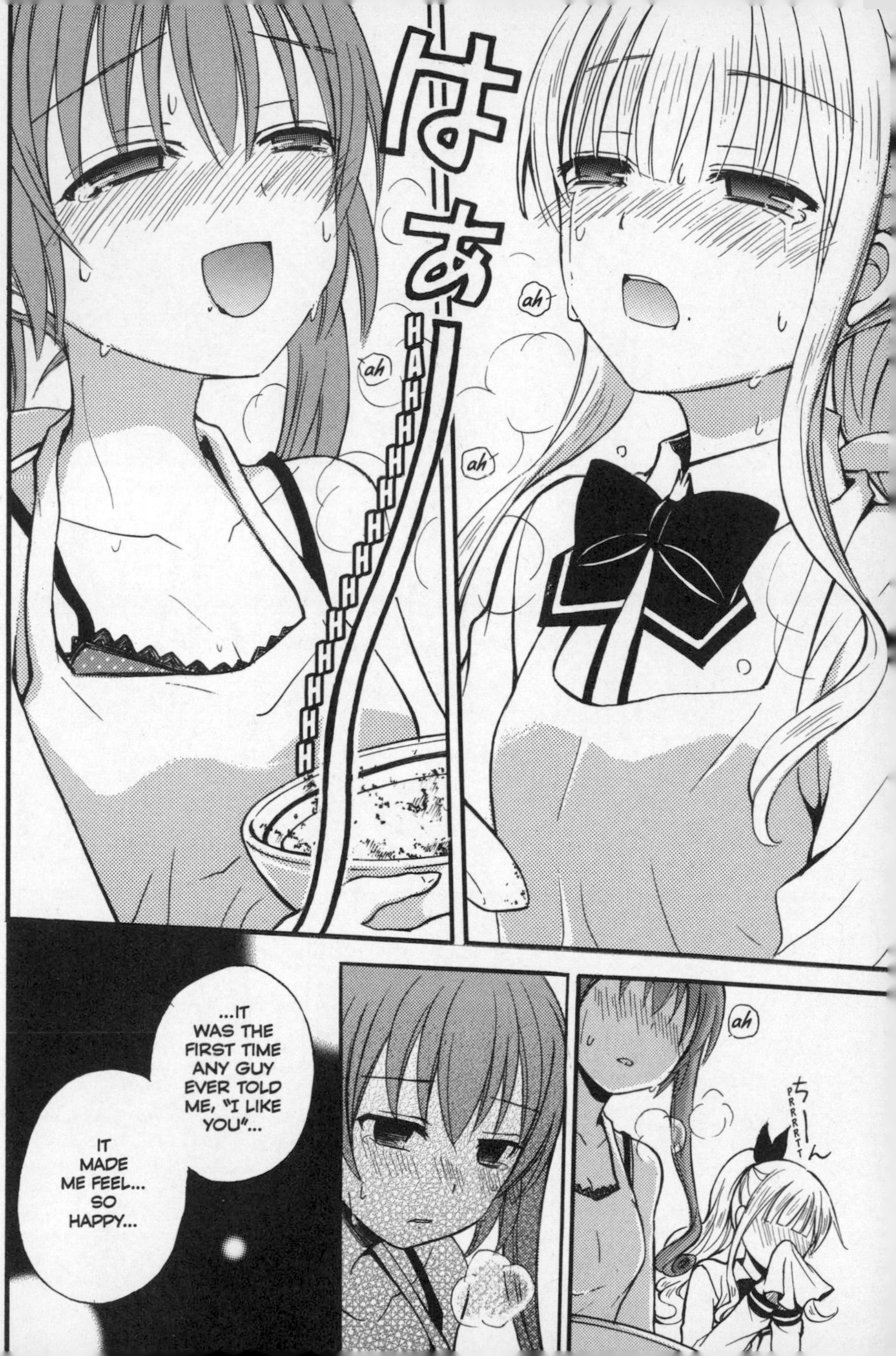

はぁ
HAHHHHHHHHHHHHHHHH
ah
ah
ah
ah
ちーん
PRRRRTT
...IT WAS THE FIRST TIME ANY GUY EVER TOLD ME, "I LIKE YOU"...
IT MADE ME FEEL... SO HAPPY...

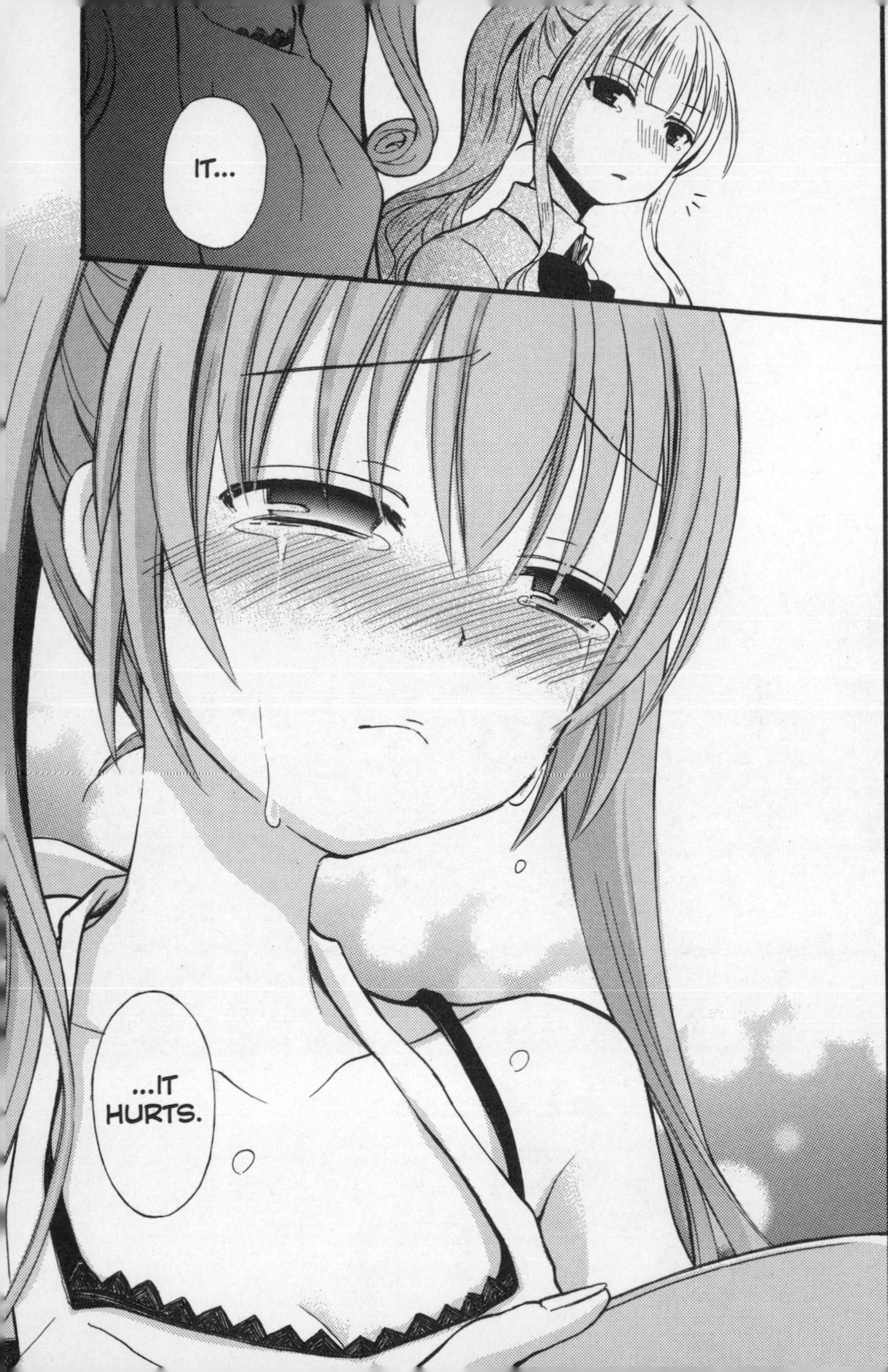
IT...
...IT HURTS.

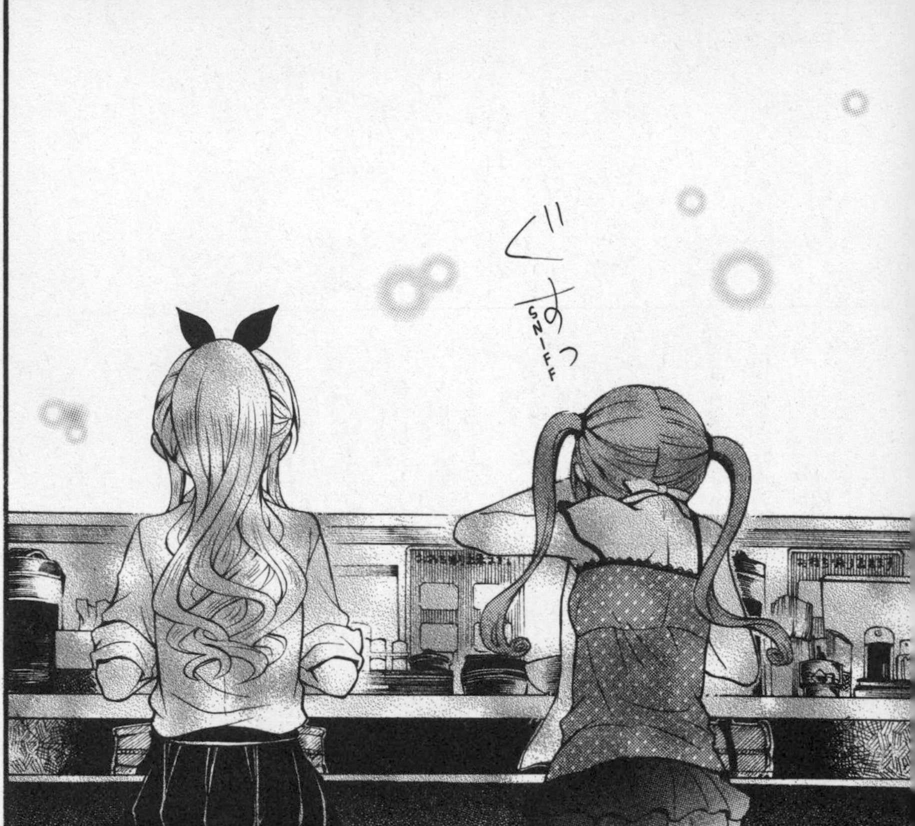
ぐすっ
SNIFF

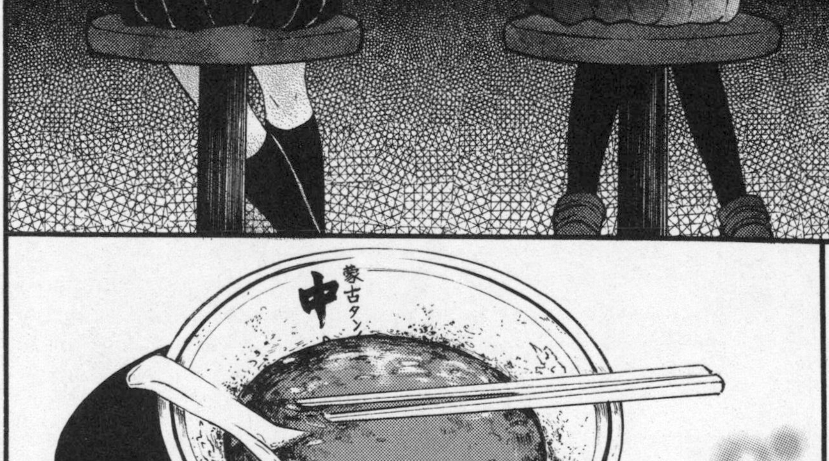
中
蒙古タン

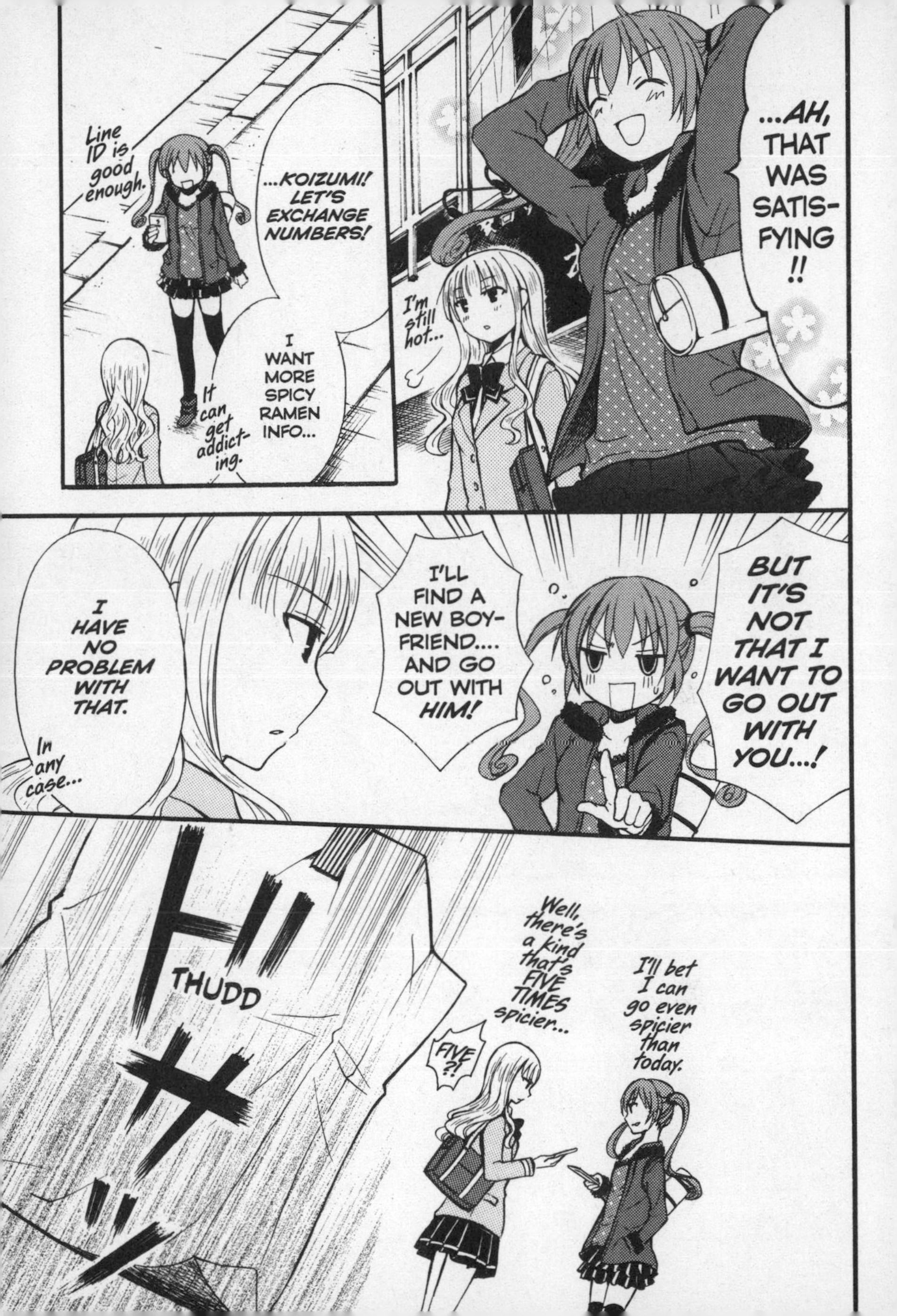
...AH, THAT WAS SATIS-FYING!!
I'm still hot...
...KOIZUMI! LET'S EXCHANGE NUMBERS!
Line ID is good enough.
I WANT MORE SPICY RAMEN INFO...
It can get addict-ing.
BUT IT'S NOT THAT I WANT TO GO OUT WITH YOU...!
I'LL FIND A NEW BOY-FRIEND.... AND GO OUT WITH HIM!
I HAVE NO PROBLEM WITH THAT.
In any case...
I'll bet I can go even spicier than today.
Well, there's a kind that's FIVE TIMES spicier...
FIVE?!
THUDD

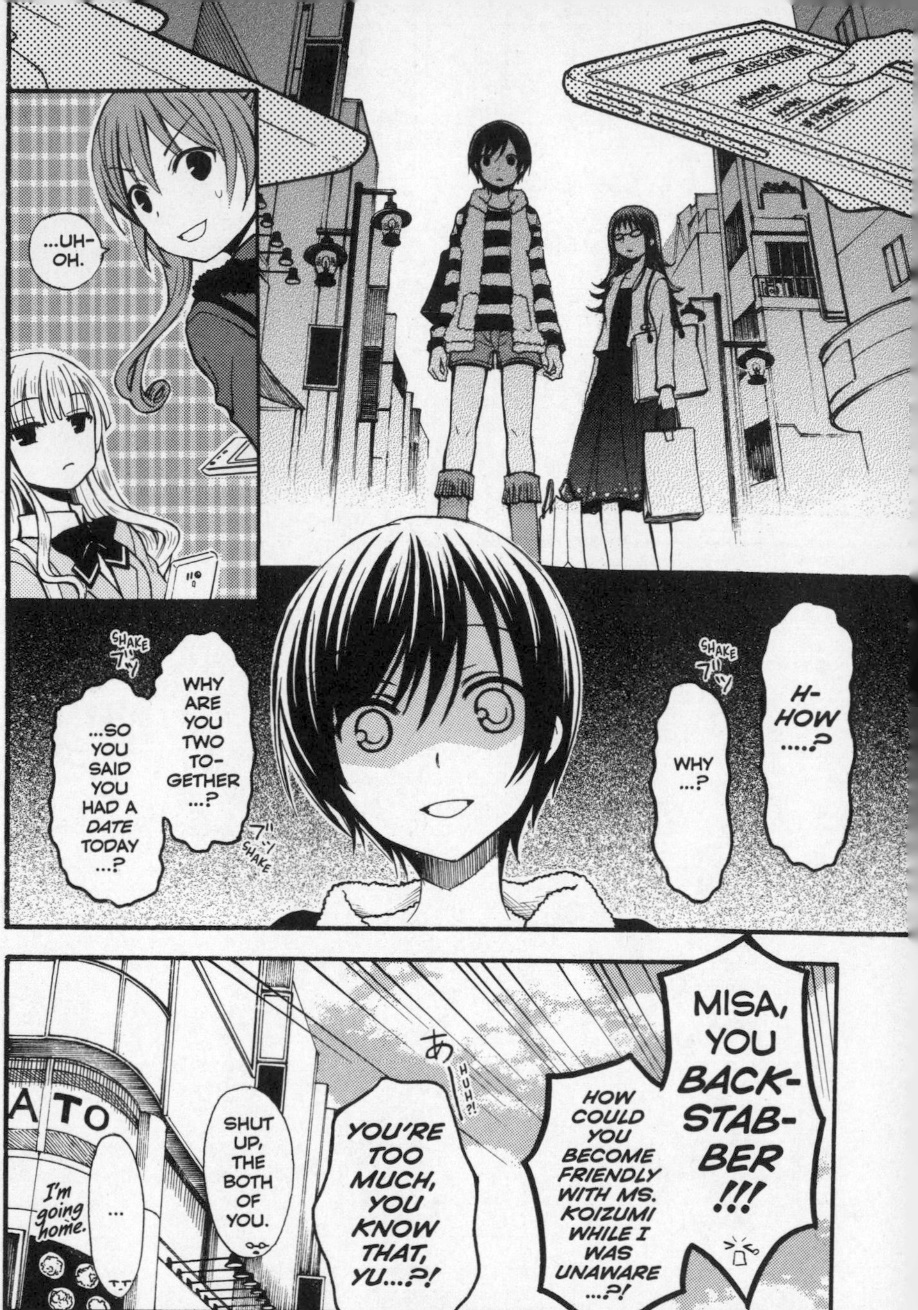
...UH-OH.
SHAKE
H-HOW ....?
WHY ...?
SHAKE
WHY ARE YOU TWO TO-GETHER ...?
...SO YOU SAID YOU HAD A DATE TODAY ...?
SHAKE
MISA, YOU BACK-STAB-BER !!!
HOW COULD YOU BECOME FRIENDLY WITH MS. KOIZUMI WHILE I WAS UNAWARE ...?!
HUH?!
YOU'RE TOO MUCH, YOU KNOW THAT, YU...?!
SHUT UP, THE BOTH OF YOU.
...
I'm going home.
ATO

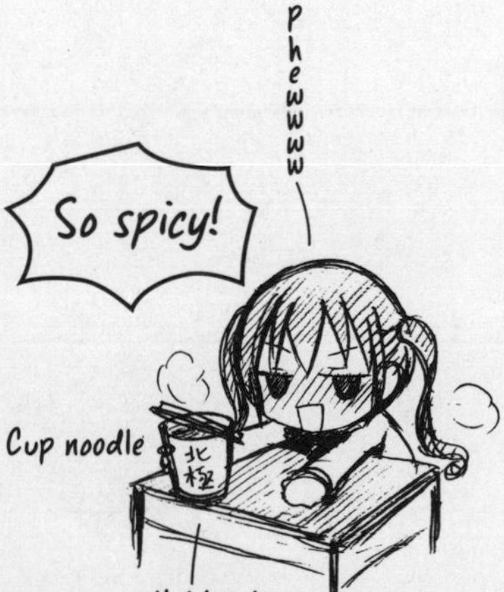
Phewwww
So spicy!
Cup noodle
北極
Hokkyoku

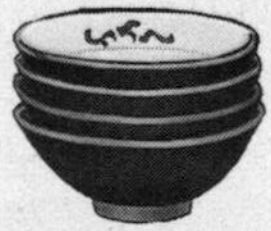

Ms. Koizumi loves
ramen noodles

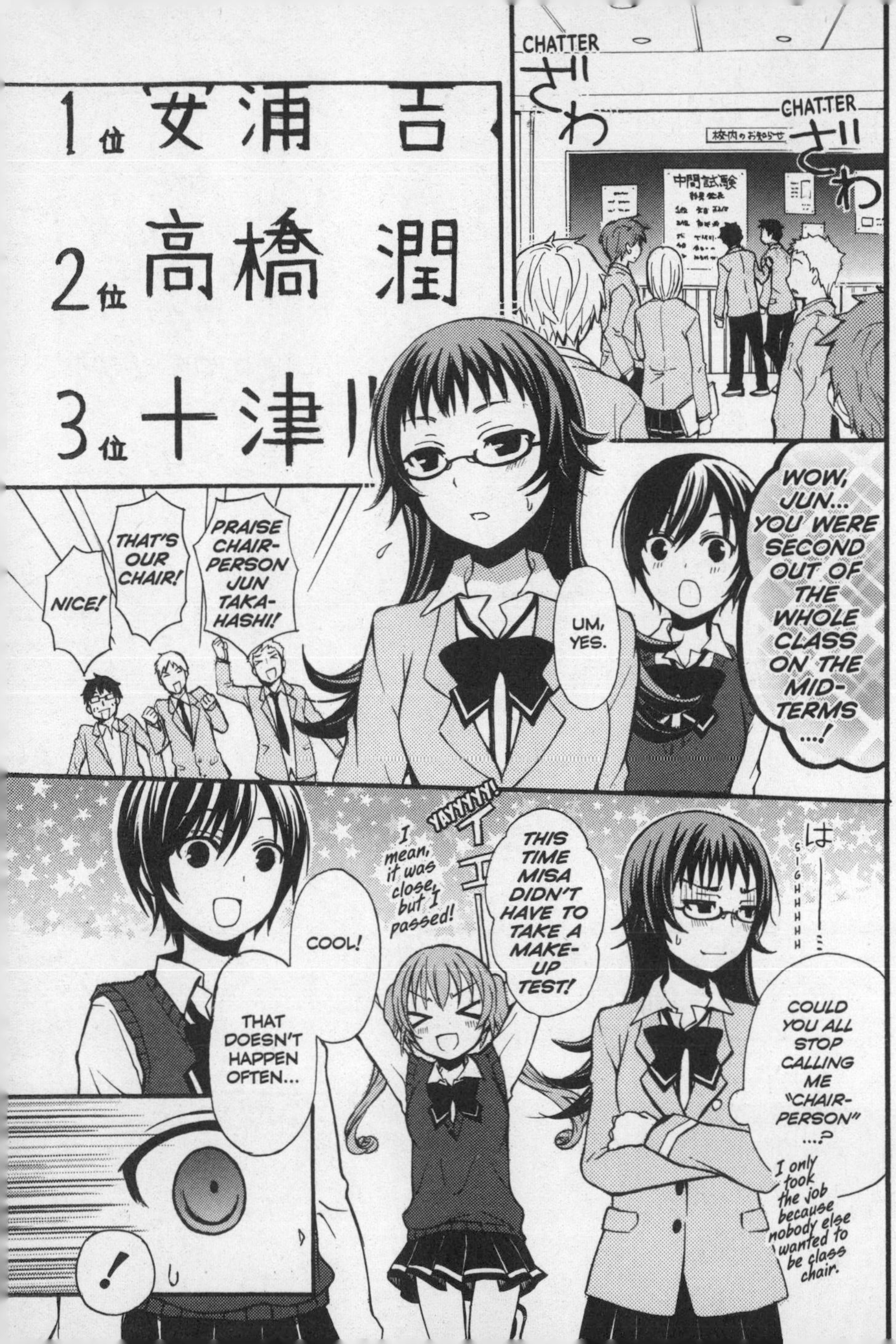
CHATTER
ざわ
CHATTER
ざわ
校内のお知らせ
中間試験
1位 安浦 吾
2位 高橋 潤
3位 十津
WOW, JUN... YOU WERE SECOND OUT OF THE WHOLE CLASS ON THE MID-TERMS...!
UM, YES.
PRAISE CHAIR-PERSON JUN TAKA-HASHI!
THAT'S OUR CHAIR!
NICE!
YAYYYYY!
THIS TIME MISA DIDN'T HAVE TO TAKE A MAKE-UP TEST!
I mean, it was close, but I passed!
COOL!
THAT DOESN'T HAPPEN OFTEN...
SIGHHHHH
COULD YOU ALL STOP CALLING ME "CHAIR-PERSON" ...?
I only took the job because nobody else wanted to be class chair.
!

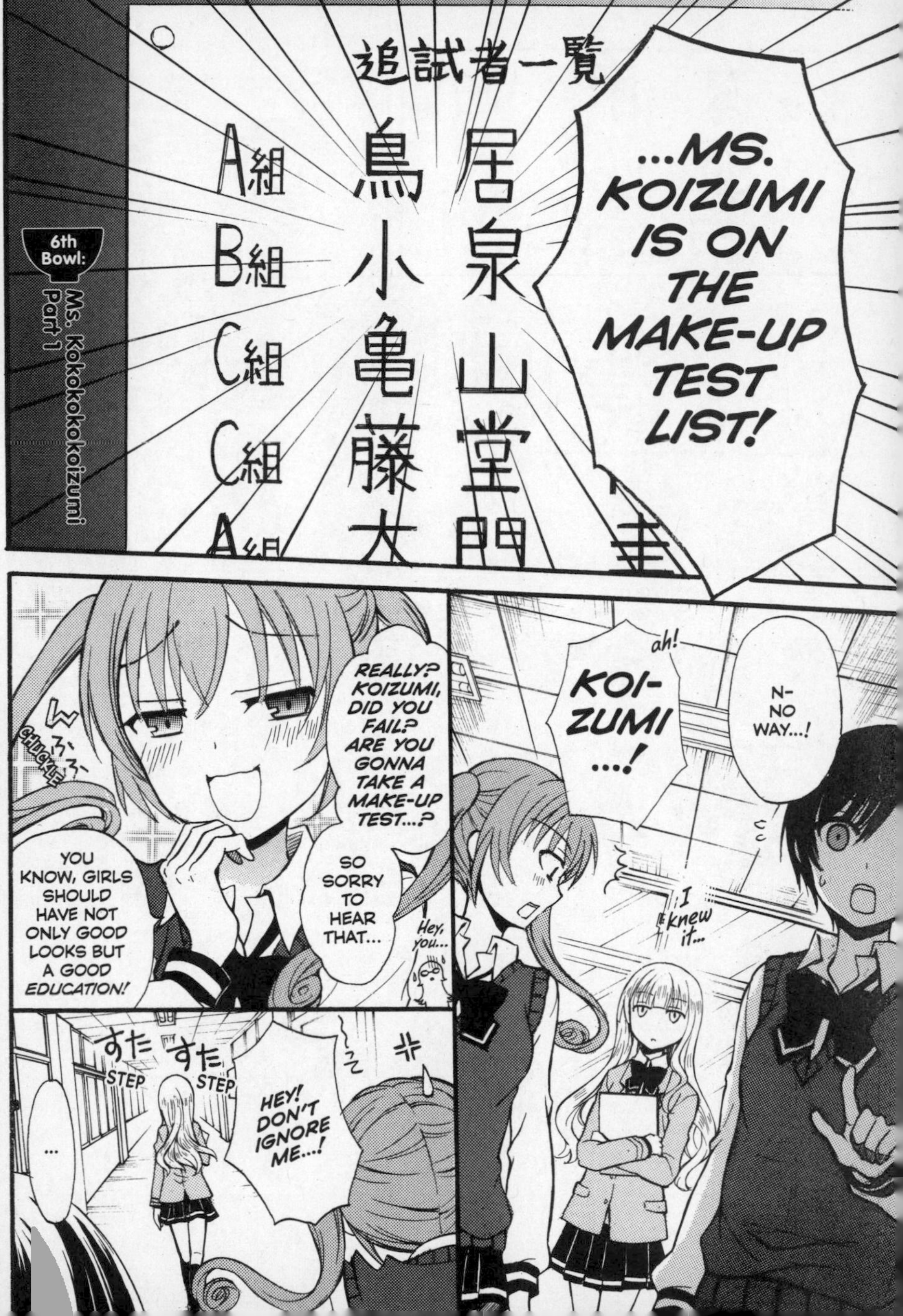
6th Bowl: Ms. Kokokokokoizumi Part 1
追試者一覧
A組 鳥居
B組 小泉
C組 亀山
C組 藤堂
...MS. KOIZUMI IS ON THE MAKE-UP TEST LIST!
N-NO WAY...!
ah!
KOI-ZUMI...!
I knew it...
REALLY? KOIZUMI, DID YOU FAIL? ARE YOU GONNA TAKE A MAKE-UP TEST...?
ふふ CHUCKLE
SO SORRY TO HEAR THAT...
YOU KNOW, GIRLS SHOULD HAVE NOT ONLY GOOD LOOKS BUT A GOOD EDUCATION!
Hey, you...
HEY! DON'T IGNORE ME...!
すた すた STEP STEP
...

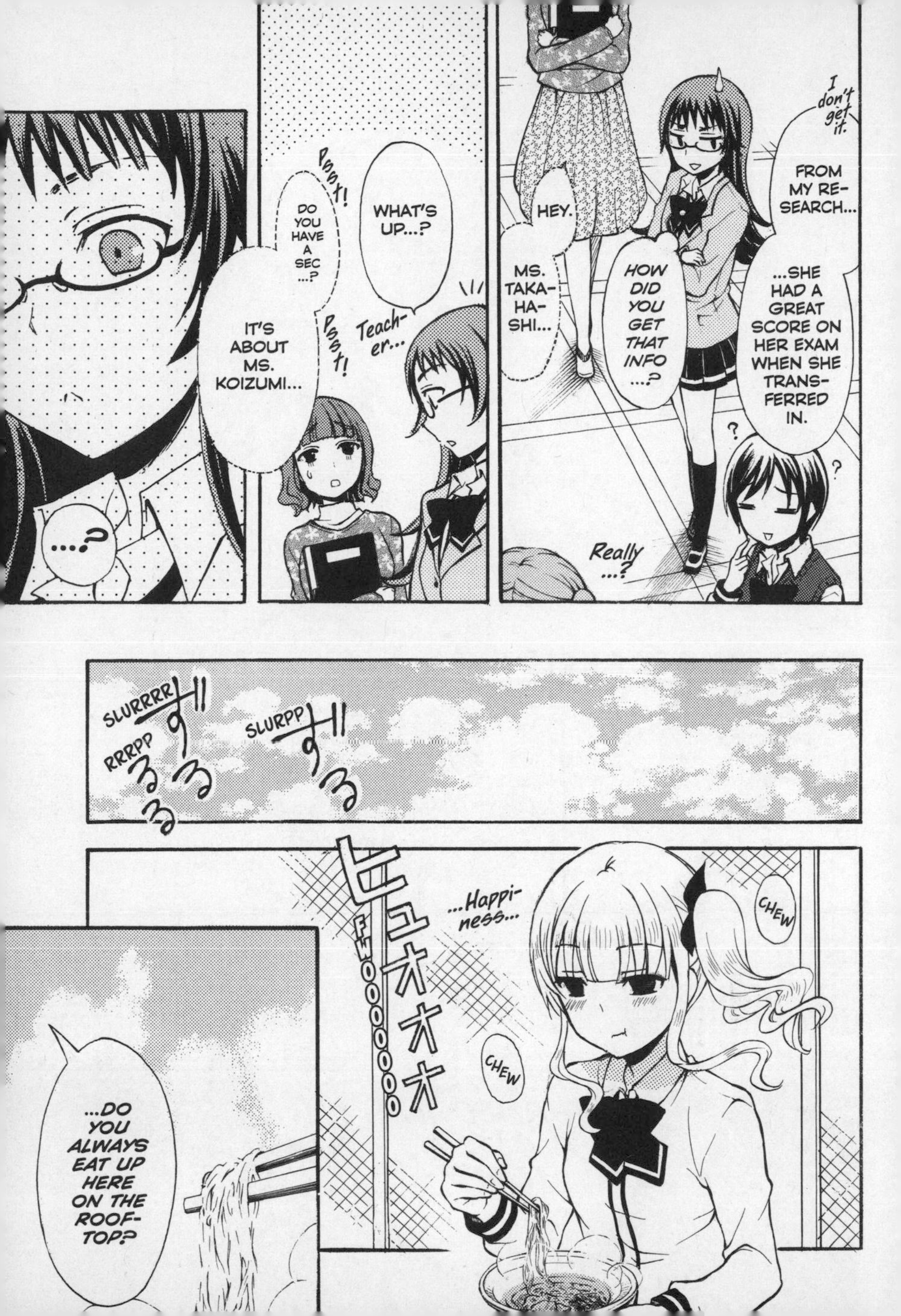
I don't get it.
FROM MY RE-SEARCH...
...SHE HAD A GREAT SCORE ON HER EXAM WHEN SHE TRANS-FERRED IN.
HEY.
HOW DID YOU GET THAT INFO ...?
MS. TAKA-HA-SHI...
?
?
Really ...?
Teach-er...
WHAT'S UP...?
Pssst!
DO YOU HAVE A SEC ...?
Pssst!
IT'S ABOUT MS. KOIZUMI...
...?
SLURPP
SLURRRR
RRRPP
CHEW
...Happi-ness...
FWOOOOOOO
CHEW
...DO YOU ALWAYS EAT UP HERE ON THE ROOF-TOP?

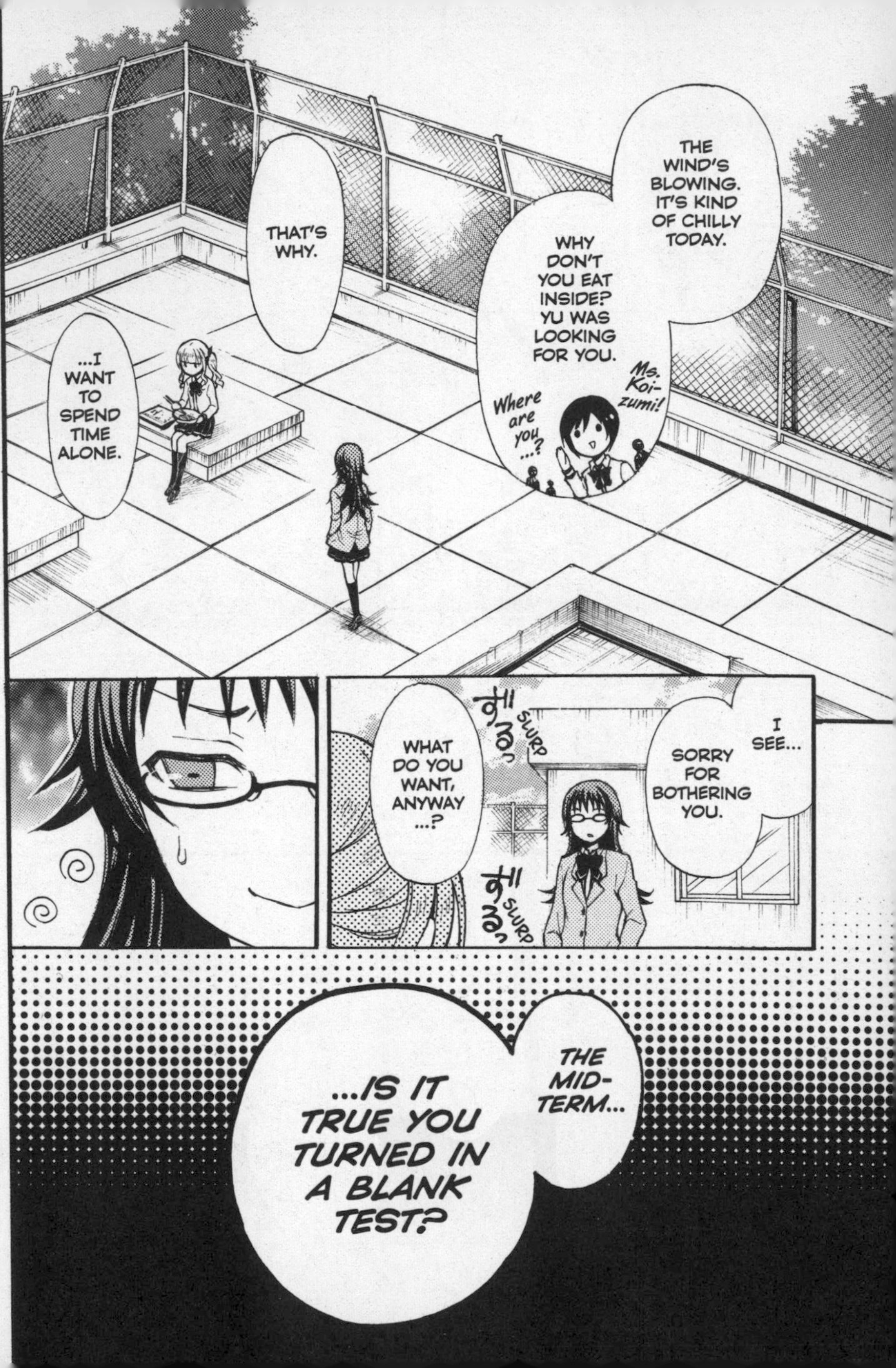
THE WIND'S BLOWING. IT'S KIND OF CHILLY TODAY.
WHY DON'T YOU EAT INSIDE? YU WAS LOOKING FOR YOU.
Ms. Koi-zumi!
Where are you ...?
THAT'S WHY.
...I WANT TO SPEND TIME ALONE.
I SEE...
SORRY FOR BOTHERING YOU.
すする SLURP
WHAT DO YOU WANT, ANYWAY ...?
すする SLURP
THE MID-TERM...
...IS IT TRUE YOU TURNED IN A BLANK TEST?

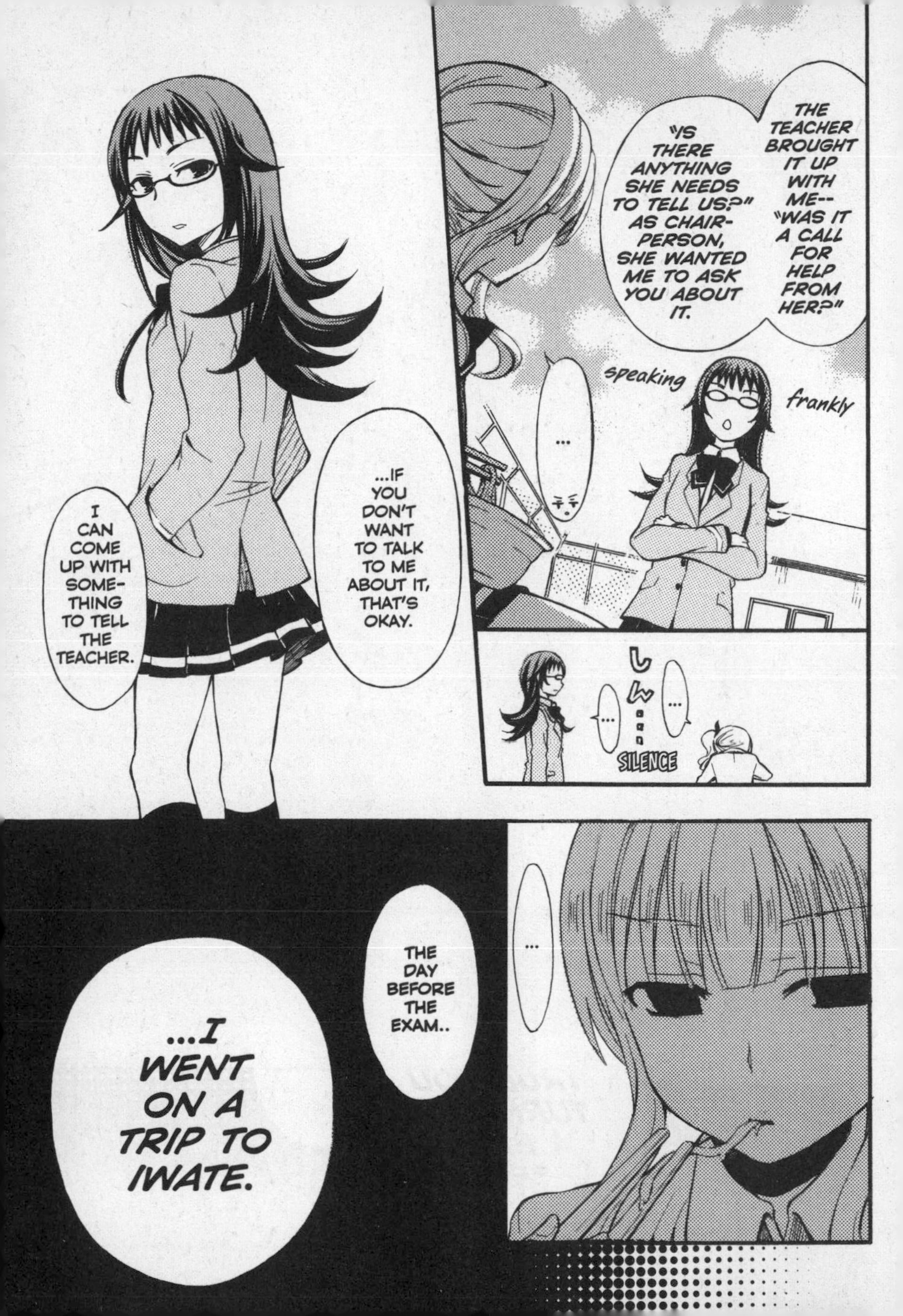

THE TEACHER BROUGHT IT UP WITH ME-- "WAS IT A CALL FOR HELP FROM HER?"
"IS THERE ANYTHING SHE NEEDS TO TELL US?" AS CHAIR-PERSON, SHE WANTED ME TO ASK YOU ABOUT IT.
speaking frankly
...
しん...
SILENCE
...
...
...IF YOU DON'T WANT TO TALK TO ME ABOUT IT, THAT'S OKAY.
I CAN COME UP WITH SOME-THING TO TELL THE TEACHER.
...
THE DAY BEFORE THE EXAM..
...I WENT ON A TRIP TO IWATE.

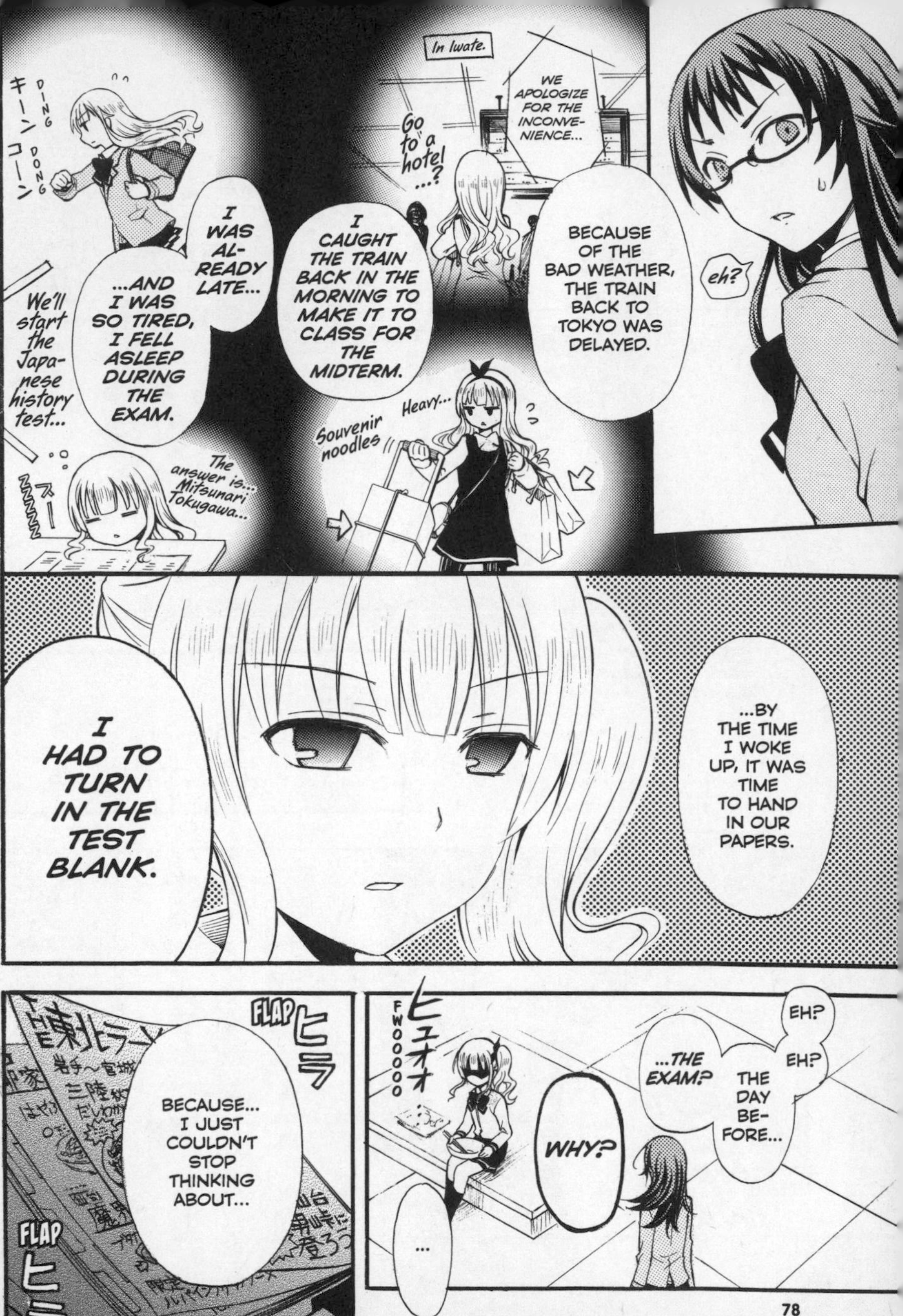
eh?
In Iwate.
BECAUSE OF THE BAD WEATHER, THE TRAIN BACK TO TOKYO WAS DELAYED.
WE APOLOGIZE FOR THE INCONVENIENCE...
Go to a hotel...?
I CAUGHT THE TRAIN BACK IN THE MORNING TO MAKE IT TO CLASS FOR THE MIDTERM.
Heavy...
Souvenir noodles
I WAS ALREADY LATE...
キーンコーン
DING DONG
...AND I WAS SO TIRED, I FELL ASLEEP DURING THE EXAM.
We'll start the Japanese history test...
The answer is... Mitsunari Tokugawa...
スー
ZZZZ
...BY THE TIME I WOKE UP, IT WAS TIME TO HAND IN OUR PAPERS.
I HAD TO TURN IN THE TEST BLANK.
EH?
EH?
...THE EXAM?
THE DAY BEFORE...
WHY?
...
ヒュオオ
FWOOOOO
FLAP
ヒラ
BECAUSE... I JUST COULDN'T STOP THINKING ABOUT...
FLAP
ヒラ

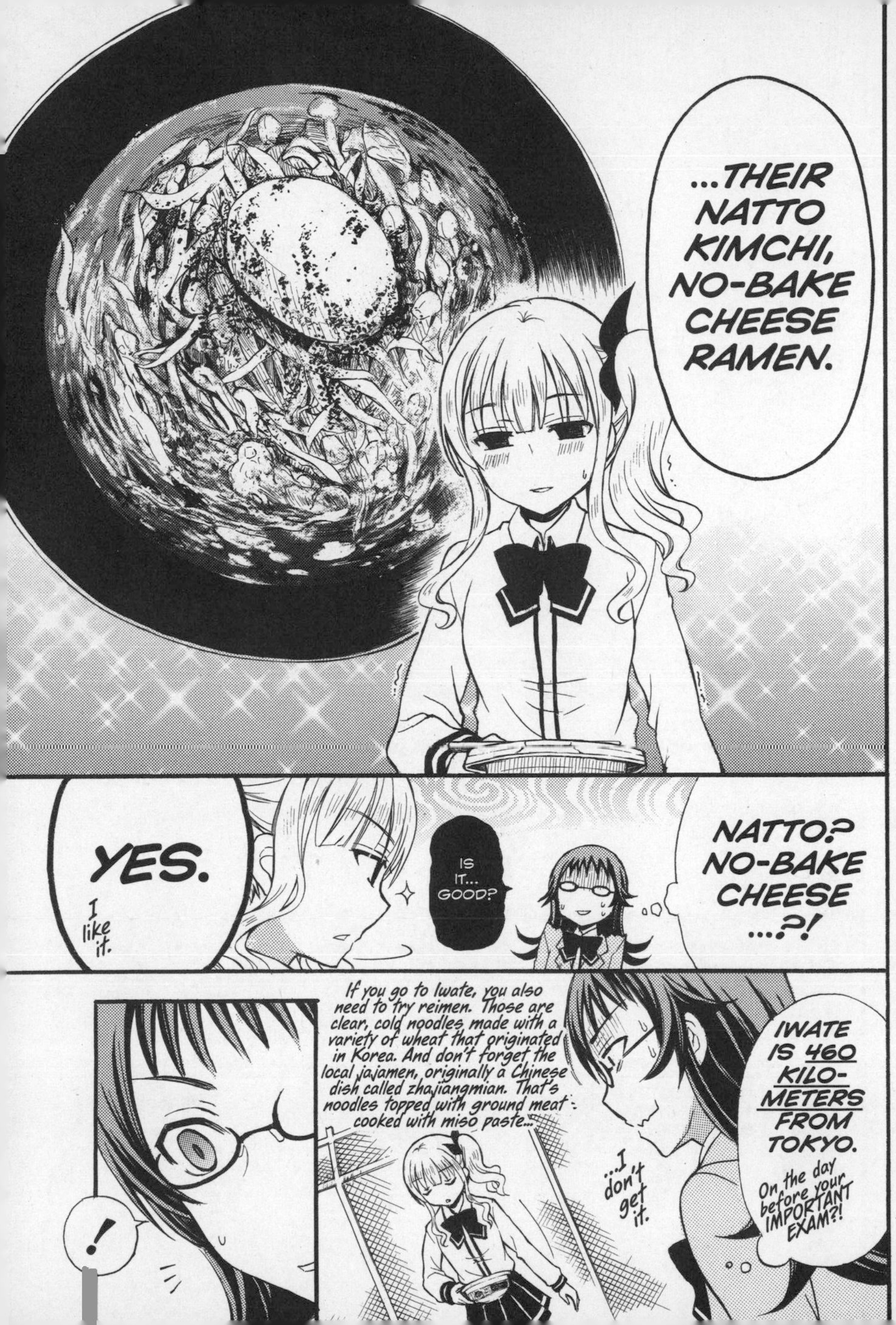
...THEIR NATTO KIMCHI, NO-BAKE CHEESE RAMEN.
NATTO? NO-BAKE CHEESE ...?!
IS IT... GOOD?
YES.
I like it.
IWATE IS 460 KILO-METERS FROM TOKYO.
On the day before your IMPORTANT EXAM?!
...I don't get it.
If you go to Iwate, you also need to try reimen. Those are clear, cold noodles made with a variety of wheat that originated in Korea. And don't forget the local jajamen, originally a Chinese dish called zhajiangmian. That's noodles topped with ground meat cooked with miso paste...
!

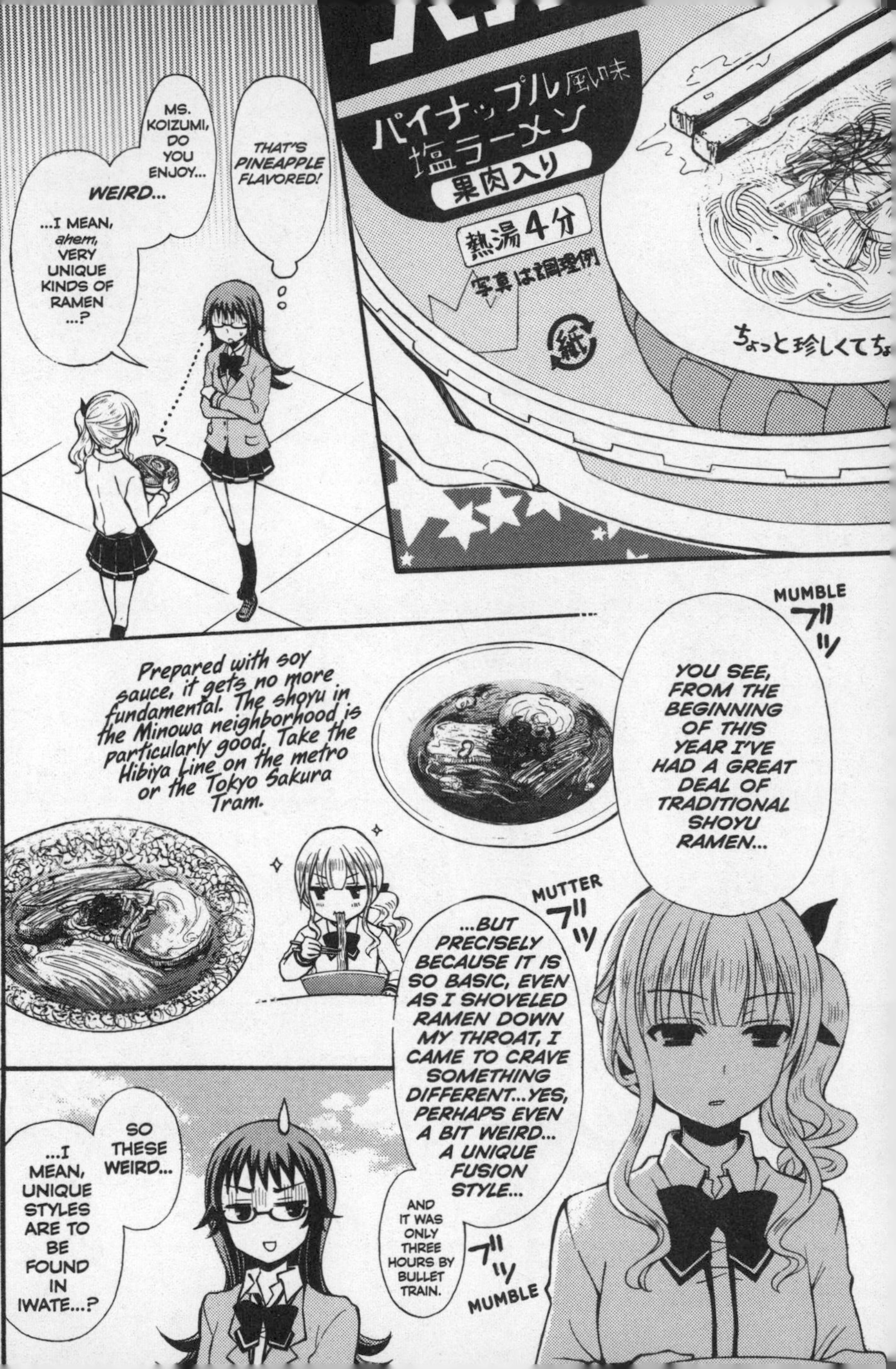

パイナップル風味
塩ラーメン
果肉入り
熱湯4分
写真は調理例
紙
ちょっと珍しくてちょ
THAT'S PINEAPPLE FLAVORED!
MS. KOIZUMI, DO YOU ENJOY... WEIRD... ...I MEAN, ahem, VERY UNIQUE KINDS OF RAMEN ...?
MUMBLE
ブツ
YOU SEE, FROM THE BEGINNING OF THIS YEAR I'VE HAD A GREAT DEAL OF TRADITIONAL SHOYU RAMEN...
MUTTER
ブツ
...BUT PRECISELY BECAUSE IT IS SO BASIC, EVEN AS I SHOVELED RAMEN DOWN MY THROAT, I CAME TO CRAVE SOMETHING DIFFERENT...YES, PERHAPS EVEN A BIT WEIRD... A UNIQUE FUSION STYLE...
AND IT WAS ONLY THREE HOURS BY BULLET TRAIN.
ブツ
MUMBLE
Prepared with soy sauce, it gets no more fundamental. The shoyu in the Minowa neighborhood is particularly good. Take the Hibiya Line on the metro or the Tokyo Sakura Tram.
SO THESE WEIRD...
...I MEAN, UNIQUE STYLES ARE TO BE FOUND IN IWATE...?

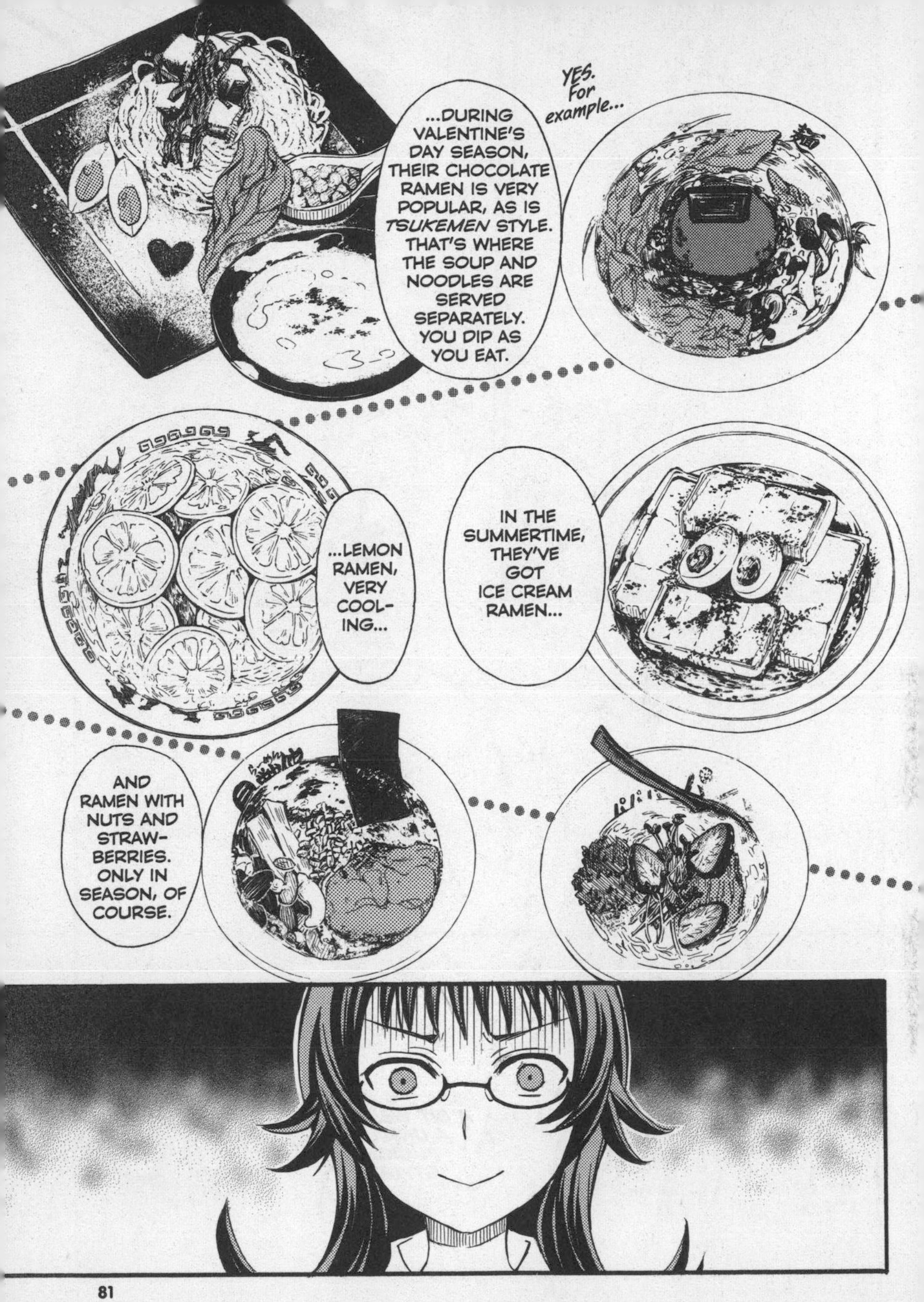
YES. For example...
...DURING VALENTINE'S DAY SEASON, THEIR CHOCOLATE RAMEN IS VERY POPULAR, AS IS *TSUKEMEN* STYLE. THAT'S WHERE THE SOUP AND NOODLES ARE SERVED SEPARATELY. YOU DIP AS YOU EAT.
IN THE SUMMERTIME, THEY'VE GOT ICE CREAM RAMEN...
...LEMON RAMEN, VERY COOL-ING...
AND RAMEN WITH NUTS AND STRAW-BERRIES. ONLY IN SEASON, OF COURSE.

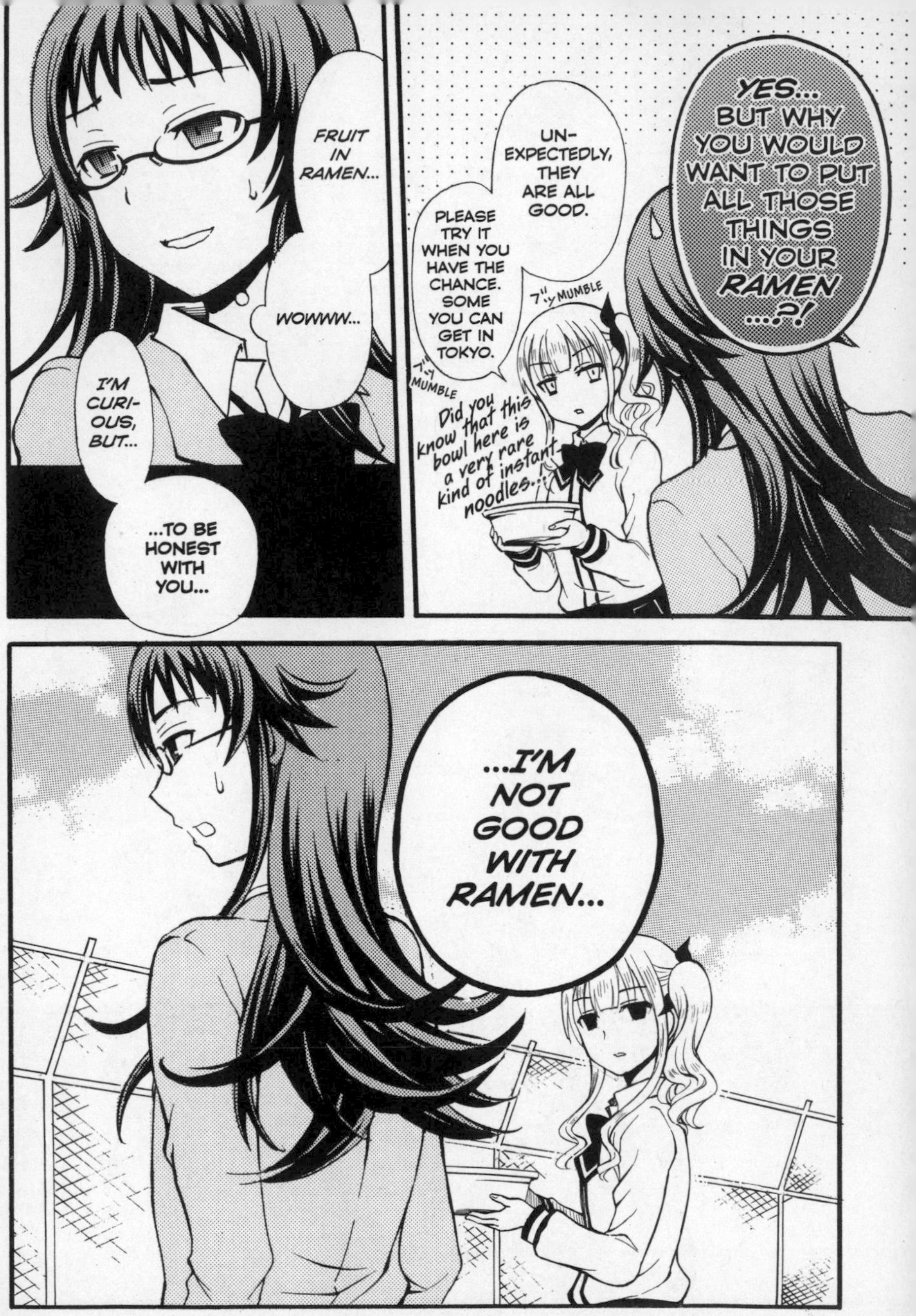
YES... BUT WHY YOU WOULD WANT TO PUT ALL THOSE THINGS IN YOUR RAMEN ...?!
UN-EXPECTEDLY, THEY ARE ALL GOOD.
PLEASE TRY IT WHEN YOU HAVE THE CHANCE. SOME YOU CAN GET IN TOKYO.
MUMBLE
MUMBLE
Did you know that this bowl here is a very rare kind of instant noodles...!
FRUIT IN RAMEN...
WOWWW...
I'M CURIOUS, BUT...
...TO BE HONEST WITH YOU...
...I'M NOT GOOD WITH RAMEN...

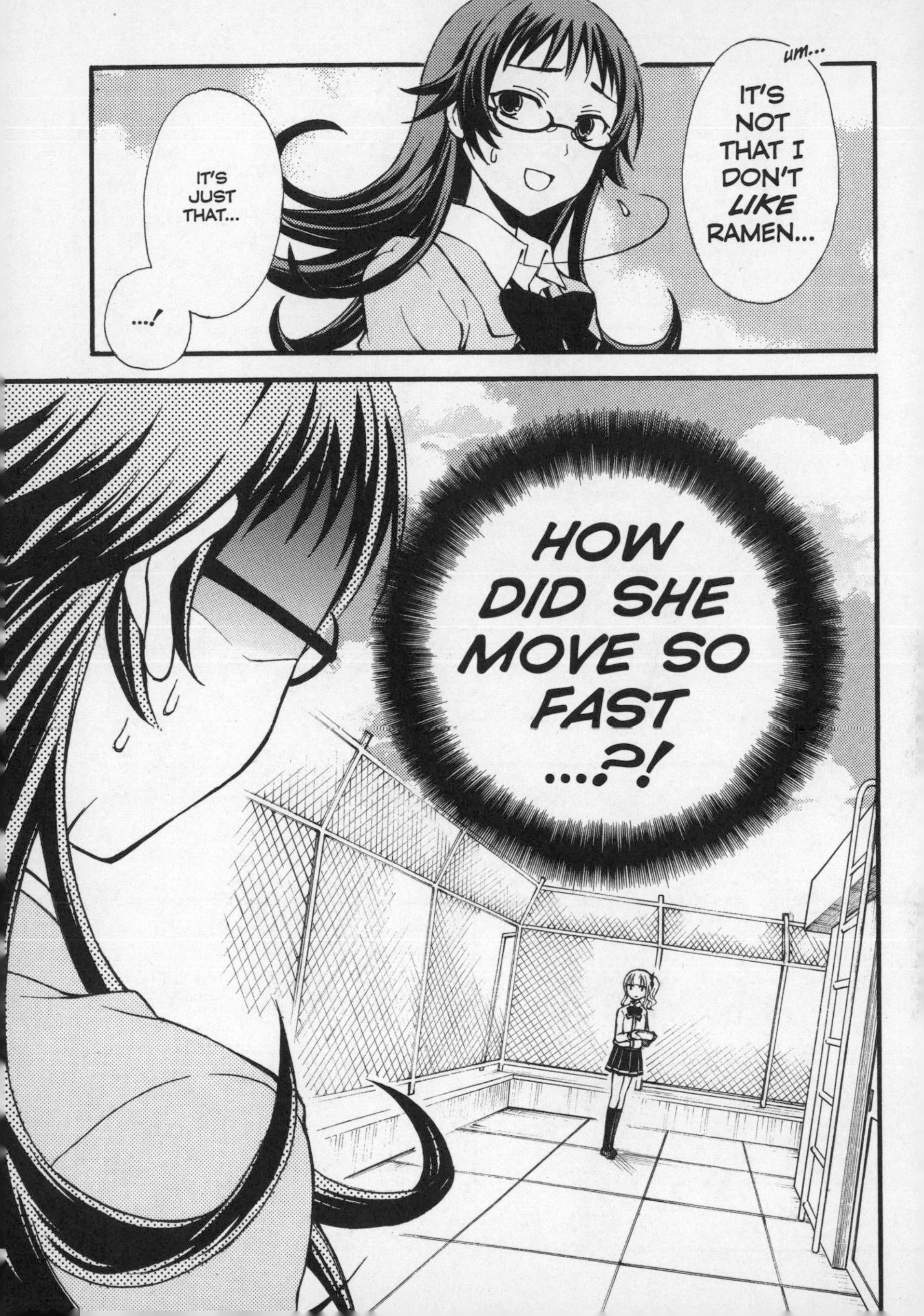
um...
IT'S NOT THAT I DON'T *LIKE* RAMEN...
IT'S JUST THAT...
...!
HOW DID SHE MOVE SO FAST ...?!

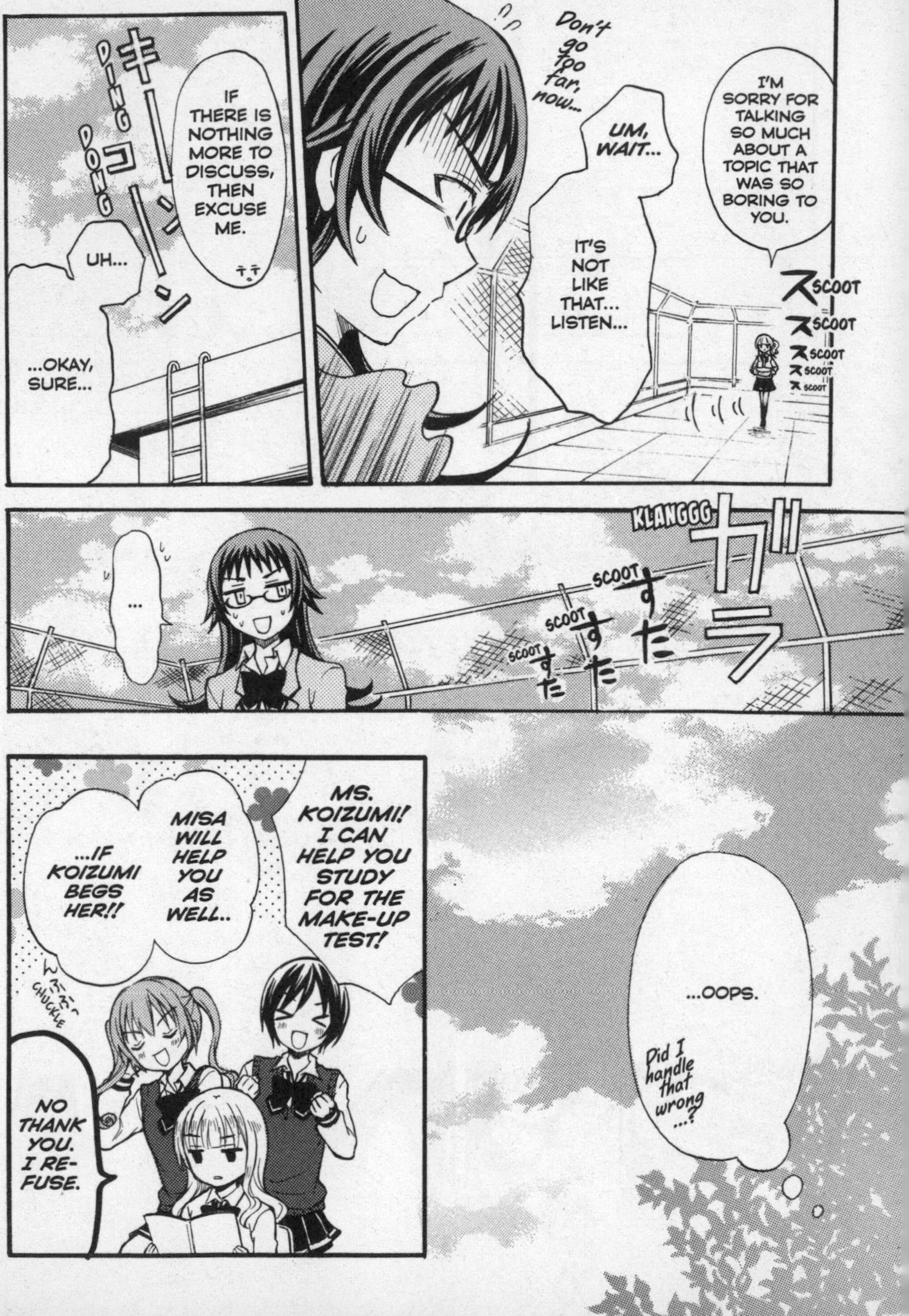
I'M SORRY FOR TALKING SO MUCH ABOUT A TOPIC THAT WAS SO BORING TO YOU.
SCOOT SCOOT SCOOT SCOOT SCOOT
Don't go too far, now...
UM, WAIT...
IT'S NOT LIKE THAT... LISTEN...
IF THERE IS NOTHING MORE TO DISCUSS, THEN EXCUSE ME.
DING DONG
UH...
...OKAY, SURE...
KLANGGG
SCOOT SCOOT SCOOT
...
...OOPS.
Did I handle that wrong...?
MS. KOIZUMI! I CAN HELP YOU STUDY FOR THE MAKE-UP TEST!
MISA WILL HELP YOU AS WELL..
...IF KOIZUMI BEGS HER!!
CHUCKLE
NO THANK YOU. I REFUSE.

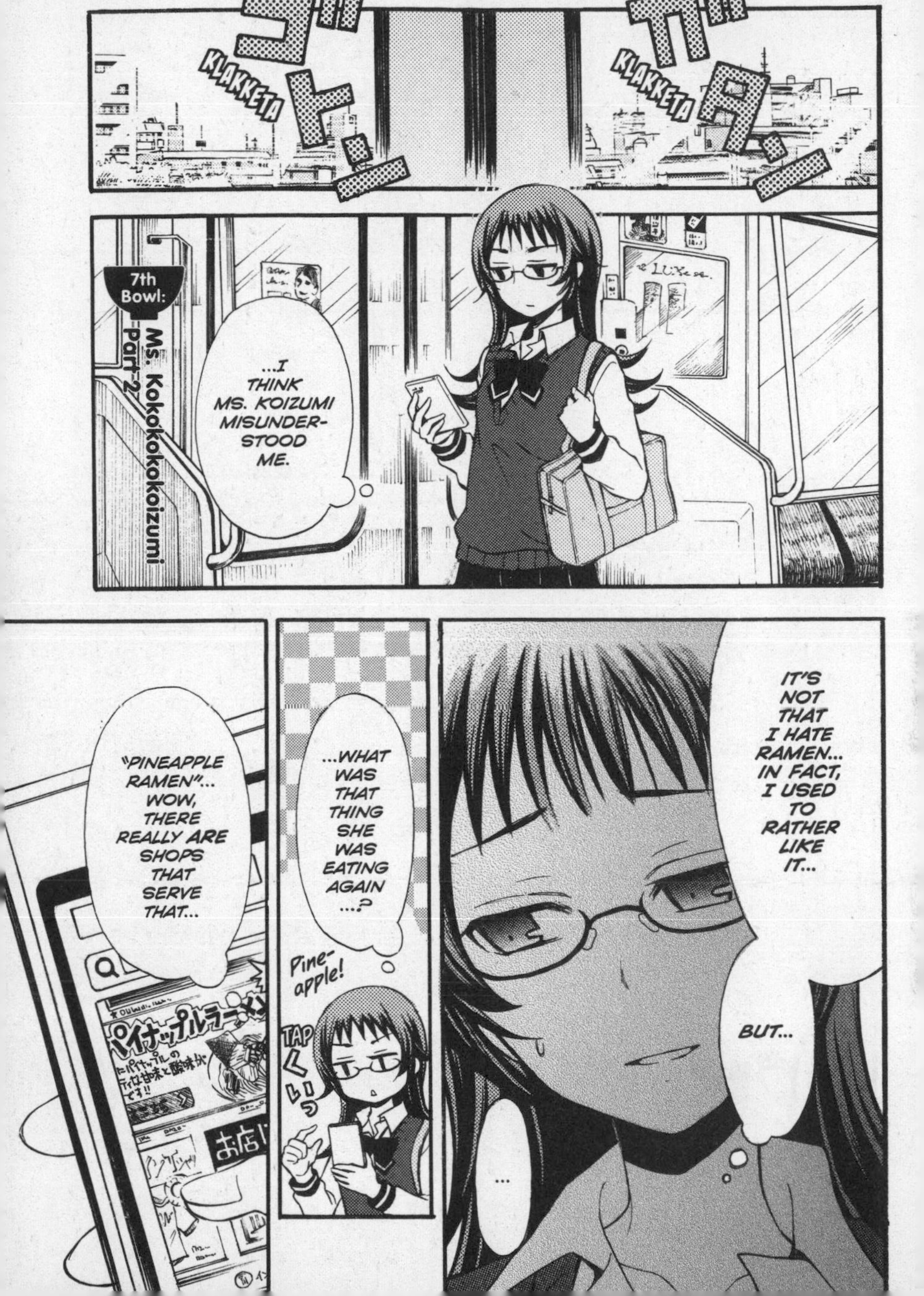
ガタン
KLAKKETA
ゴトン
KLAKKETA
7th Bowl: Ms. Kokokokokoizumi Part 2
...I THINK MS. KOIZUMI MISUNDERSTOOD ME.
IT'S NOT THAT I HATE RAMEN... IN FACT, I USED TO RATHER LIKE IT...
BUT...
...
...WHAT WAS THAT THING SHE WAS EATING AGAIN ...?
Pine-apple!
TAP
"PINEAPPLE RAMEN"... WOW, THERE REALLY ARE SHOPS THAT SERVE THAT...

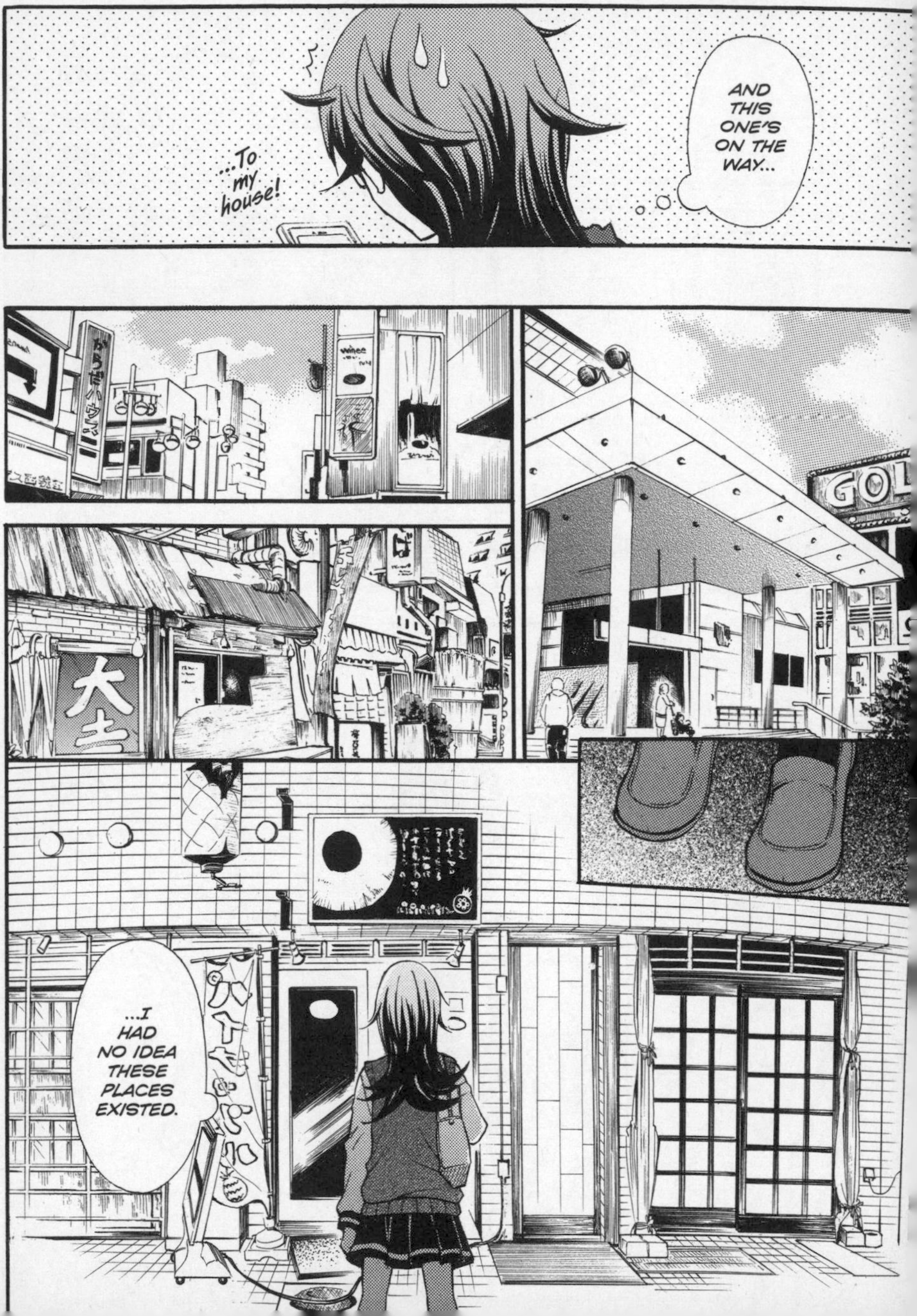
AND THIS ONE'S ON THE WAY...
...To my house!
...I HAD NO IDEA THESE PLACES EXISTED.

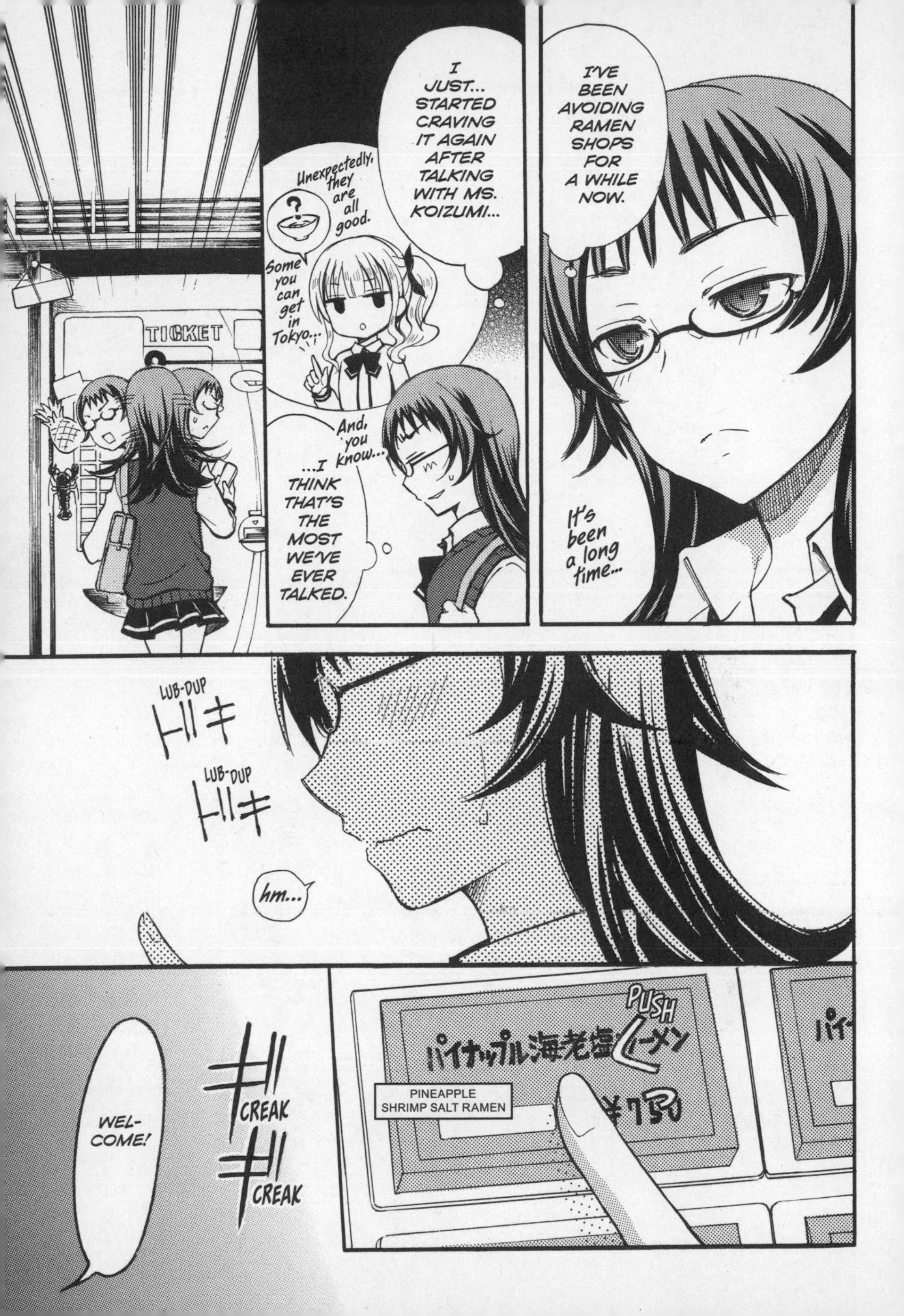
I'VE BEEN AVOIDING RAMEN SHOPS FOR A WHILE NOW.
It's been a long time...
I JUST... STARTED CRAVING IT AGAIN AFTER TALKING WITH MS. KOIZUMI...
Unexpectedly, they are all good.
Some you can get in Tokyo...
And, you know...
...I THINK THAT'S THE MOST WE'VE EVER TALKED.
TICKET
LUB-DUP
LUB-DUP
hm...
PUSH
PINEAPPLE SHRIMP SALT RAMEN
¥730
CREAK
CREAK
WEL-COME!

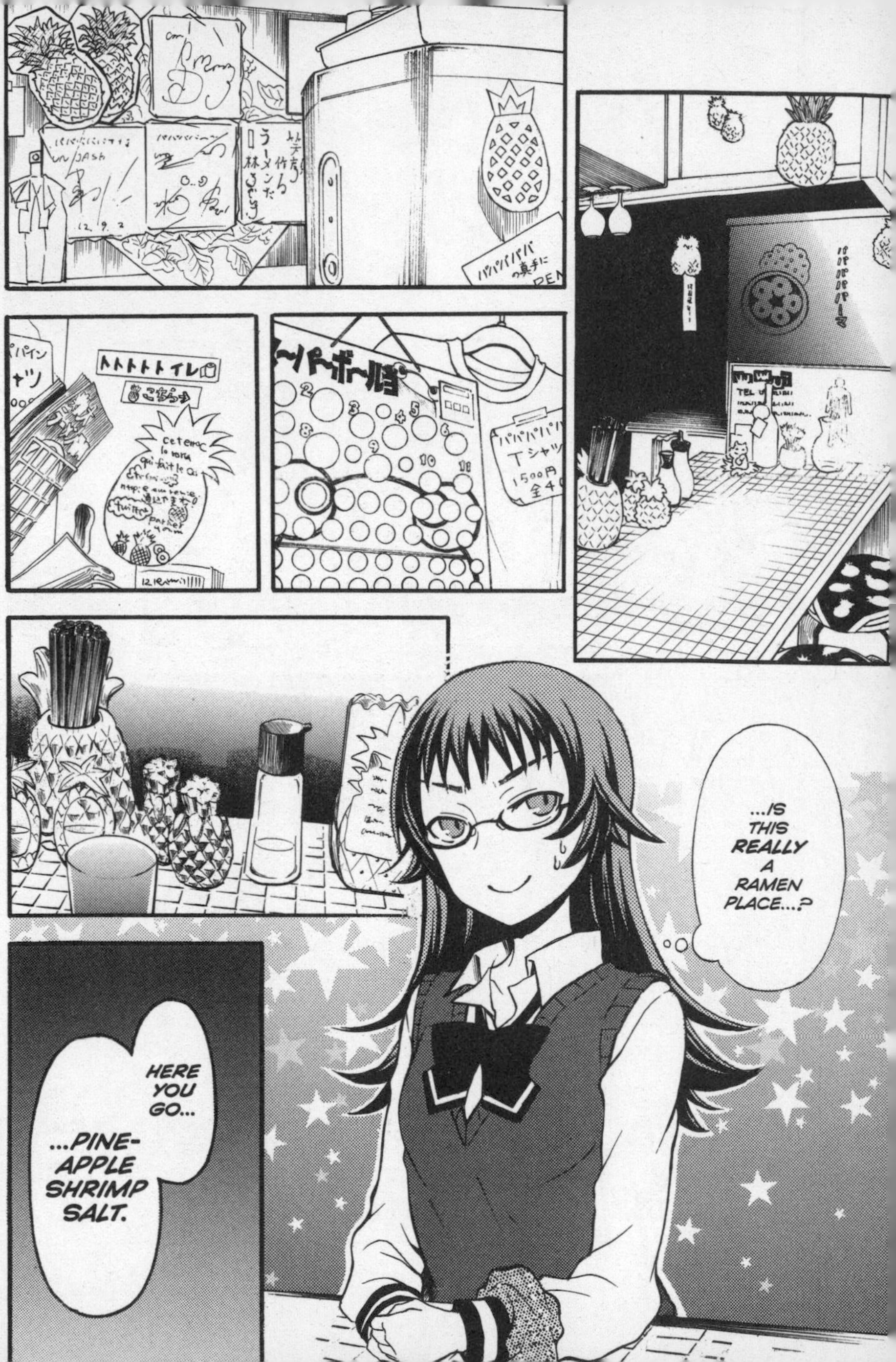

トトトトトイレ
...IS THIS REALLY A RAMEN PLACE...?
HERE YOU GO...
...PINE-APPLE SHRIMP SALT.

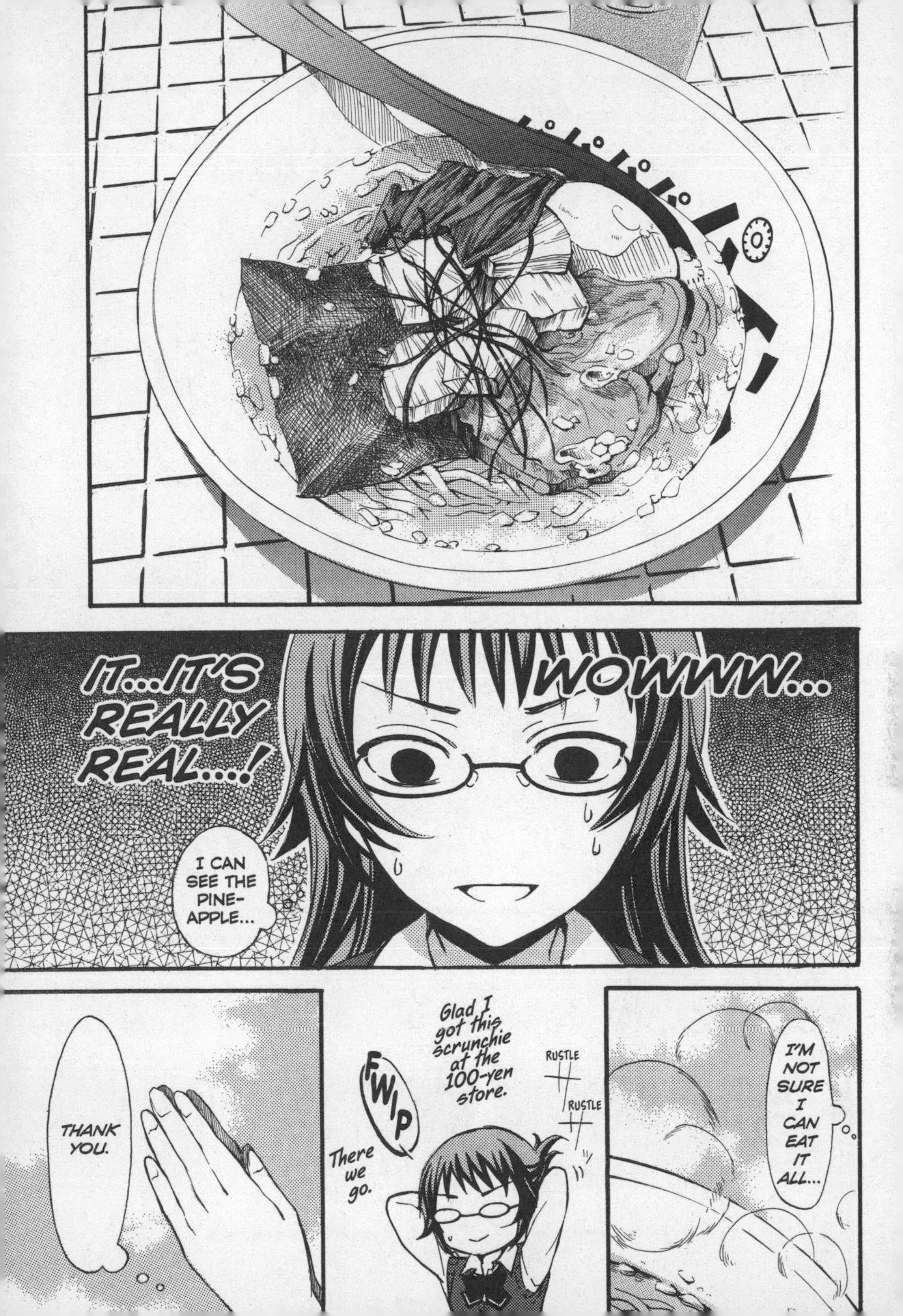
WOWWW...
IT...IT'S REALLY REAL...!
I CAN SEE THE PINE-APPLE...
I'M NOT SURE I CAN EAT IT ALL...
Glad I got this scrunchie at the 100-yen store.
RUSTLE
RUSTLE
FWIP
There we go.
THANK YOU.

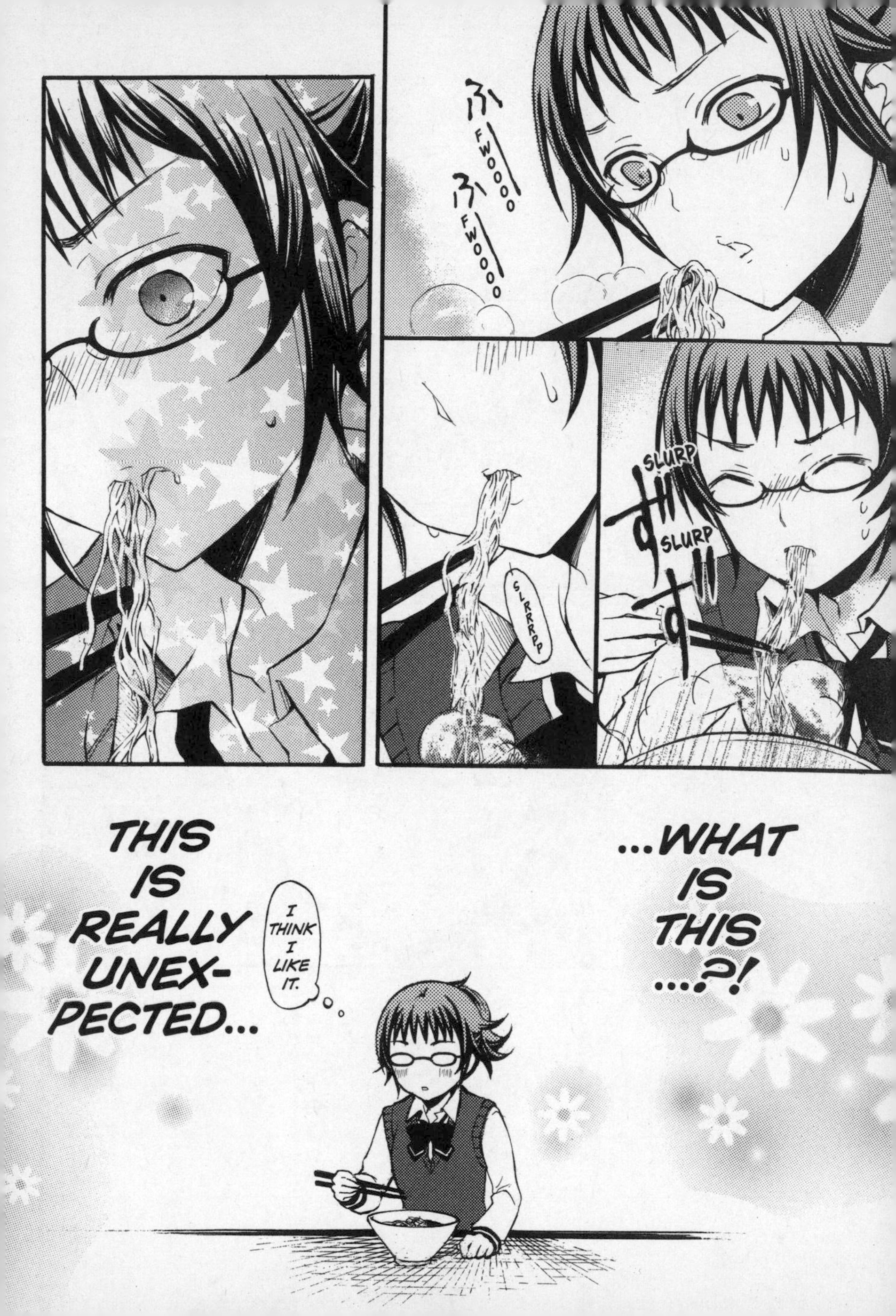

ふ
FWOOOOO
ふ
FWOOOOO
SLURP
SLURP
SLRRRP
...WHAT IS THIS ...?!
THIS IS REALLY UNEX-PECTED...
I THINK I LIKE IT.

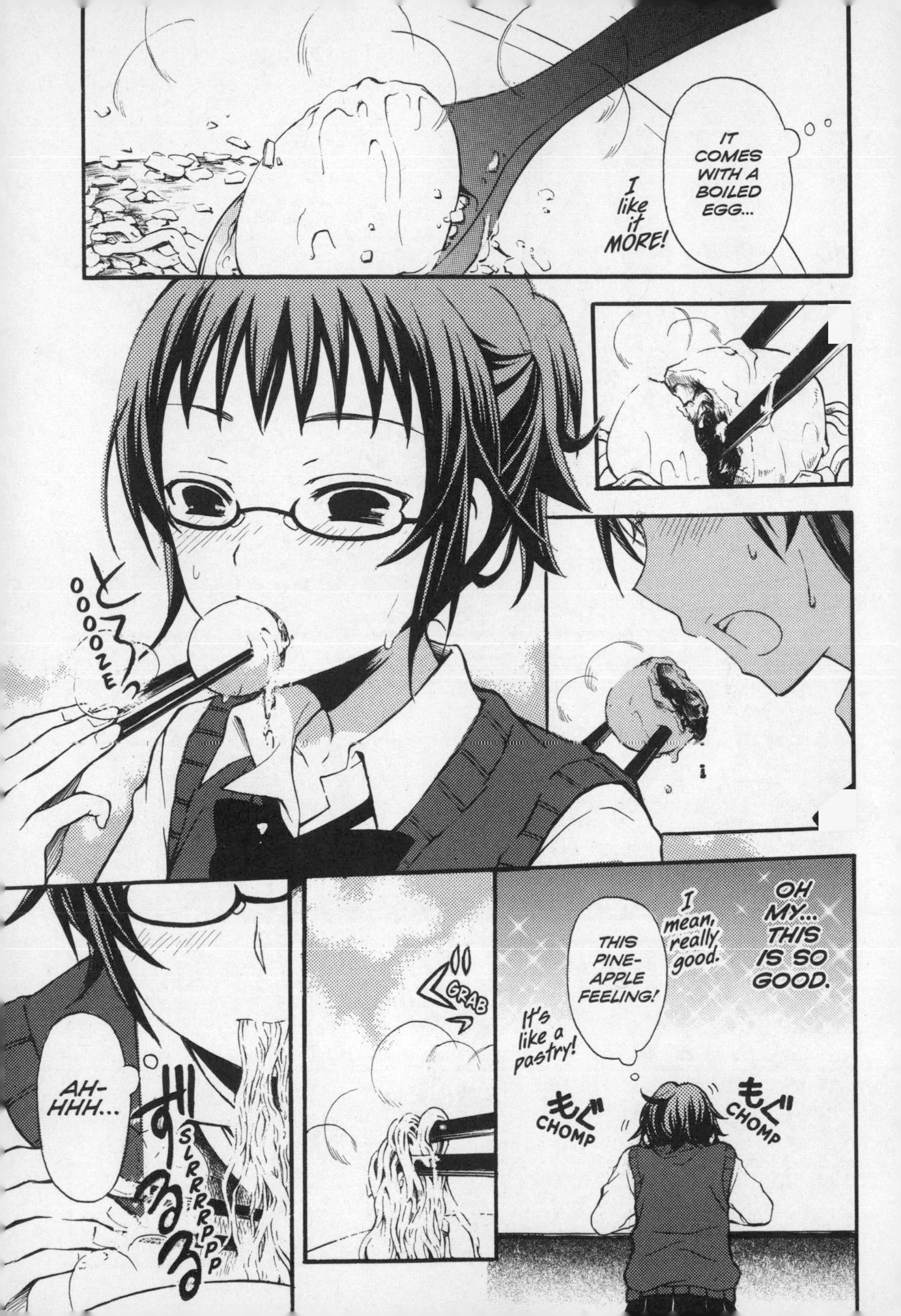
IT COMES WITH A BOILED EGG...
I like it MORE!
OOOOOZE
OH MY... THIS IS SO GOOD.
I mean, really good.
THIS PINE-APPLE FEELING!
It's like a pastry!
もぐ CHOMP
もぐ CHOMP
GRAB
AH-HHH...
ずるる SLRRRRPPP

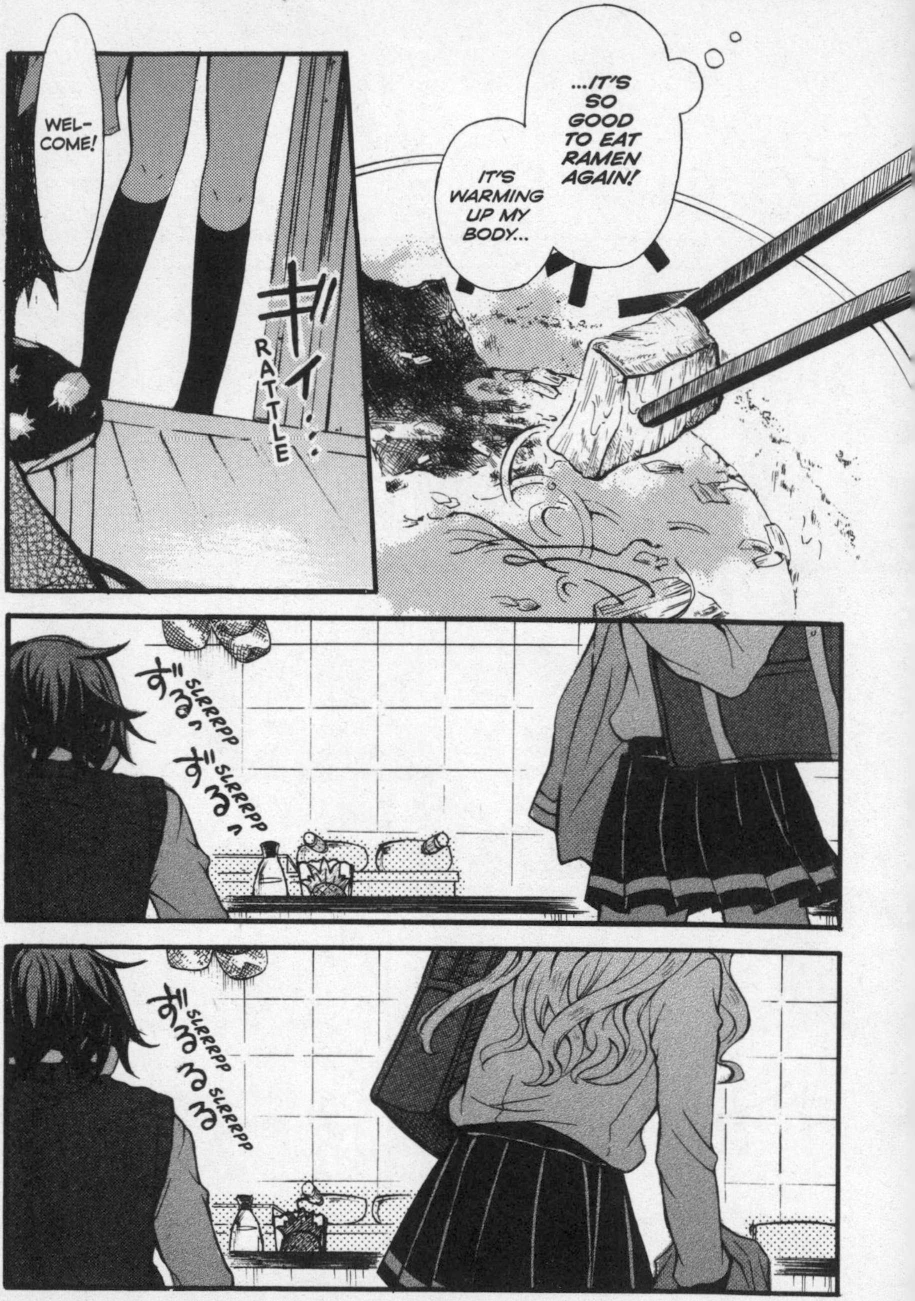
...IT'S SO GOOD TO EAT RAMEN AGAIN!
IT'S WARMING UP MY BODY...
ギイ…
RATTLE
WEL-COME!
ずるっ
SLRRPP
ずるっ
SLRRPP
ずるるる
SLRRPP
SLRRPP

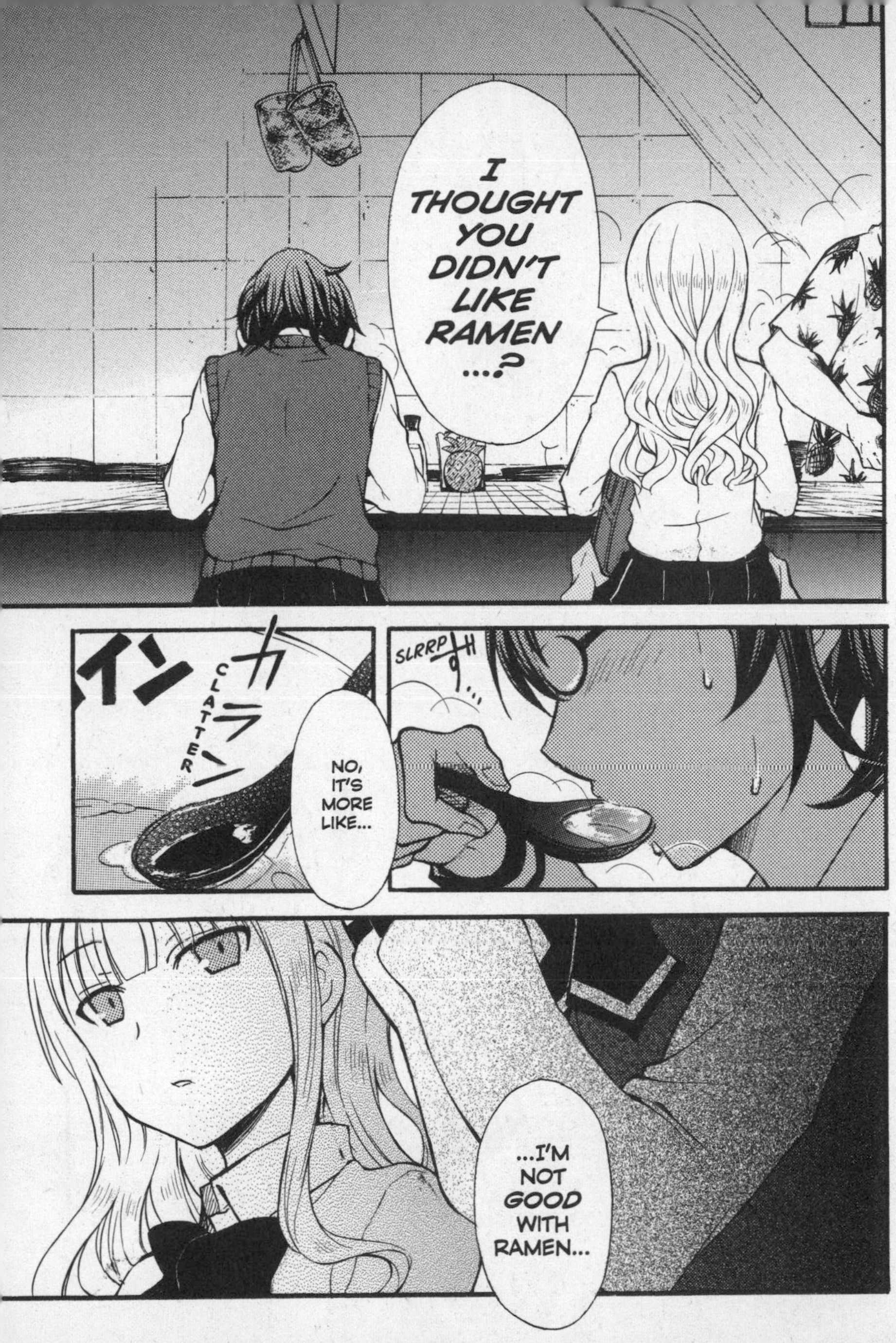
I THOUGHT YOU DIDN'T LIKE RAMEN ...?
SLRRP
NO, IT'S MORE LIKE...
CLATTER
...I'M NOT GOOD WITH RAMEN...

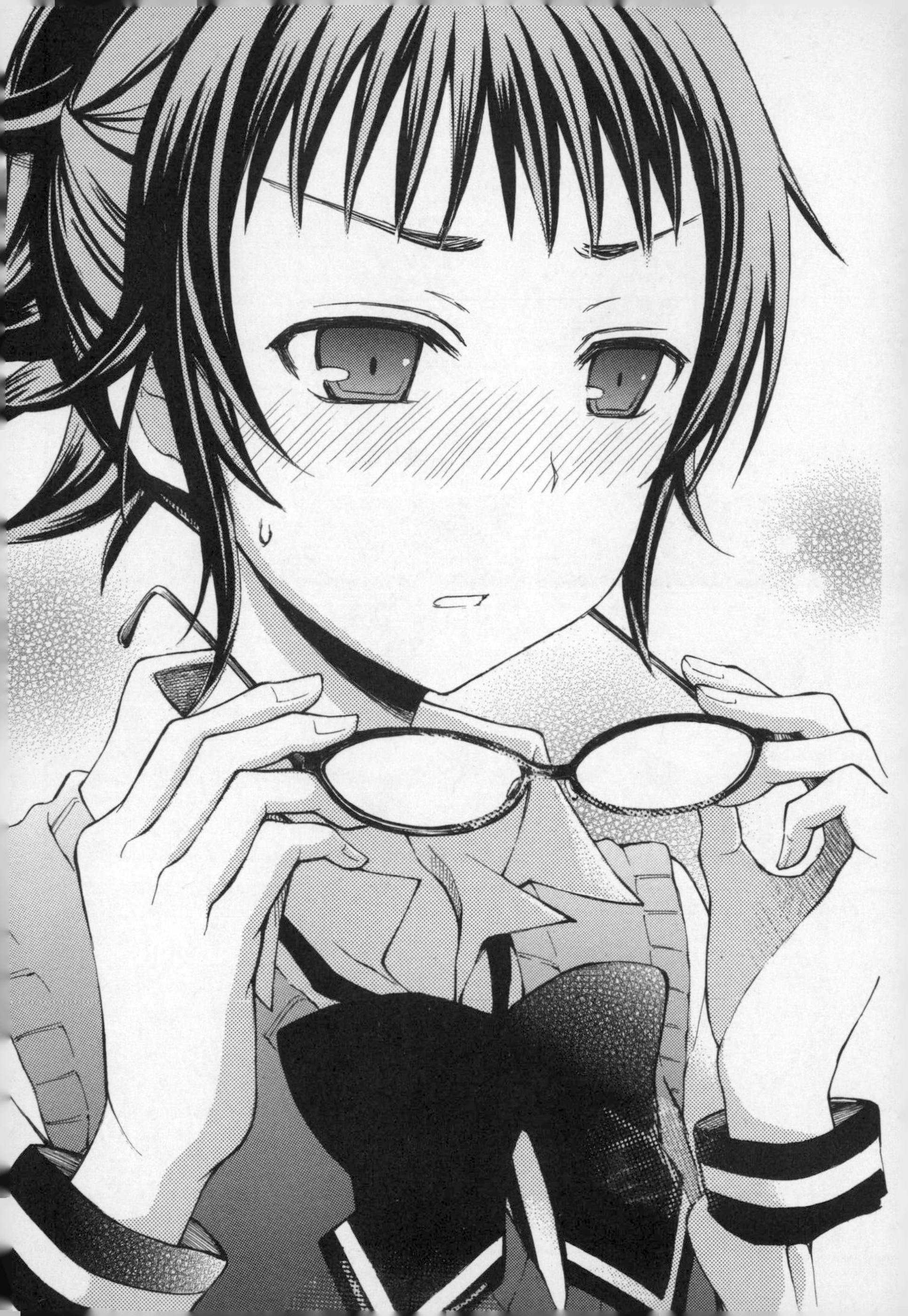

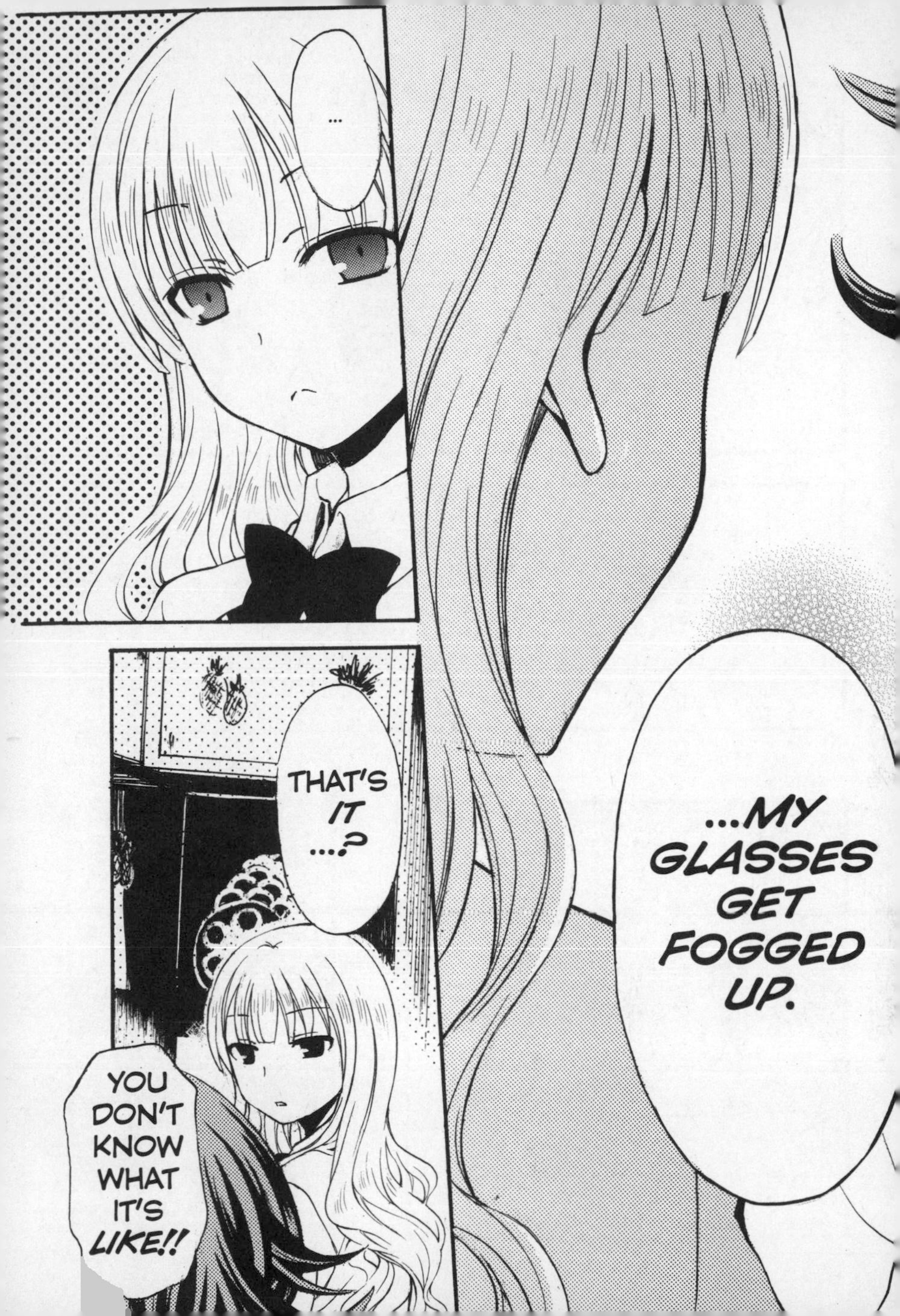
...MY GLASSES GET FOGGED UP.
...
THAT'S *IT* ...?
YOU DON'T KNOW WHAT IT'S *LIKE!!*

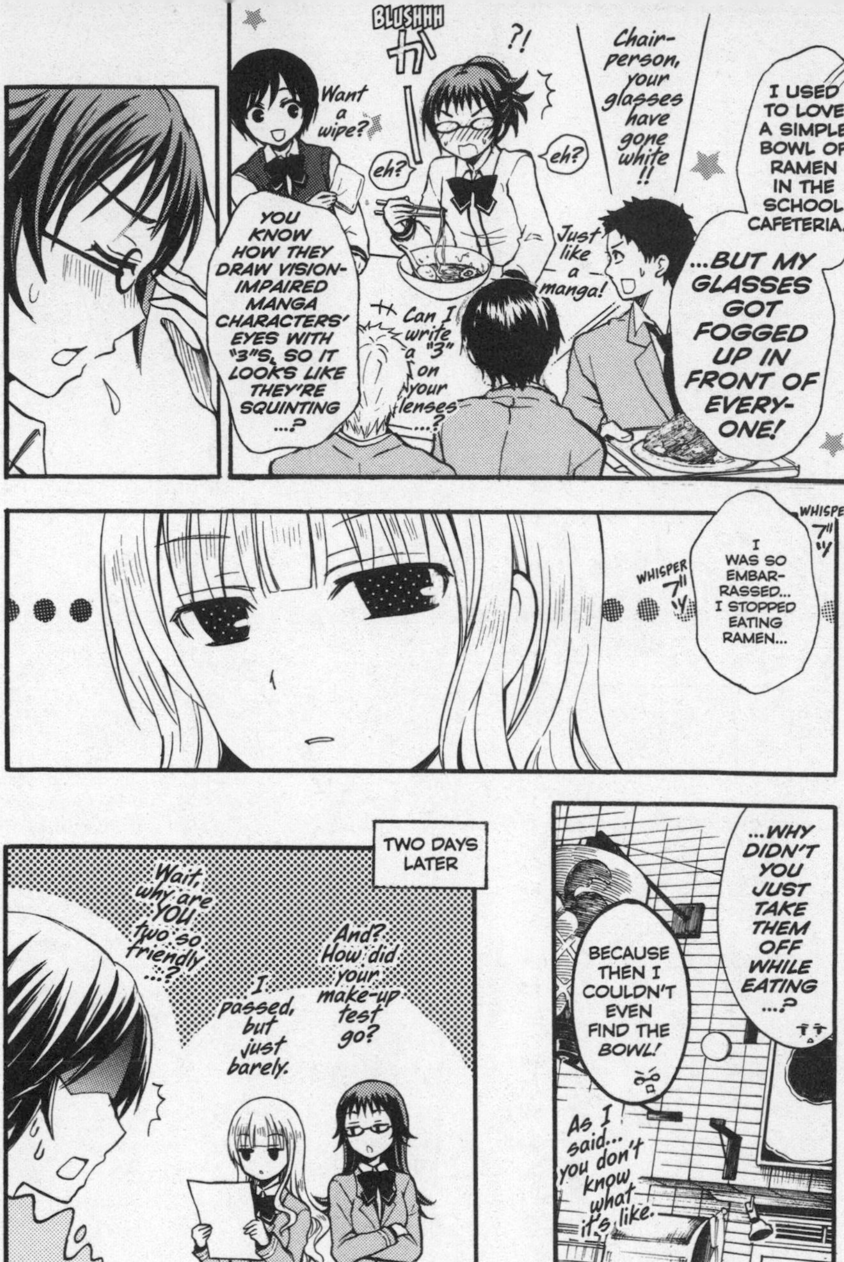
I USED TO LOVE A SIMPLE BOWL OF RAMEN IN THE SCHOOL CAFETERIA...
...BUT MY GLASSES GOT FOGGED UP IN FRONT OF EVERY-ONE!
Chair-person, your glasses have gone white!!
?!
BLUSHHH
eh?
Just like a manga!
Want a wipe?
eh?
Can I write a "3" on your lenses...?
YOU KNOW HOW THEY DRAW VISION-IMPAIRED MANGA CHARACTERS' EYES WITH "3"S, SO IT LOOKS LIKE THEY'RE SQUINTING...?
WHISPER
I WAS SO EMBAR-RASSED... I STOPPED EATING RAMEN...
WHISPER
...WHY DIDN'T YOU JUST TAKE THEM OFF WHILE EATING...?
BECAUSE THEN I COULDN'T EVEN FIND THE BOWL!
As I said... you don't know what it's like.
TWO DAYS LATER
And? How did your make-up test go?
I passed, but just barely.
Wait, why are YOU two so friendly...?

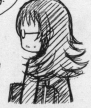

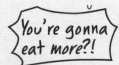

Eh?
The station's the other way.
I'm walking to the next station. There's a good ramen place along the way.
You're gonna eat more?!
They've got shaved ice.

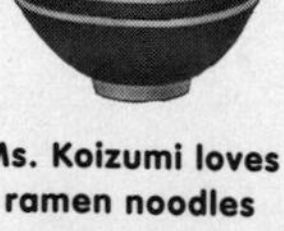

Ms. Koizumi loves ramen noodles

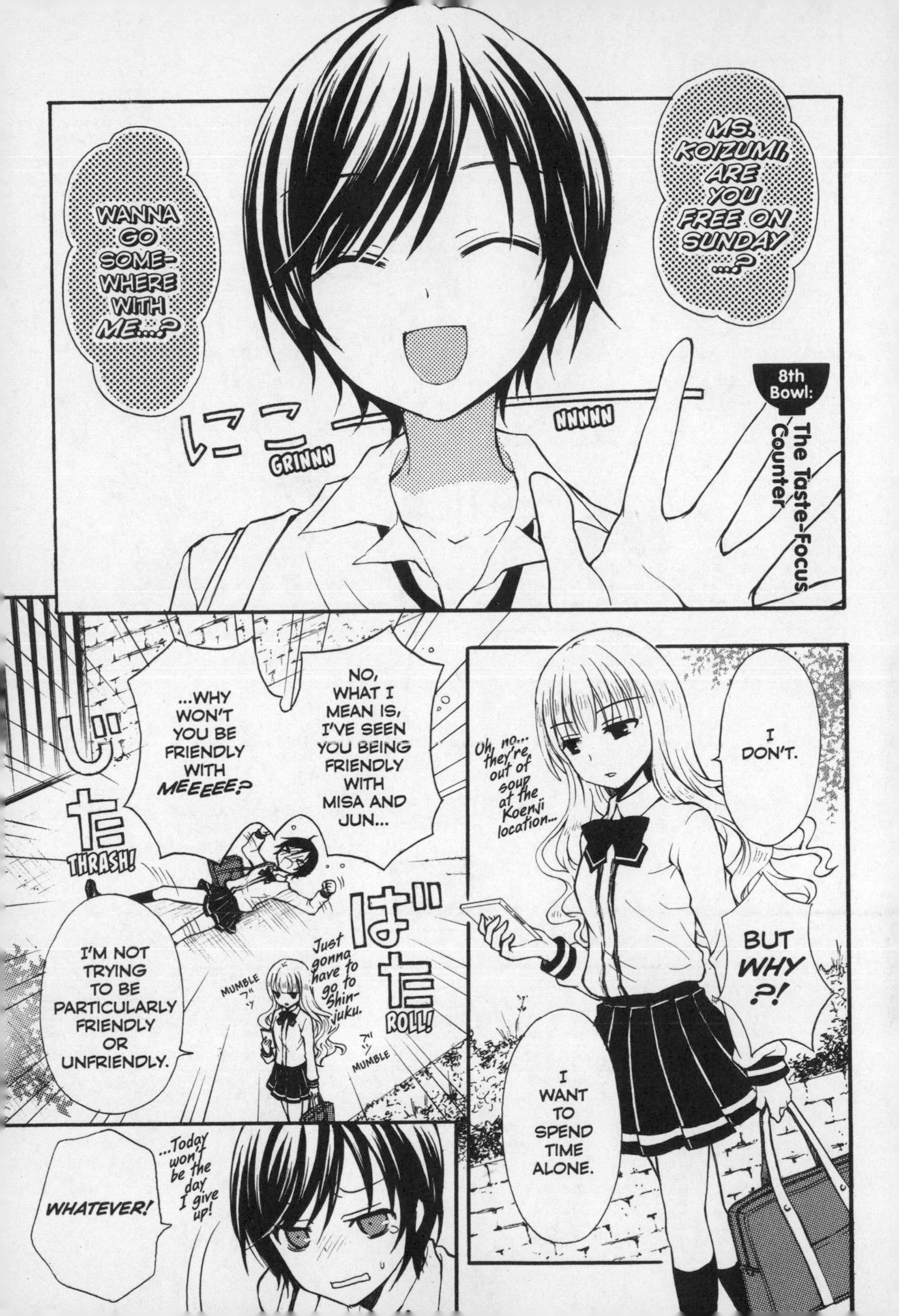
MS. KOIZUMI, ARE YOU FREE ON SUNDAY ...?
8th Bowl: The Taste-Focus Counter
NNNNN
WANNA GO SOME-WHERE WITH ME...?
にこー
GRINNN
I DON'T.
Oh, no... they're out of soup at the Koenji location...
BUT WHY ?!
I WANT TO SPEND TIME ALONE.
NO, WHAT I MEAN IS, I'VE SEEN YOU BEING FRIENDLY WITH MISA AND JUN...
...WHY WON'T YOU BE FRIENDLY WITH MEEEEE?
じた
THRASH!
ばた
ROLL!
Just gonna have to go to Shin-juku.
MUMBLE
MUMBLE
I'M NOT TRYING TO BE PARTICULARLY FRIENDLY OR UNFRIENDLY.
...Today won't be the day I give up!
WHATEVER!

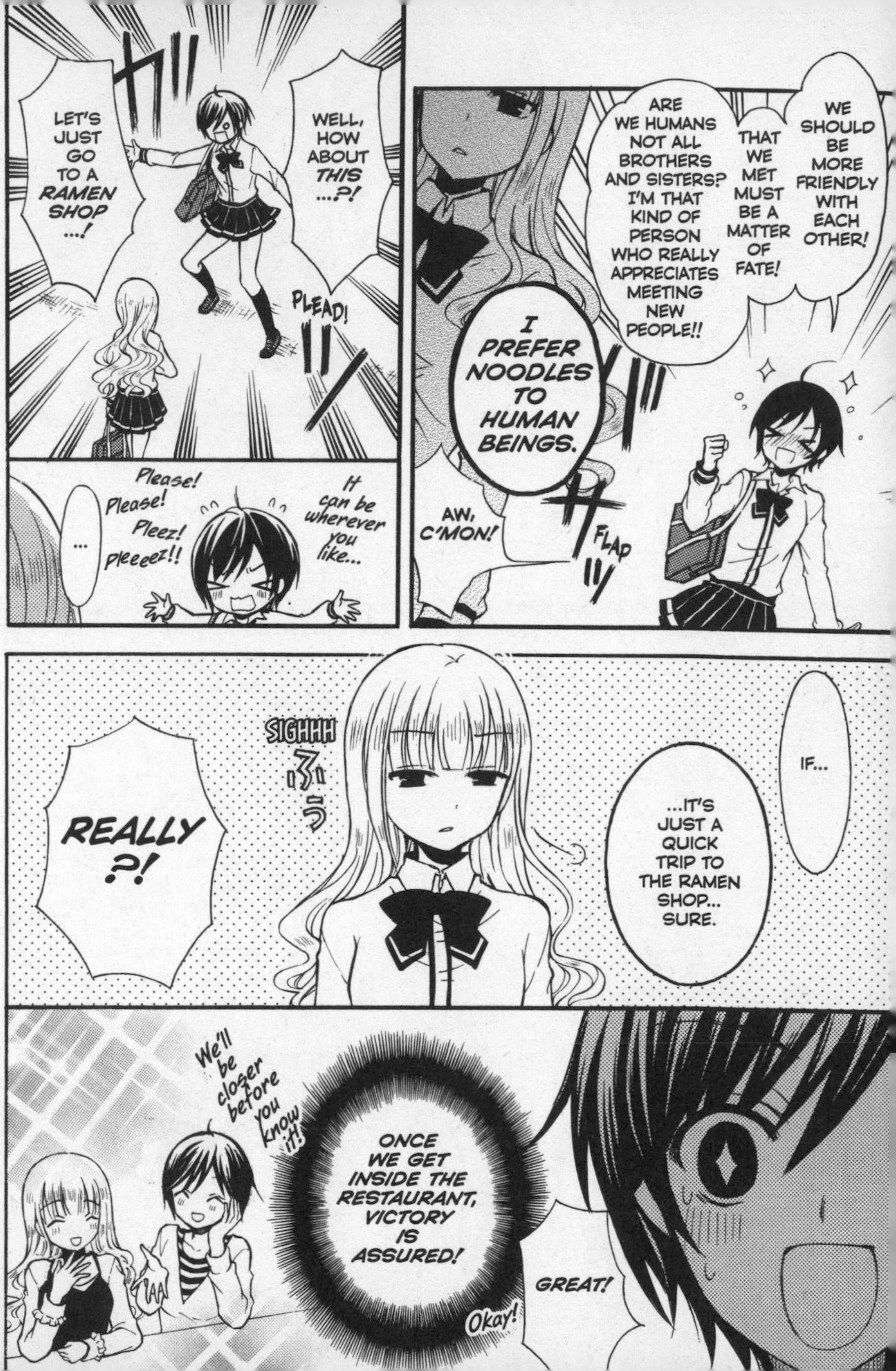
WE SHOULD BE MORE FRIENDLY WITH EACH OTHER!
THAT WE MET MUST BE A MATTER OF FATE!
ARE WE HUMANS NOT ALL BROTHERS AND SISTERS? I'M THAT KIND OF PERSON WHO REALLY APPRECIATES MEETING NEW PEOPLE!!
I PREFER NOODLES TO HUMAN BEINGS.
FLAP
AW, C'MON!
WELL, HOW ABOUT THIS ...?!
LET'S JUST GO TO A RAMEN SHOP ...!
PLEAD!
It can be wherever you like...
Please! Please! Pleez! Pleeeez!!
...
IF...
...IT'S JUST A QUICK TRIP TO THE RAMEN SHOP... SURE.
SIGHHH
REALLY ?!
GREAT!
Okay!
ONCE WE GET INSIDE THE RESTAURANT, VICTORY IS ASSURED!
We'll be closer before you know it!

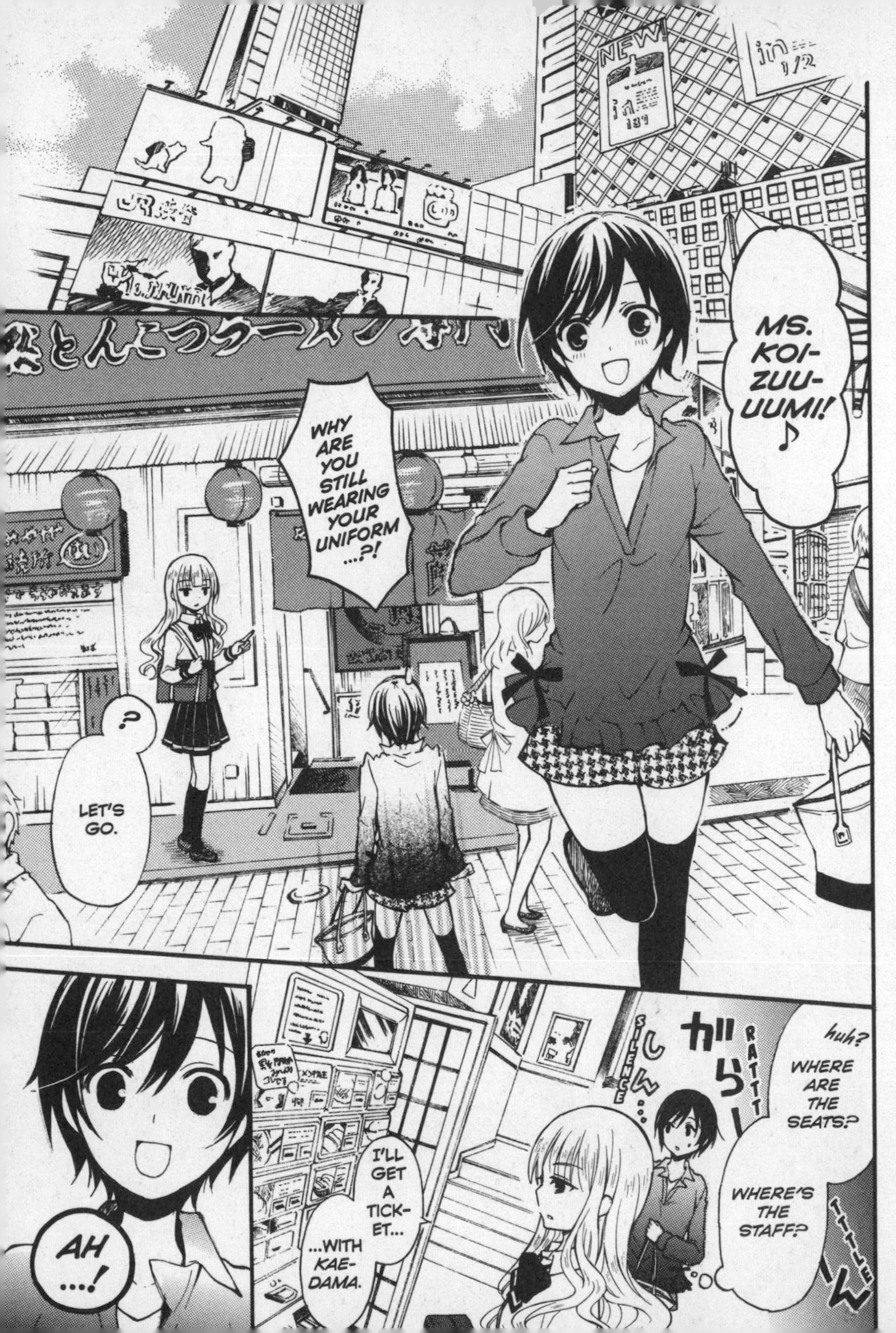
MS. KOI-ZUUU-UUMI! ♪
WHY ARE YOU STILL WEARING YOUR UNIFORM ...?!
?
LET'S GO.
huh? WHERE ARE THE SEATS?
WHERE'S THE STAFF?
ガラ
RATTT
TTTLE
しーん...
SILENCE
I'LL GET A TICK-ET...
...WITH KAE-DAMA.
AH ....!

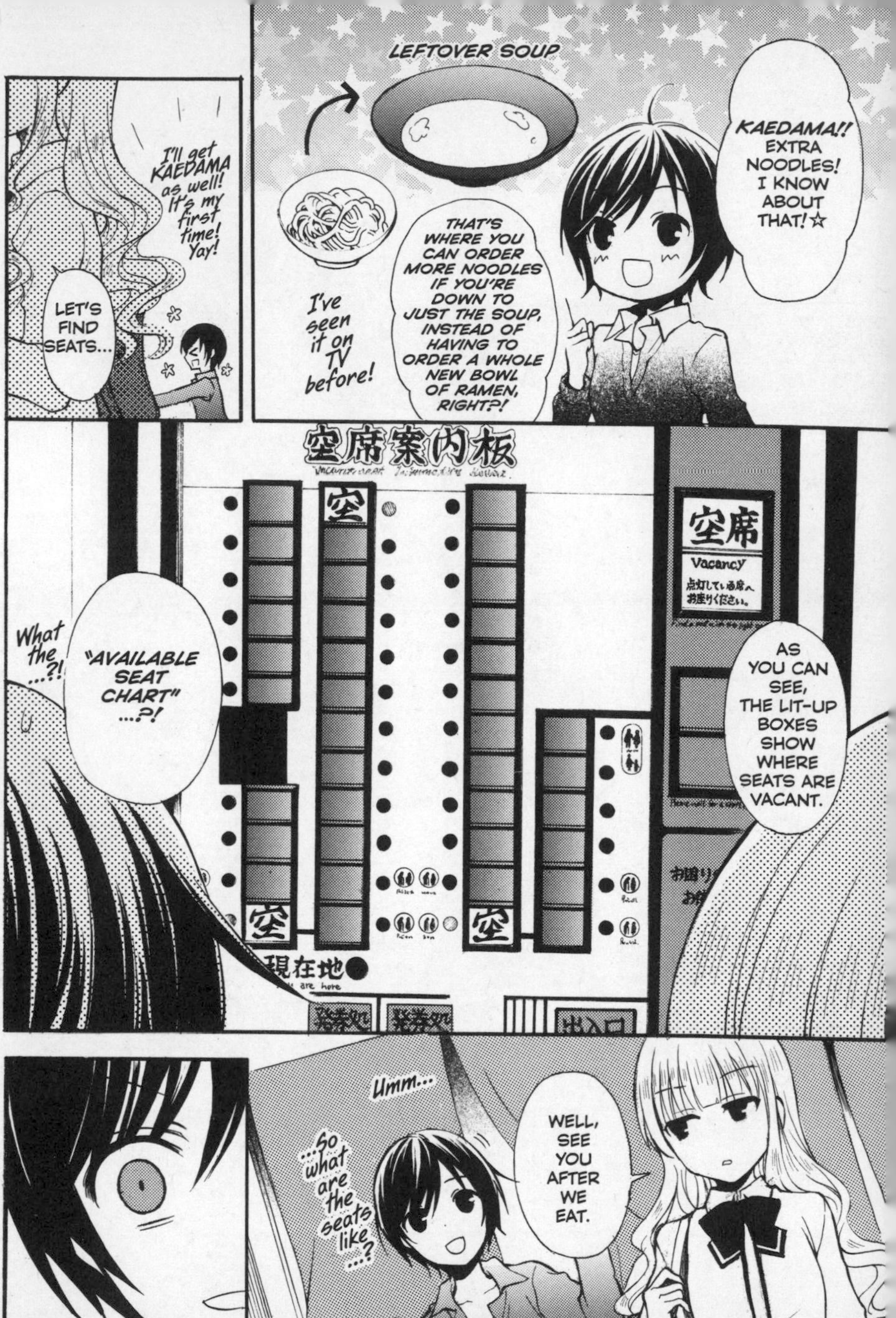
LEFTOVER SOUP
KAEDAMA!! EXTRA NOODLES! I KNOW ABOUT THAT!☆
THAT'S WHERE YOU CAN ORDER MORE NOODLES IF YOU'RE DOWN TO JUST THE SOUP, INSTEAD OF HAVING TO ORDER A WHOLE NEW BOWL OF RAMEN, RIGHT?!
I've seen it on TV before!
I'll get KAEDAMA as well! It's my first time! Yay!
LET'S FIND SEATS...
空席案内板
空席
Vacancy
点灯している席へお座りください。
現在地
AS YOU CAN SEE, THE LIT-UP BOXES SHOW WHERE SEATS ARE VACANT.
"AVAILABLE SEAT CHART" ...?!
What the...?!
WELL, SEE YOU AFTER WE EAT.
Umm...
...So what are the seats like...?

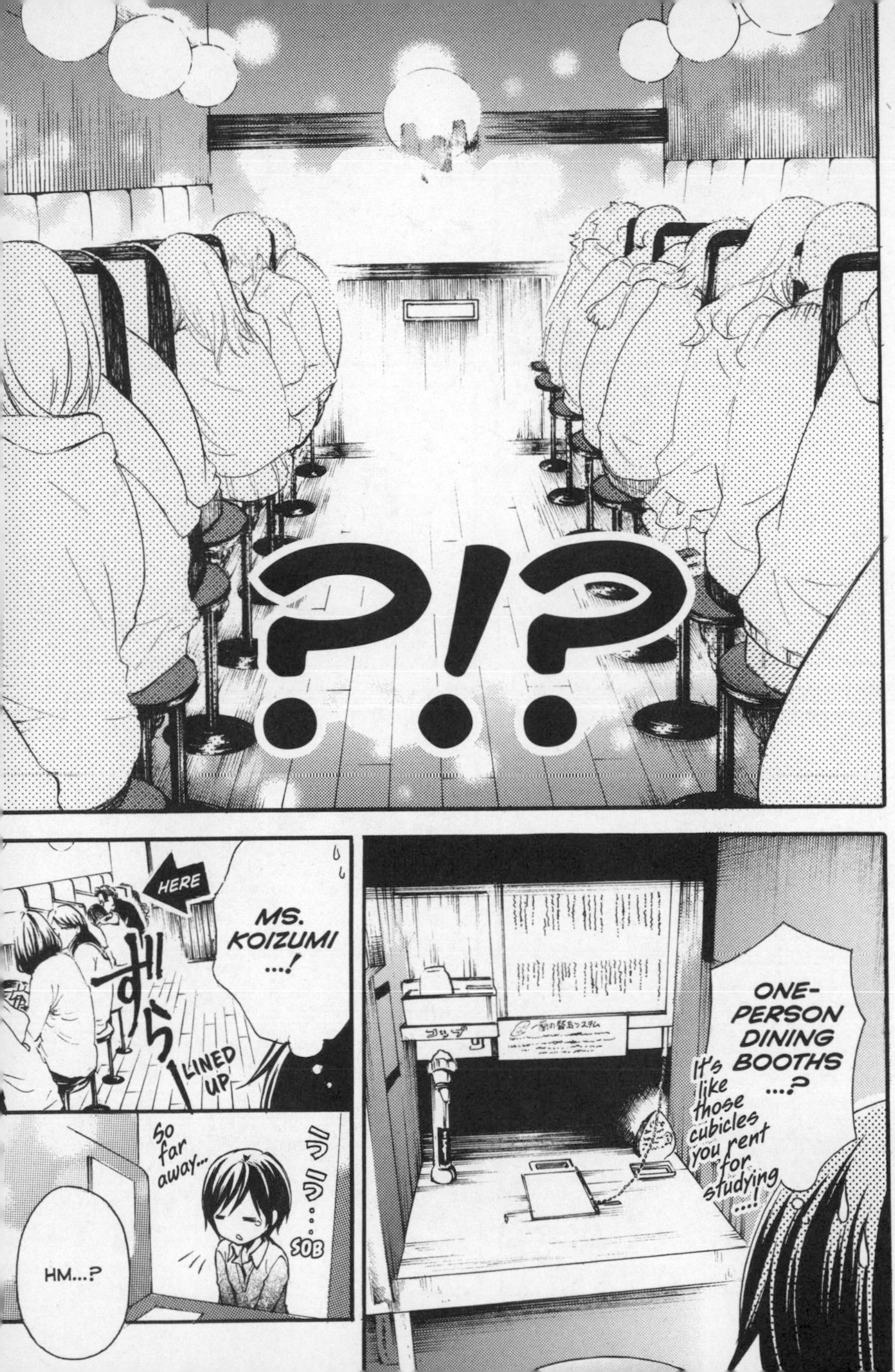
?!?
ONE-PERSON DINING BOOTHS ...?
It's like those cubicles you rent for studying ...!
HERE
MS. KOIZUMI ...!
LINED UP
So far away...
SOB
HM...?

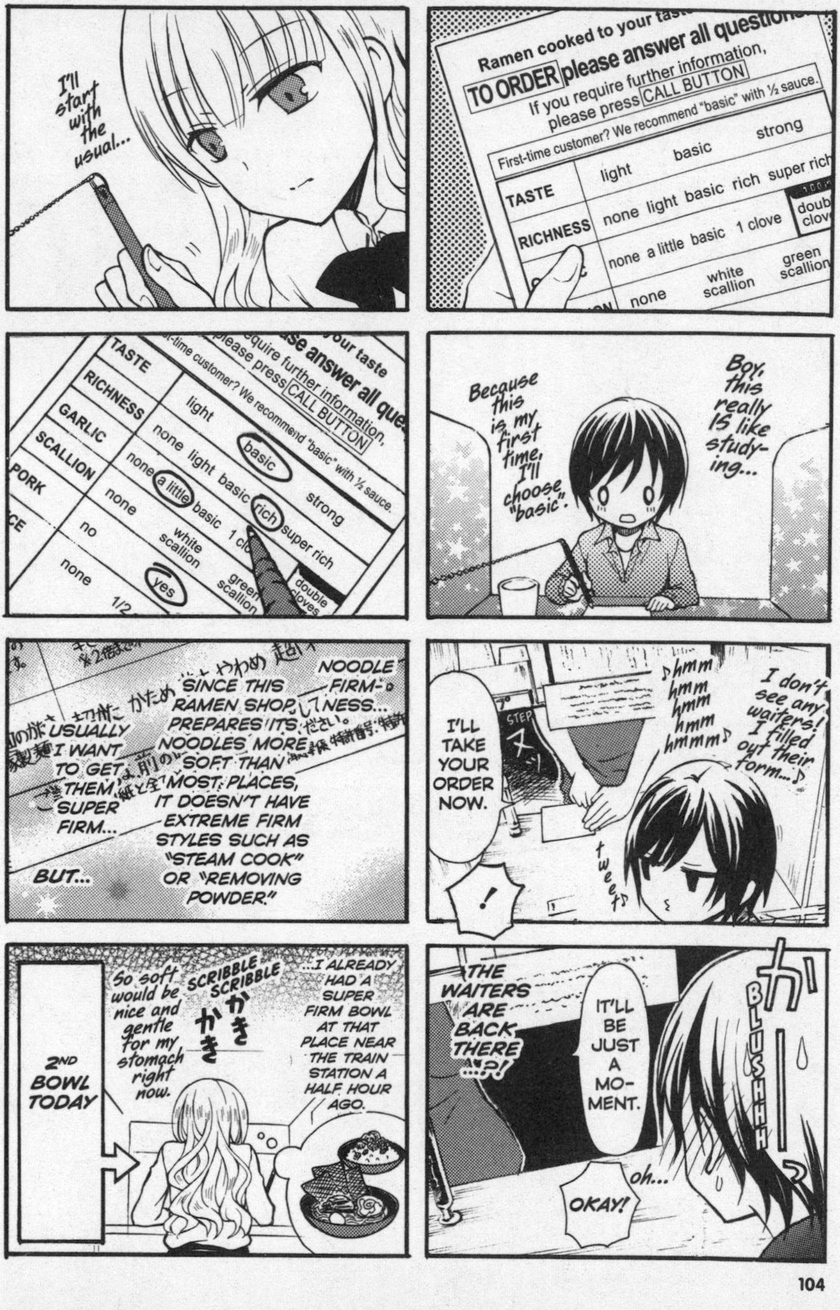
Ramen cooked to your taste
TO ORDER please answer all questions
If you require further information, please press CALL BUTTON
First-time customer? We recommend "basic" with ½ sauce.
TASTE light basic strong
RICHNESS none light basic rich super rich
none a little basic 1 clove double cloves
none white scallion green scallion
I'll start with the usual...
Boy, this really IS like studying...
Because this is my first time, I'll choose "basic".
TASTE
RICHNESS
GARLIC
SCALLION
PORK
please answer all questions
If you require further information, please press CALL BUTTON
First-time customer? We recommend "basic" with ½ sauce.
light basic strong
none light basic rich super rich
none a little basic 1 clove double cloves
none white scallion green scallion
no yes
none 1/2
I don't see any waiters! I filled out their form...♪
♪hmm hmm hmm hmm hmmm♪
I'LL TAKE YOUR ORDER NOW.
tweet♪
!
NOODLE FIRMNESS...
USUALLY I WANT TO GET THEM SUPER FIRM...
SINCE THIS RAMEN SHOP PREPARES ITS NOODLES MORE SOFT THAN MOST PLACES, IT DOESN'T HAVE EXTREME FIRM STYLES SUCH AS "STEAM COOK" OR "REMOVING POWDER."
BUT...
THE WAITERS ARE BACK THERE...?!
IT'LL BE JUST A MOMENT.
か一
BLUSHHH
oh...
OKAY!
...I ALREADY HAD A SUPER FIRM BOWL AT THAT PLACE NEAR THE TRAIN STATION A HALF HOUR AGO.
SCRIBBLE SCRIBBLE
かき かき
So soft would be nice and gentle for my stomach right now.
2ND BOWL TODAY

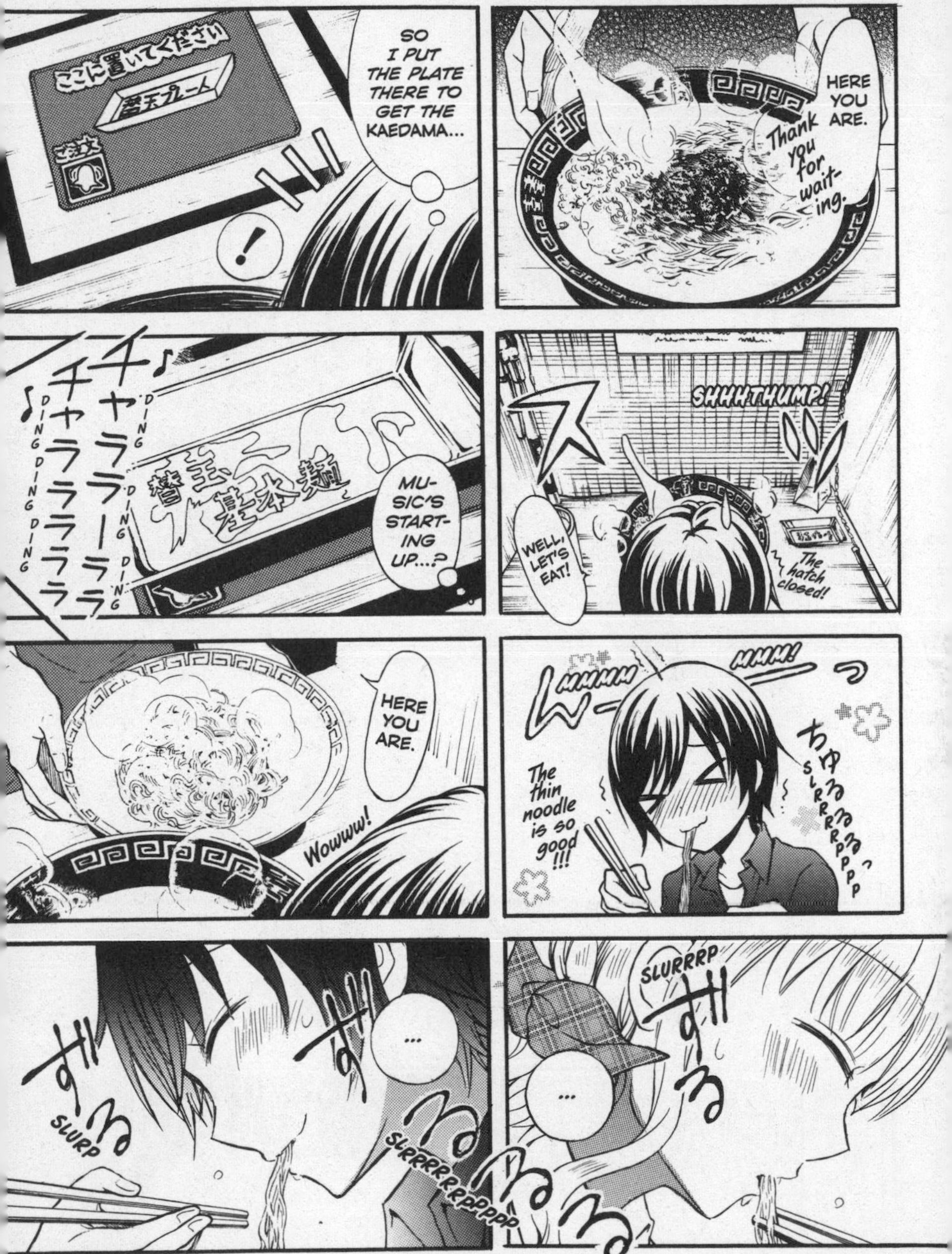
HERE YOU ARE.
Thank you for wait-ing.
ここに置いてください
替玉プレート
ご注文
SO I PUT THE PLATE THERE TO GET THE KAEDAMA...
!
SHHHTHUMP!
ス
WELL, LET'S EAT!
The hatch closed!
チャラララーララ♪
DING DING DING DING
チャララララララ♪
DING DING DING DING
MU-SIC'S START-ING UP...?
MMMM
ん—
MMM!
っ
ちゅるるるるる
SLRRRRPPPP
The thin noodle is so good!!!
HERE YOU ARE.
Wowww!
SLURRRP
ずる
...
ずる
SLURP
...
ずるるるる
SLRRRRRRPPPPP

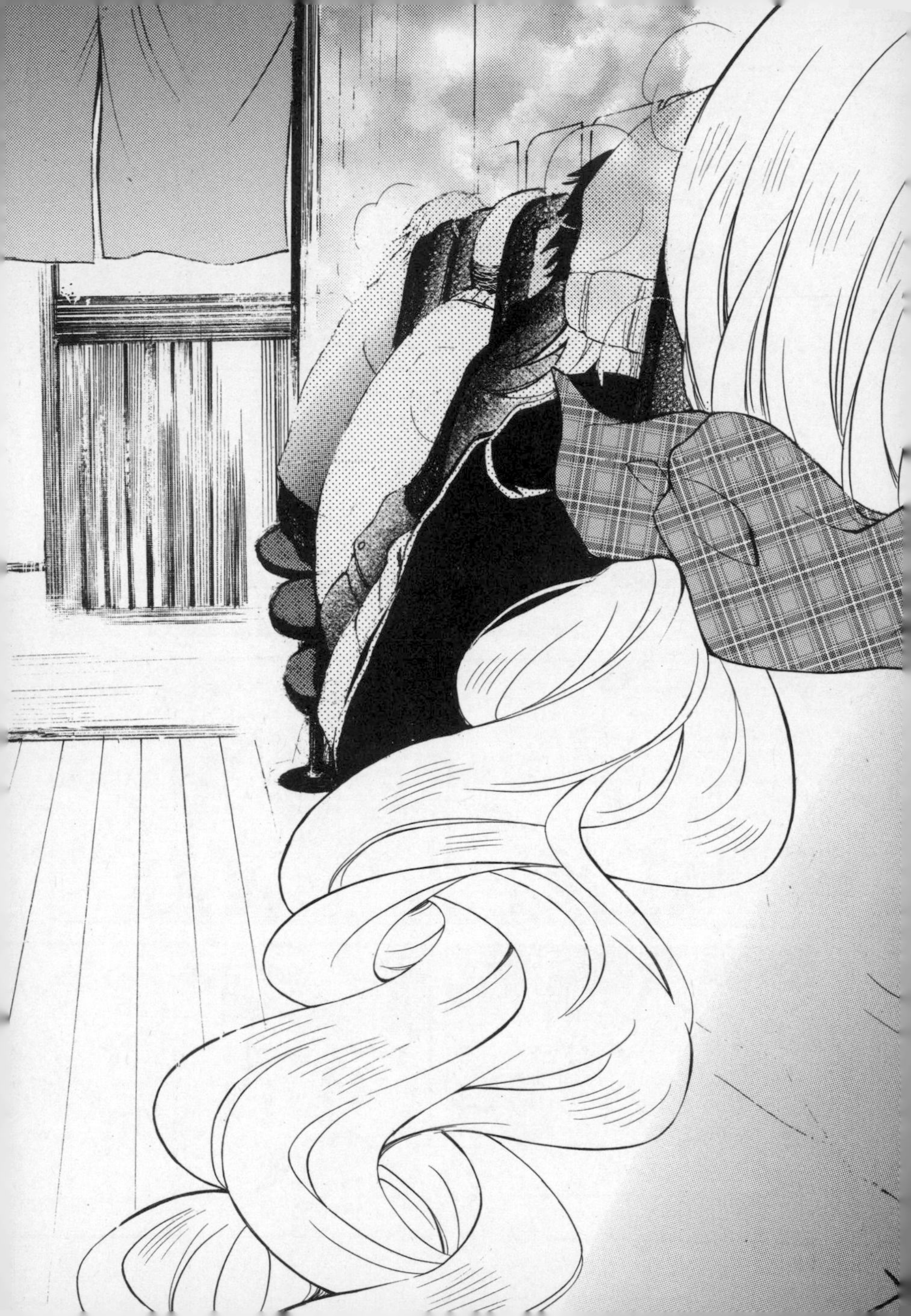

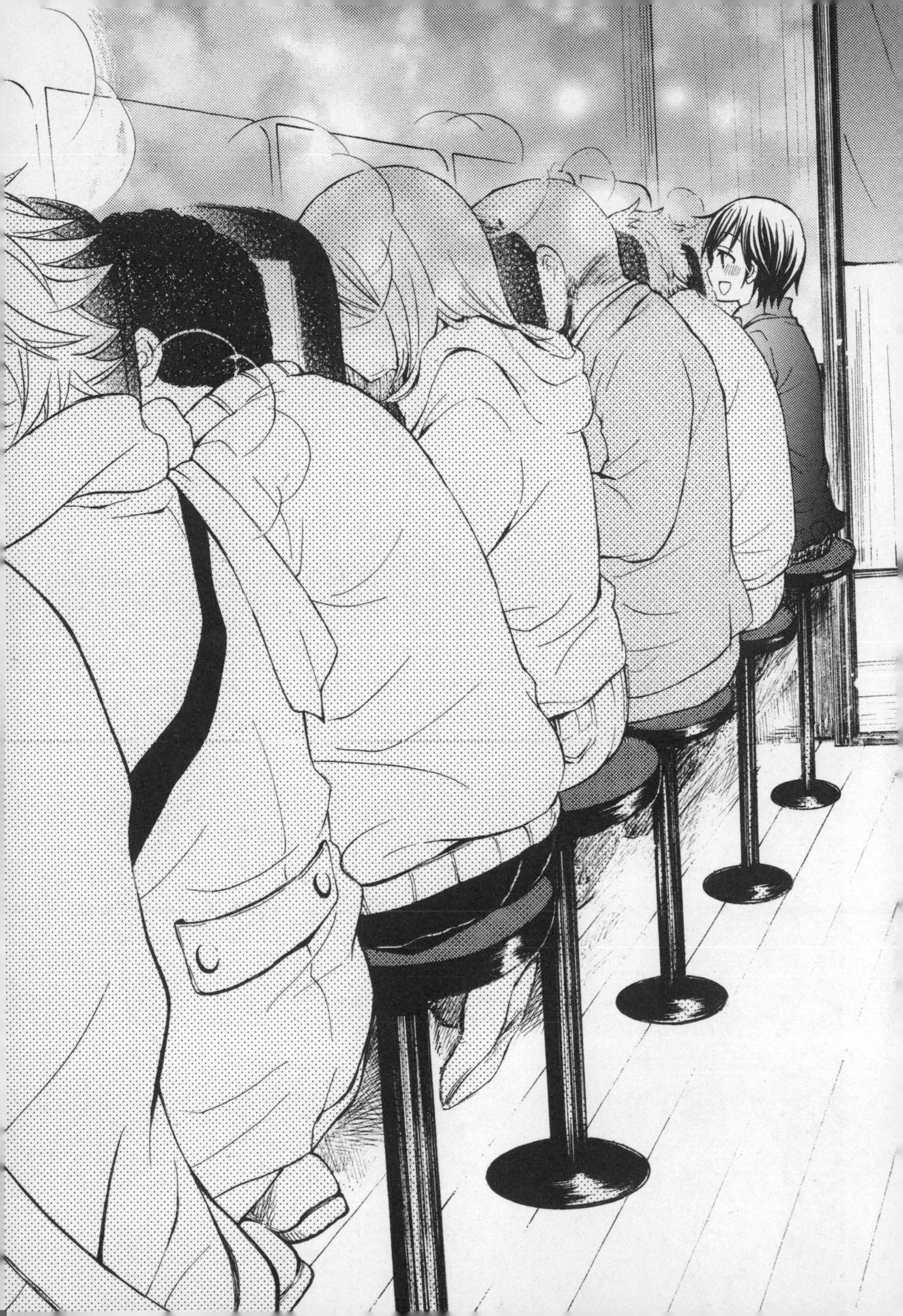

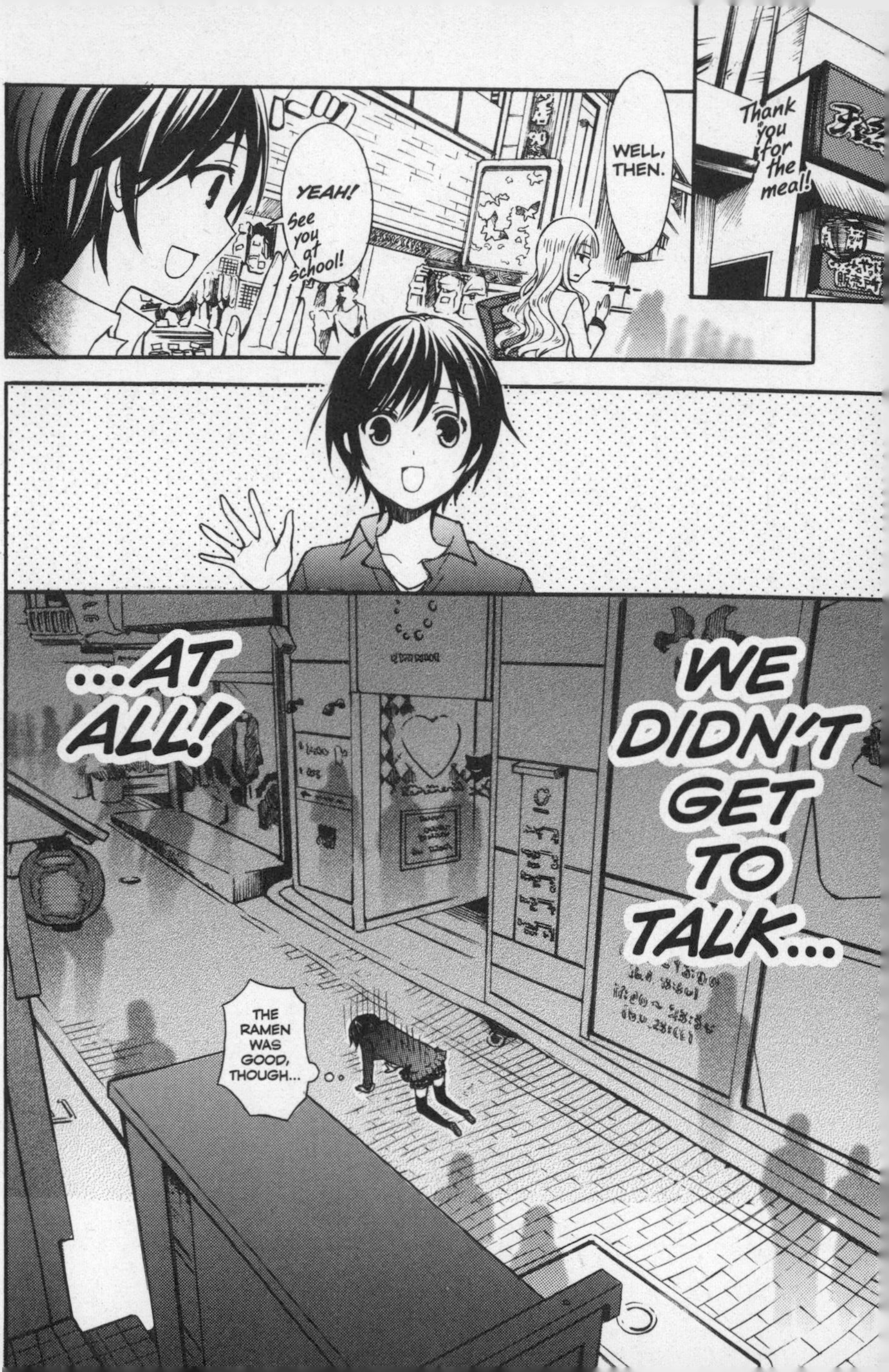
Thank you for the meal!
WELL, THEN.
YEAH! See you at school!
WE DIDN'T GET TO TALK...
...AT ALL!
THE RAMEN WAS GOOD, THOUGH...

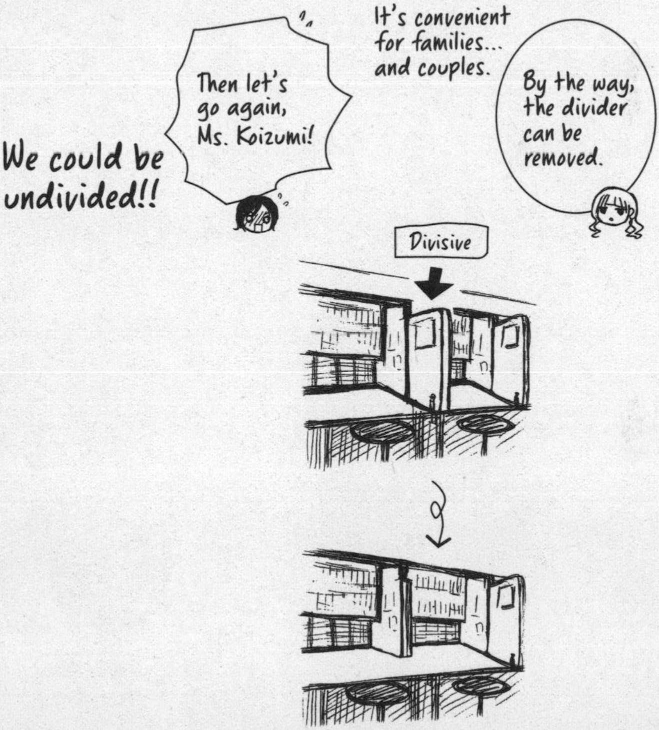
By the way, the divider can be removed.
It's convenient for families... and couples.
Then let's go again, Ms. Koizumi!
We could be undivided!!
Divisive

**Ms. Koizumi loves
ramen noodles**

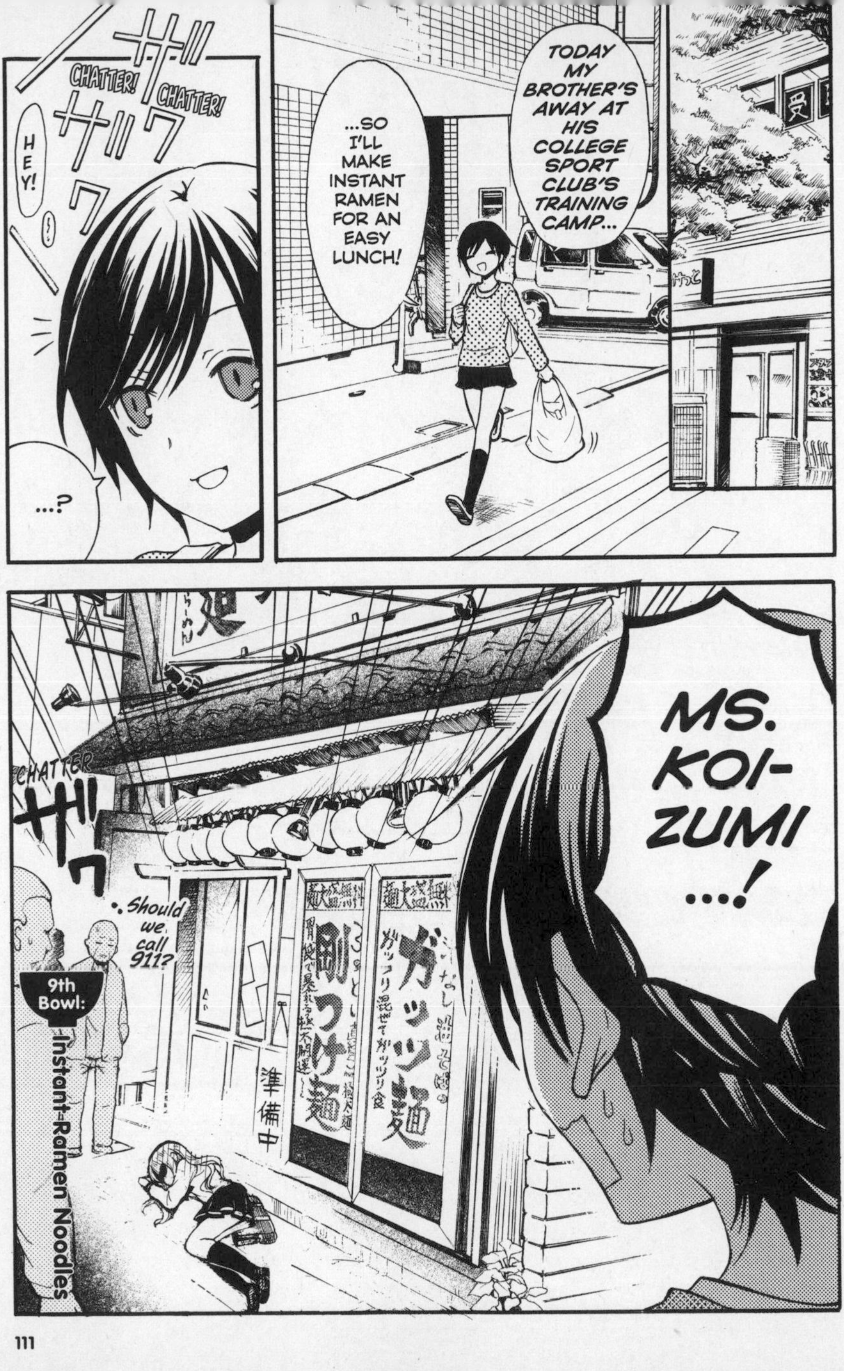
TODAY MY BROTHER'S AWAY AT HIS COLLEGE SPORT CLUB'S TRAINING CAMP...
...SO I'LL MAKE INSTANT RAMEN FOR AN EASY LUNCH!
CHATTER! CHATTER!
HEY!
!?
...?
MS. KOI-ZUMI ...!
準備中
ガッツ麺
CHATTER
...Should we call 911?
9th Bowl:
Instant-Ramen Noodles

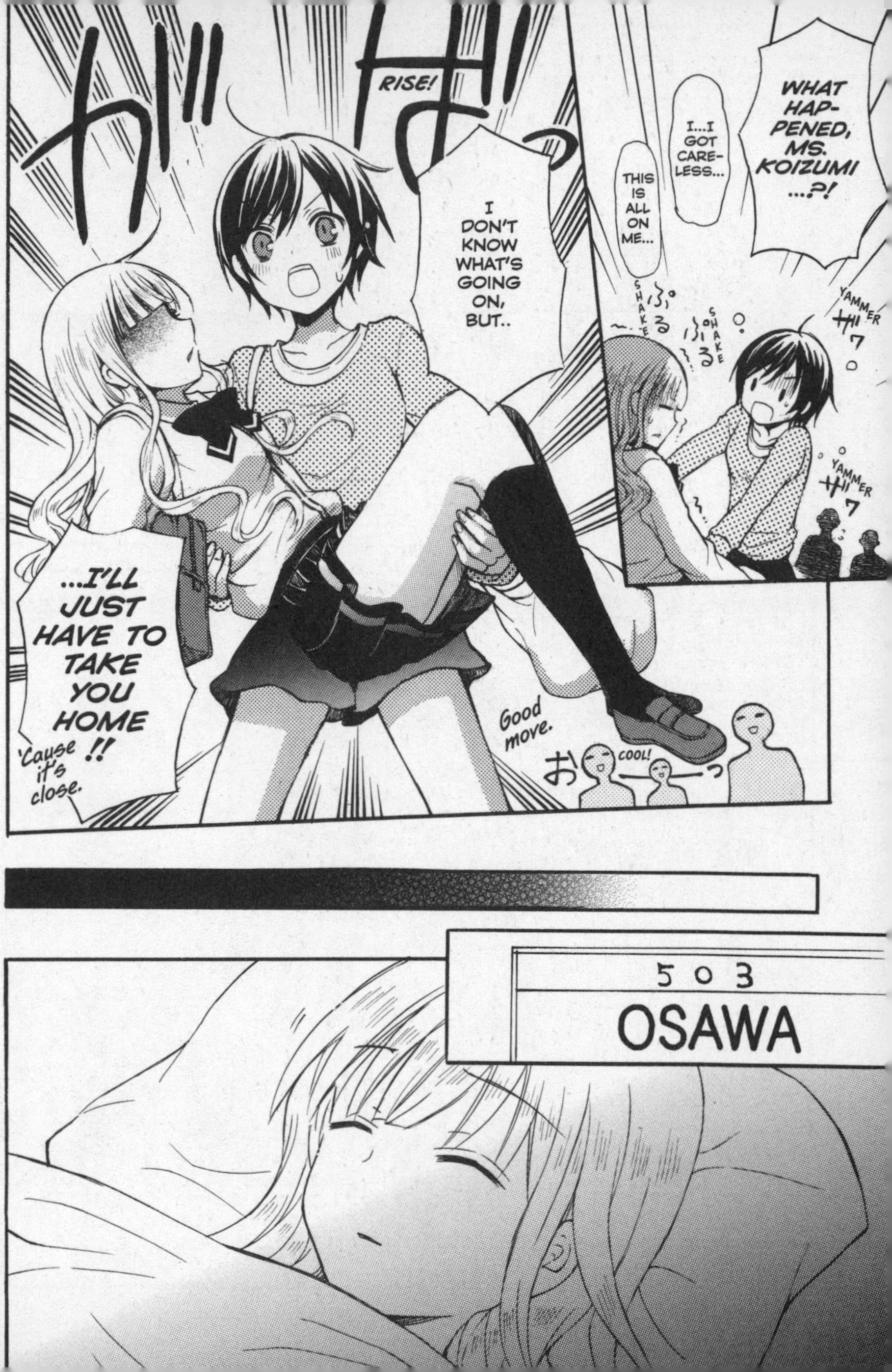
WHAT HAPPENED, MS. KOIZUMI ...?!
I...I GOT CARELESS...
THIS IS ALL ON ME...
SHAKE
SHAKE
YAMMER
YAMMER
RISE!
I DON'T KNOW WHAT'S GOING ON, BUT..
...I'LL JUST HAVE TO TAKE YOU HOME!!
'Cause it's close.
Good move.
COOL!
503
OSAWA

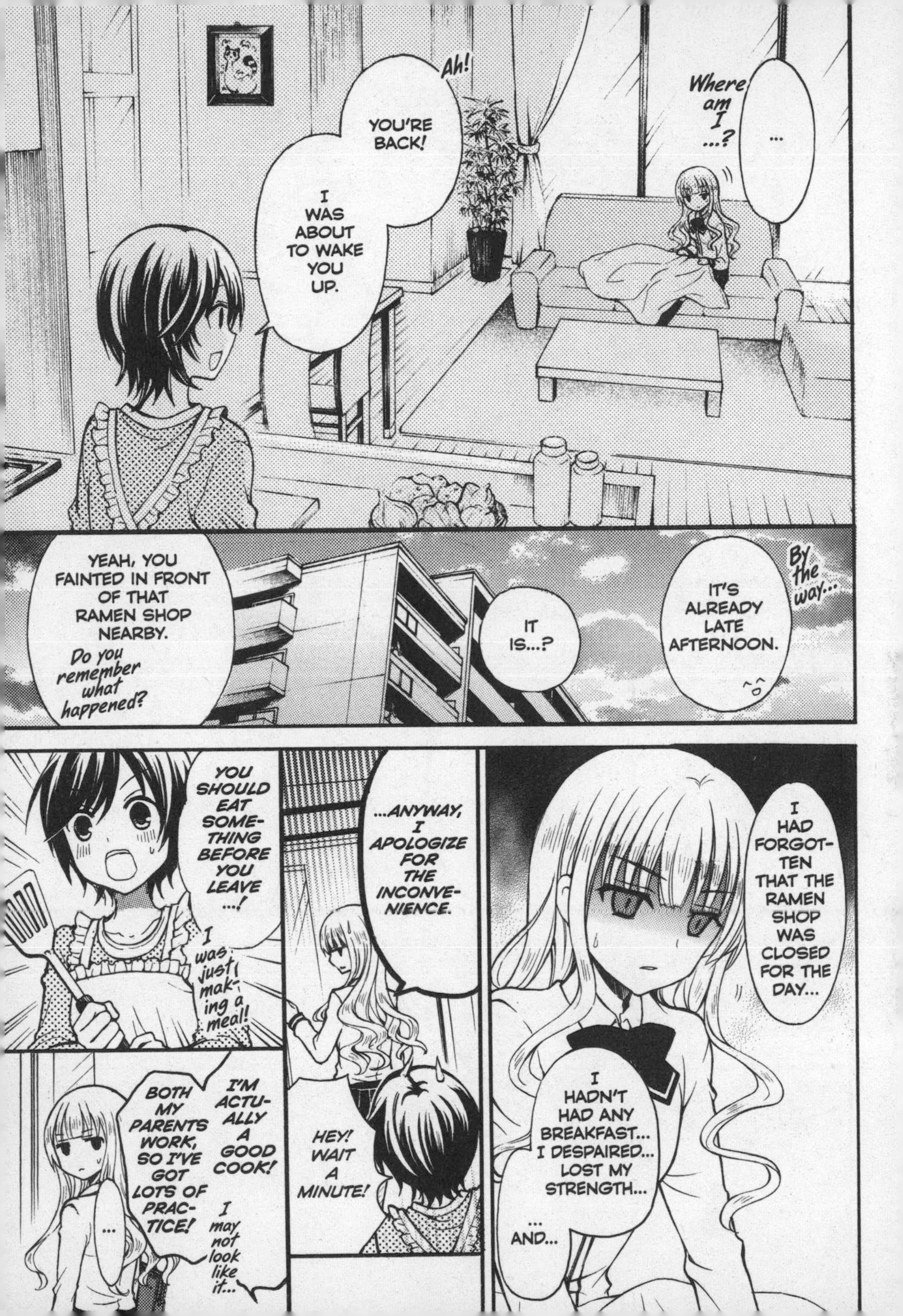
Where am I ...?
...
Ah!
YOU'RE BACK!
I WAS ABOUT TO WAKE YOU UP.
By the way...
IT'S ALREADY LATE AFTERNOON.
IT IS...?
YEAH, YOU FAINTED IN FRONT OF THAT RAMEN SHOP NEARBY.
Do you remember what happened?
I HAD FORGOTTEN THAT THE RAMEN SHOP WAS CLOSED FOR THE DAY...
I HADN'T HAD ANY BREAKFAST... I DESPAIRED... LOST MY STRENGTH...
... AND...
...ANYWAY, I APOLOGIZE FOR THE INCONVENIENCE.
YOU SHOULD EAT SOMETHING BEFORE YOU LEAVE ...!
I was just making a meal!
HEY! WAIT A MINUTE!
I'M ACTUALLY A GOOD COOK!
I may not look like it...
BOTH MY PARENTS WORK, SO I'VE GOT LOTS OF PRACTICE!
...

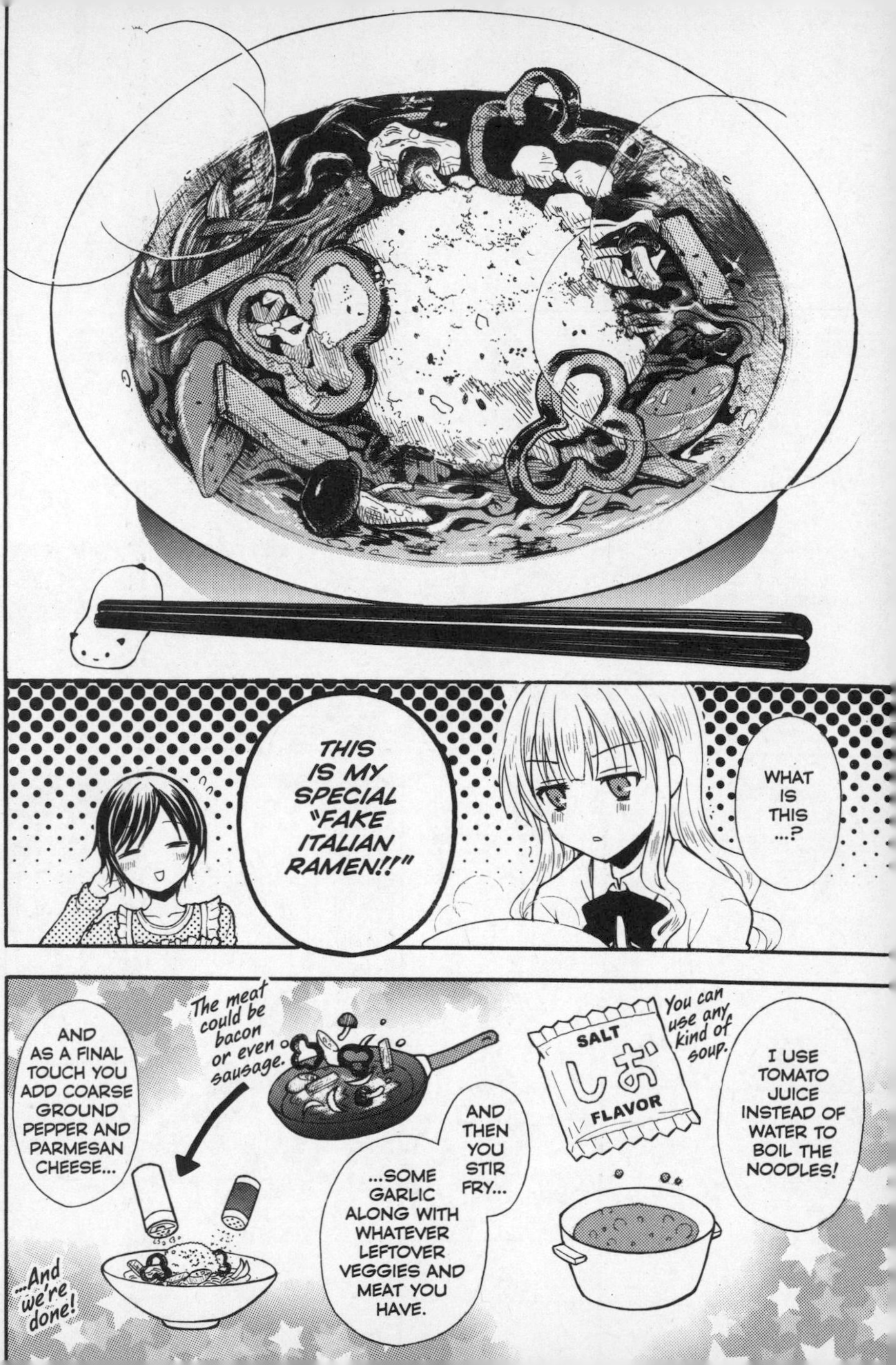
WHAT IS THIS ...?
THIS IS MY SPECIAL "FAKE ITALIAN RAMEN!!"
I USE TOMATO JUICE INSTEAD OF WATER TO BOIL THE NOODLES!
You can use any kind of soup.
SALT しお FLAVOR
AND THEN YOU STIR FRY...
...SOME GARLIC ALONG WITH WHATEVER LEFTOVER VEGGIES AND MEAT YOU HAVE.
The meat could be bacon or even sausage.
AND AS A FINAL TOUCH YOU ADD COARSE GROUND PEPPER AND PARMESAN CHEESE...
...And we're done!

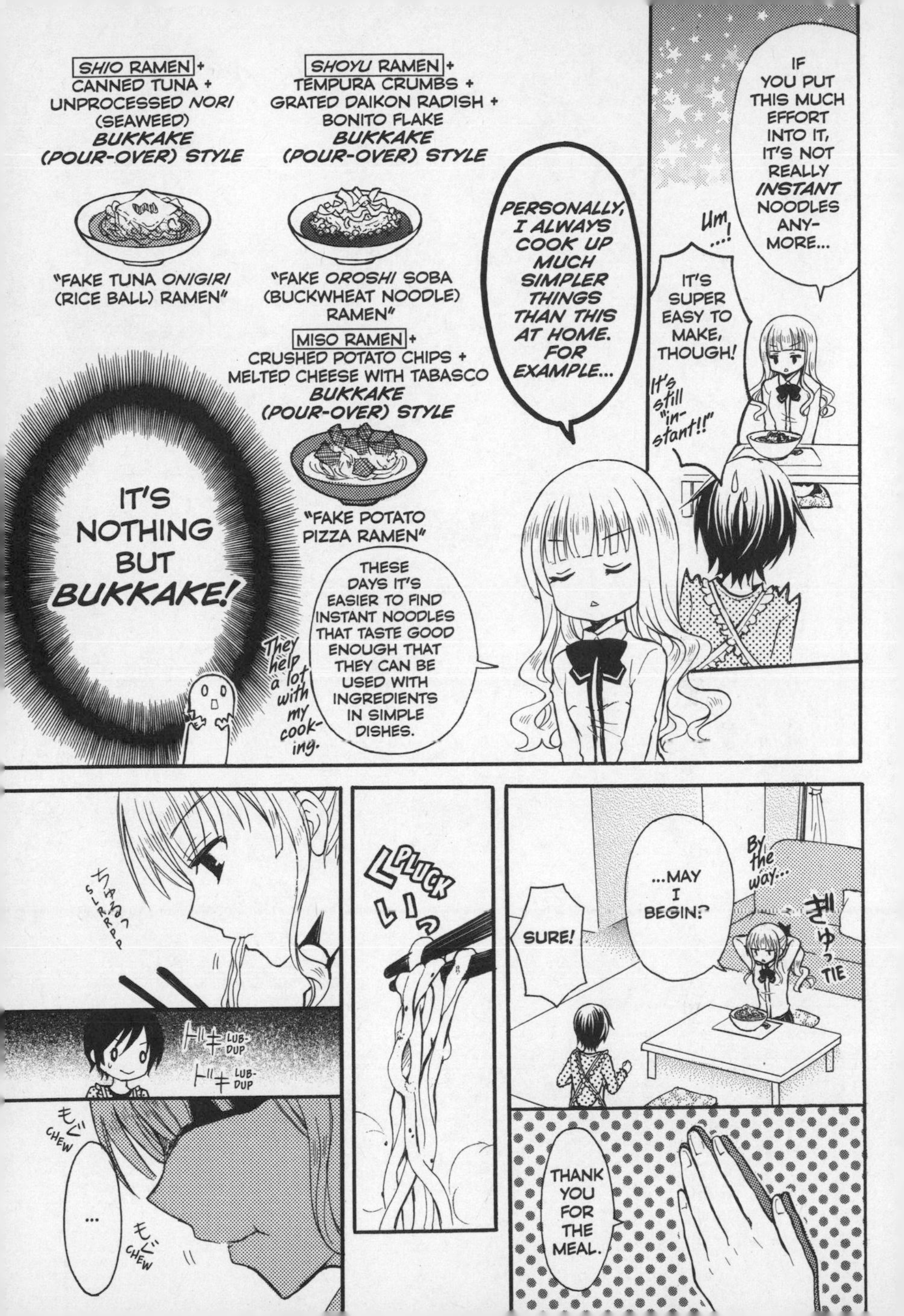

IF YOU PUT THIS MUCH EFFORT INTO IT, IT'S NOT REALLY INSTANT NOODLES ANYMORE...
Um, ...!
IT'S SUPER EASY TO MAKE, THOUGH!
It's still "instant!!"
PERSONALLY, I ALWAYS COOK UP MUCH SIMPLER THINGS THAN THIS AT HOME. FOR EXAMPLE...
SHOYU RAMEN + TEMPURA CRUMBS + GRATED DAIKON RADISH + BONITO FLAKE BUKKAKE (POUR-OVER) STYLE
"FAKE OROSHI SOBA (BUCKWHEAT NOODLE) RAMEN"
SHIO RAMEN + CANNED TUNA + UNPROCESSED NORI (SEAWEED) BUKKAKE (POUR-OVER) STYLE
"FAKE TUNA ONIGIRI (RICE BALL) RAMEN"
MISO RAMEN + CRUSHED POTATO CHIPS + MELTED CHEESE WITH TABASCO BUKKAKE (POUR-OVER) STYLE
"FAKE POTATO PIZZA RAMEN"
THESE DAYS IT'S EASIER TO FIND INSTANT NOODLES THAT TASTE GOOD ENOUGH THAT THEY CAN BE USED WITH INGREDIENTS IN SIMPLE DISHES.
They help a lot with my cooking.
IT'S NOTHING BUT BUKKAKE!
By the way...
...MAY I BEGIN?
SURE!
ぎゅっ TIE
THANK YOU FOR THE MEAL.
PLUCK
SLURRPP
LUB-DUP
LUB-DUP
もぐ CHEW
...
もぐ CHEW

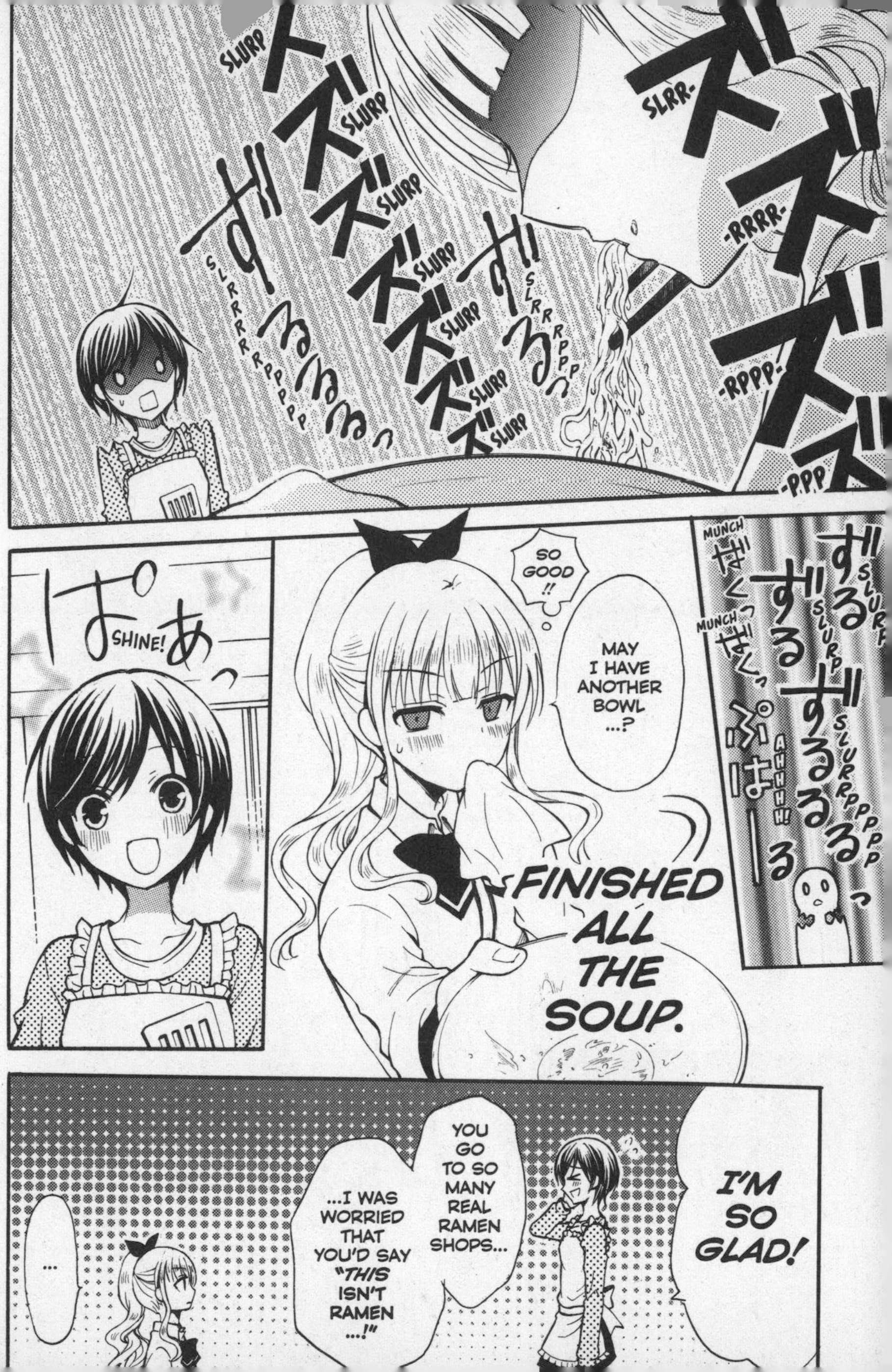

SLRR-
-RRRR-
-RPPP-
-PPP
SLRRRPPP
SLURP
SLURP
SLURP
SLURP
SLURP
SLURP
SLURP
SLRRRRRPPPPPP
SLURP
SLURP
SLURRPPPP
MUNCH
MUNCH
AHHHH!!
SO GOOD!!
MAY I HAVE ANOTHER BOWL ...?
FINISHED ALL THE SOUP.
SHINE!
I'M SO GLAD!
YOU GO TO SO MANY REAL RAMEN SHOPS...
...I WAS WORRIED THAT YOU'D SAY "THIS ISN'T RAMEN ...!"
...

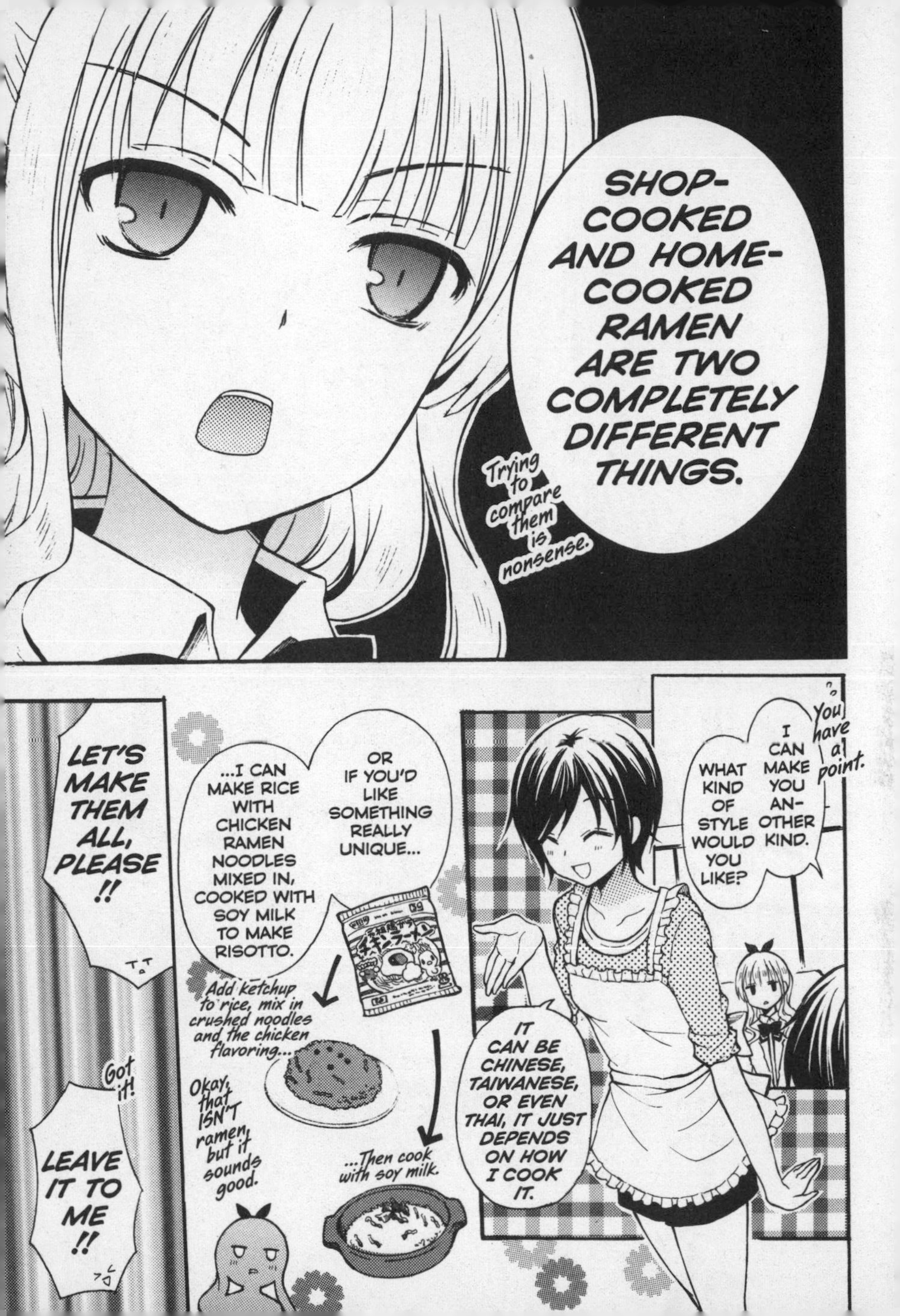
SHOP-COOKED AND HOME-COOKED RAMEN ARE TWO COMPLETELY DIFFERENT THINGS.
Trying to compare them is nonsense.
You have a point.
I CAN MAKE YOU AN-OTHER KIND.
WHAT KIND OF STYLE WOULD YOU LIKE?
IT CAN BE CHINESE, TAIWANESE, OR EVEN THAI, IT JUST DEPENDS ON HOW I COOK IT.
OR IF YOU'D LIKE SOMETHING REALLY UNIQUE...
...I CAN MAKE RICE WITH CHICKEN RAMEN NOODLES MIXED IN, COOKED WITH SOY MILK TO MAKE RISOTTO.
Add ketchup to rice, mix in crushed noodles and the chicken flavoring...
...Then cook with soy milk.
Okay, that ISN'T ramen, but it sounds good.
LET'S MAKE THEM ALL, PLEASE!!
Got it!
LEAVE IT TO ME!!

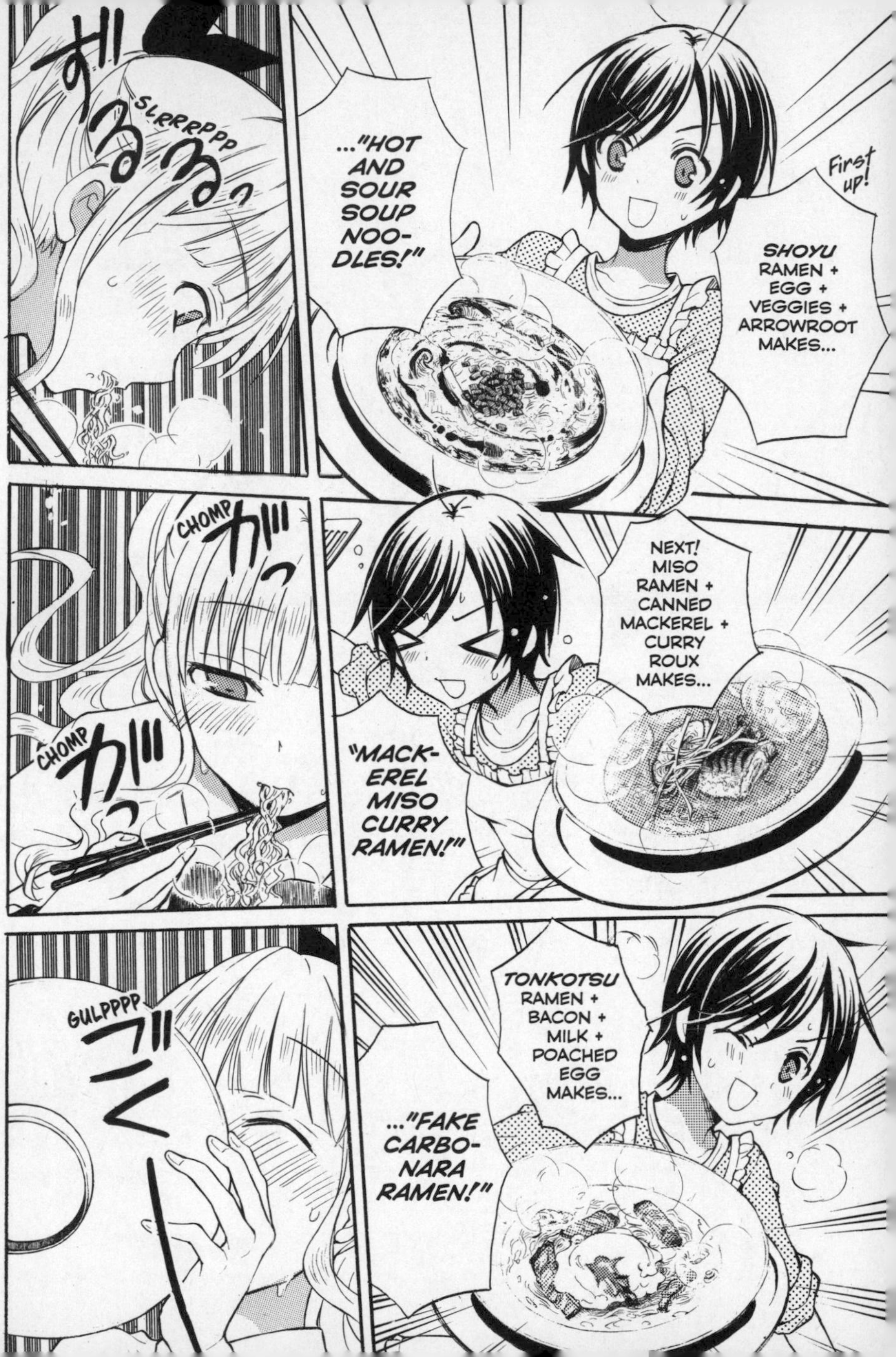
First up!
SHOYU RAMEN + EGG + VEGGIES + ARROWROOT MAKES...
..."HOT AND SOUR SOUP NOODLES!"
SLRRRPPP
ずるるるっ
NEXT! MISO RAMEN + CANNED MACKEREL + CURRY ROUX MAKES...
"MACKEREL MISO CURRY RAMEN!"
CHOMP
がっ
CHOMP
がっ
TONKOTSU RAMEN + BACON + MILK + POACHED EGG MAKES...
..."FAKE CARBONARA RAMEN!"
GULPPPP
ごく

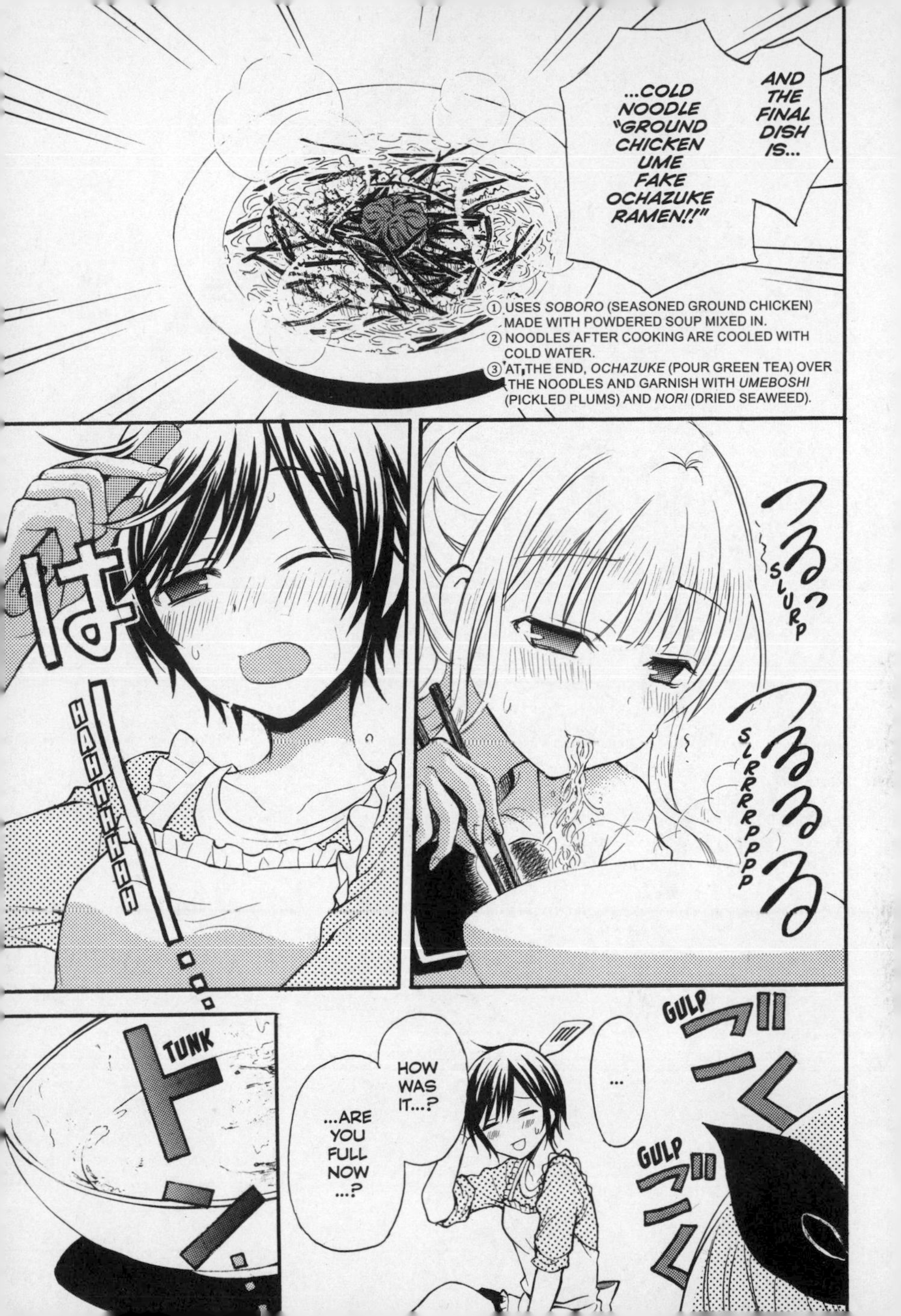
AND THE FINAL DISH IS...
...COLD NOODLE "GROUND CHICKEN UME FAKE OCHAZUKE RAMEN!!"
① USES SOBORO (SEASONED GROUND CHICKEN) MADE WITH POWDERED SOUP MIXED IN.
② NOODLES AFTER COOKING ARE COOLED WITH COLD WATER.
③ AT THE END, OCHAZUKE (POUR GREEN TEA) OVER THE NOODLES AND GARNISH WITH UMEBOSHI (PICKLED PLUMS) AND NORI (DRIED SEAWEED).
つるっ SLURP
つるるるる SLRRRPPPP
は HAHHHHHHH
GULP ごく
GULP ごく
...
HOW WAS IT...?
...ARE YOU FULL NOW...?
TUNK ト

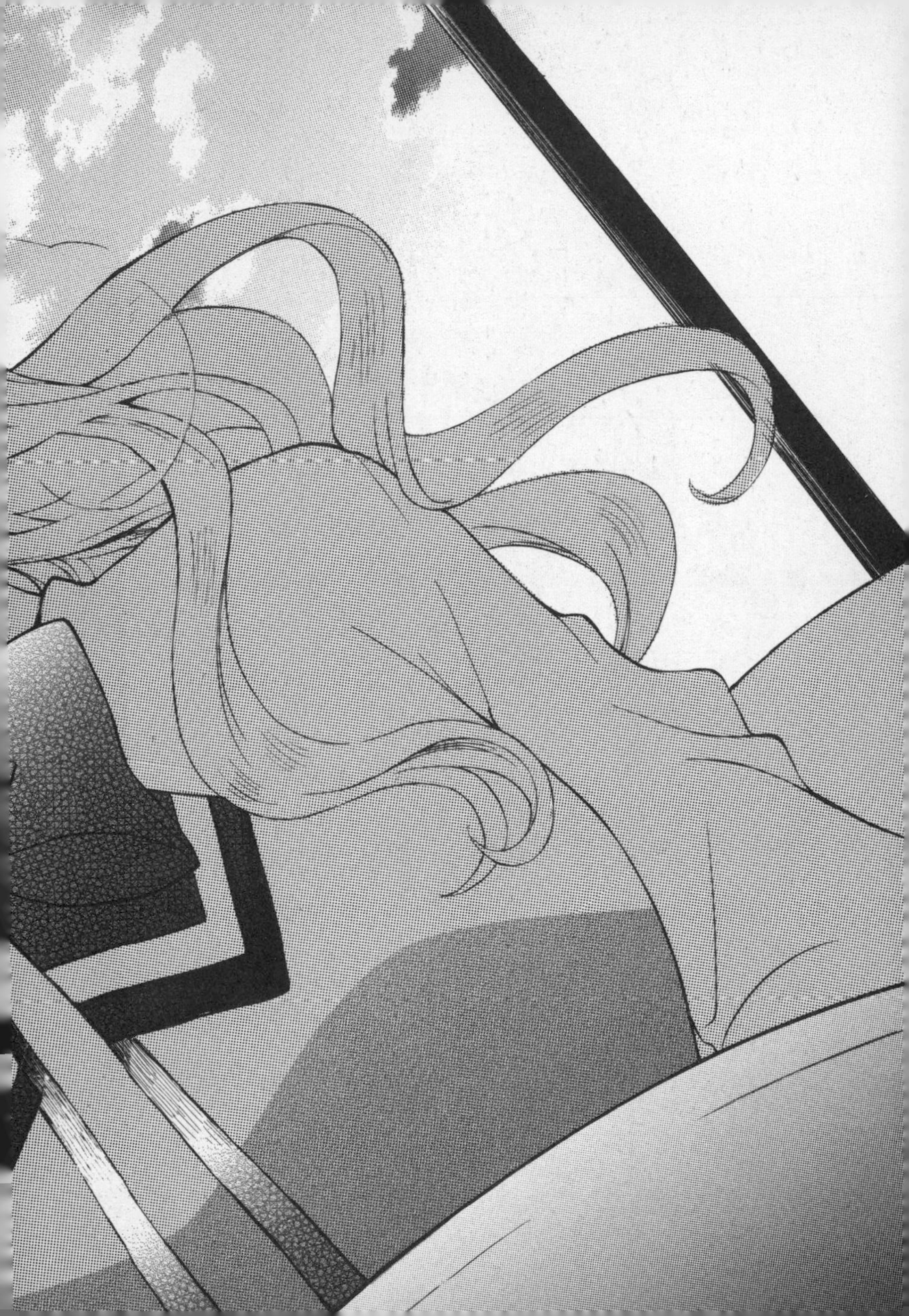

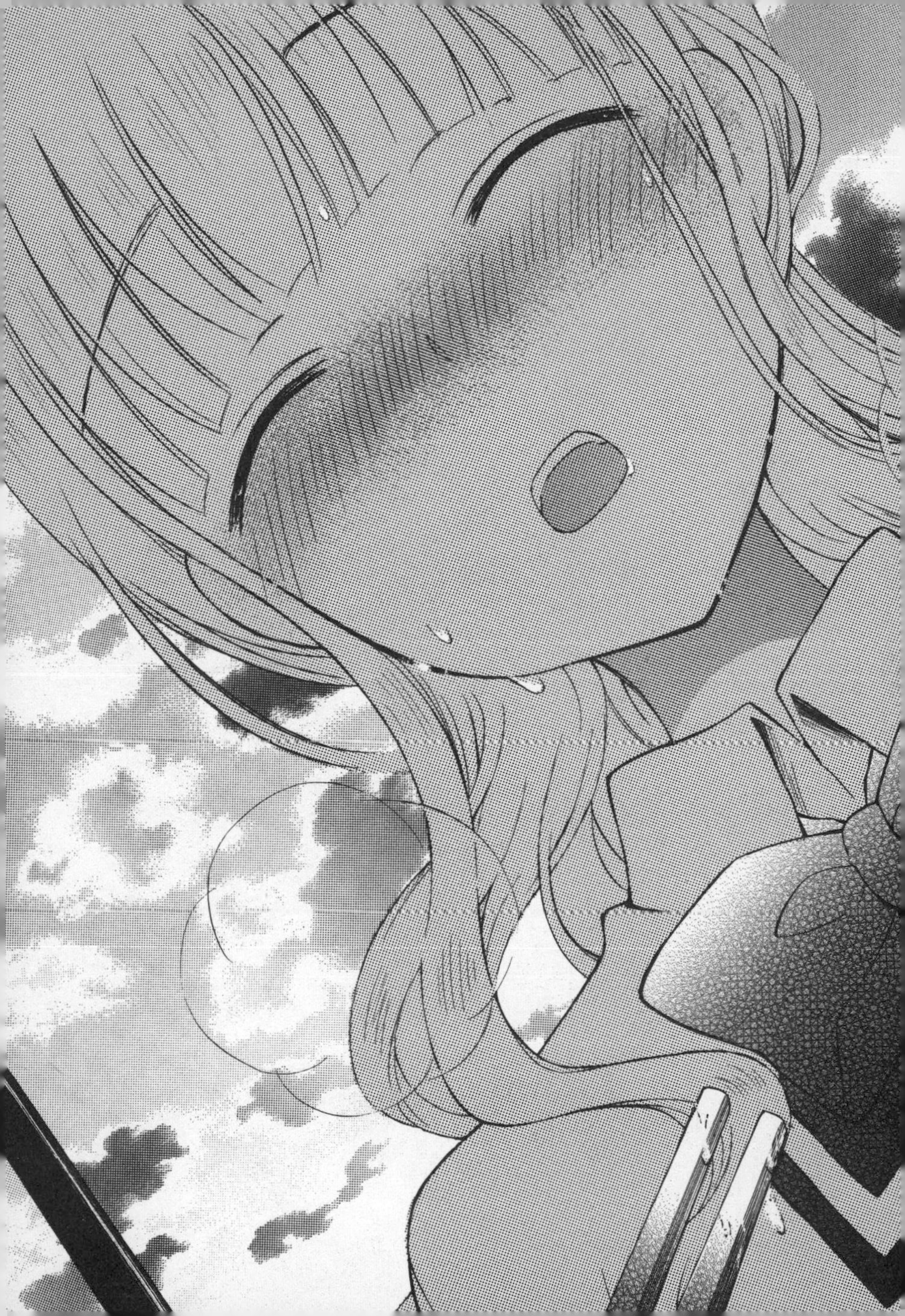

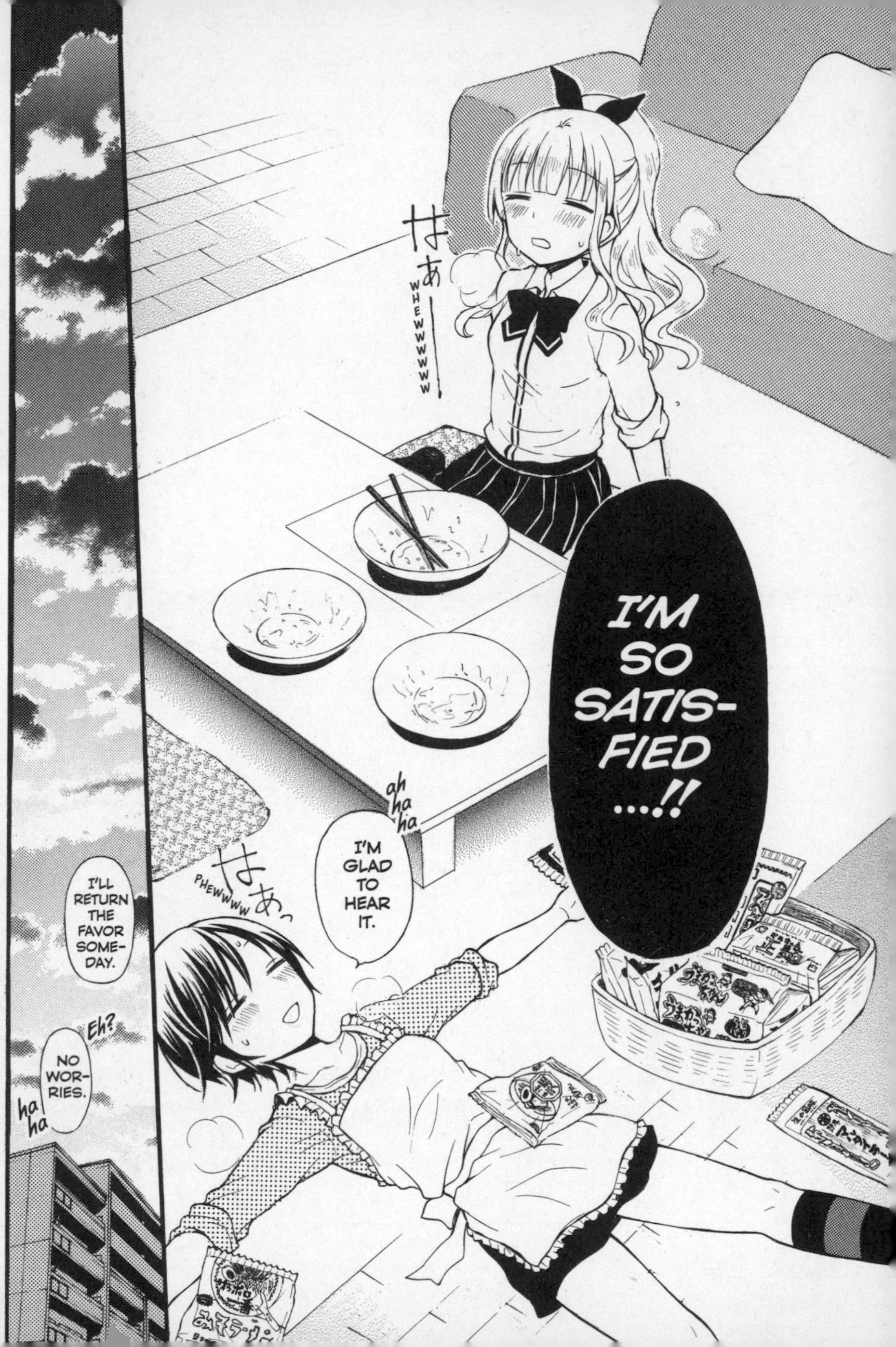

はあ—
WHEWWWWWWW
I'M SO SATISFIED....!!
ah ha ha
I'M GLAD TO HEAR IT.
はあっ
PHEWWWW
I'LL RETURN THE FAVOR SOMEDAY.
Eh?
NO WORRIES.
ha ha

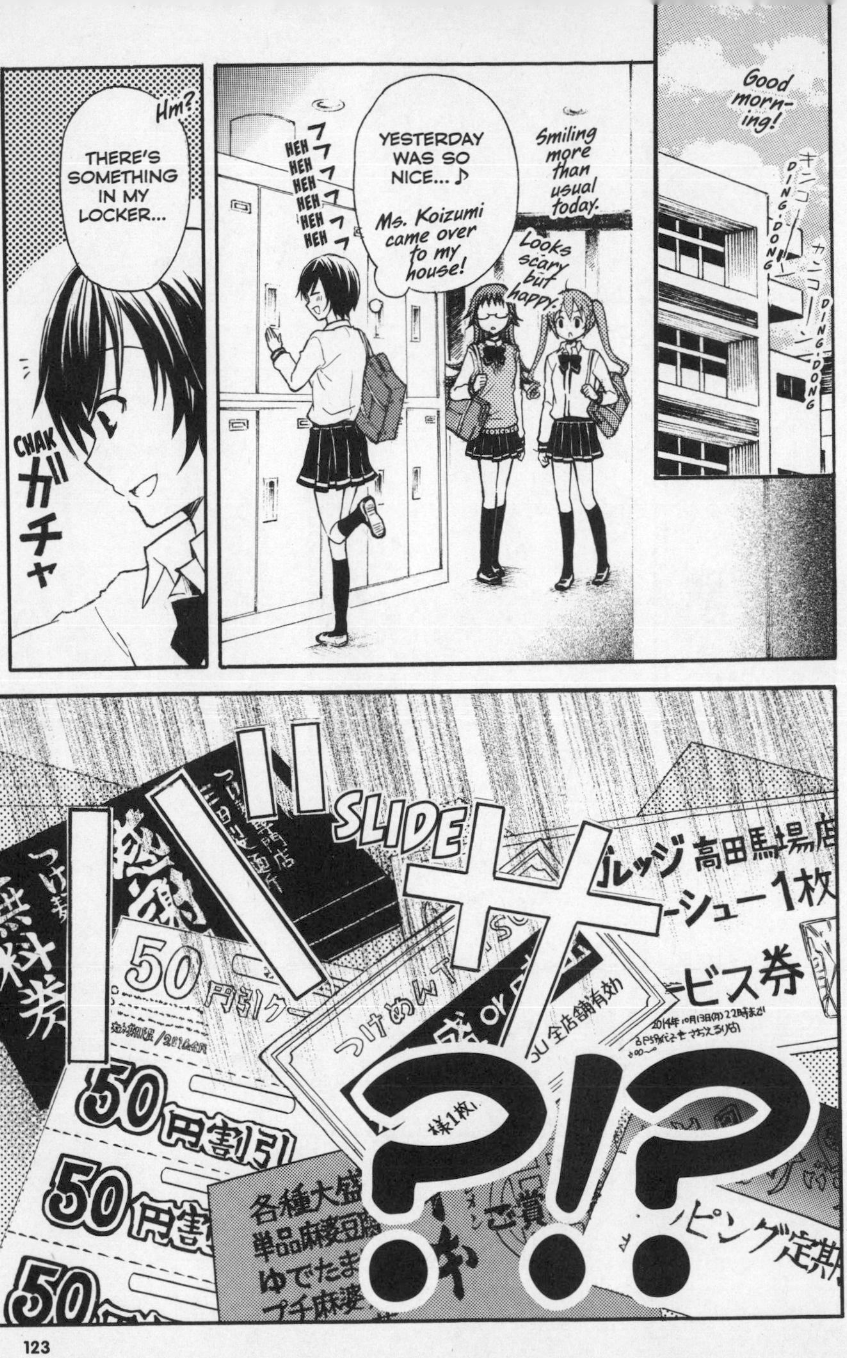
Good morning!
キンコーン
DING-DONG
カンコーン
DING-DONG
Smiling more than usual today.
Looks scary but happy.
YESTERDAY WAS SO NICE... ♪
Ms. Koizumi came over to my house!
フフフフフフ
HEH HEH HEH HEH HEH HEH
Hm?
THERE'S SOMETHING IN MY LOCKER...
CHAK
ガチャ
SLIDE
ッ!?
無料券
50円引クー
50円割引
50円害
高田馬場店
ーシュー1枚
ービス券
全店舗有効
つけめん
各種大盛
単品麻婆豆腐
ゆでたま
プチ麻婆
ピング定期

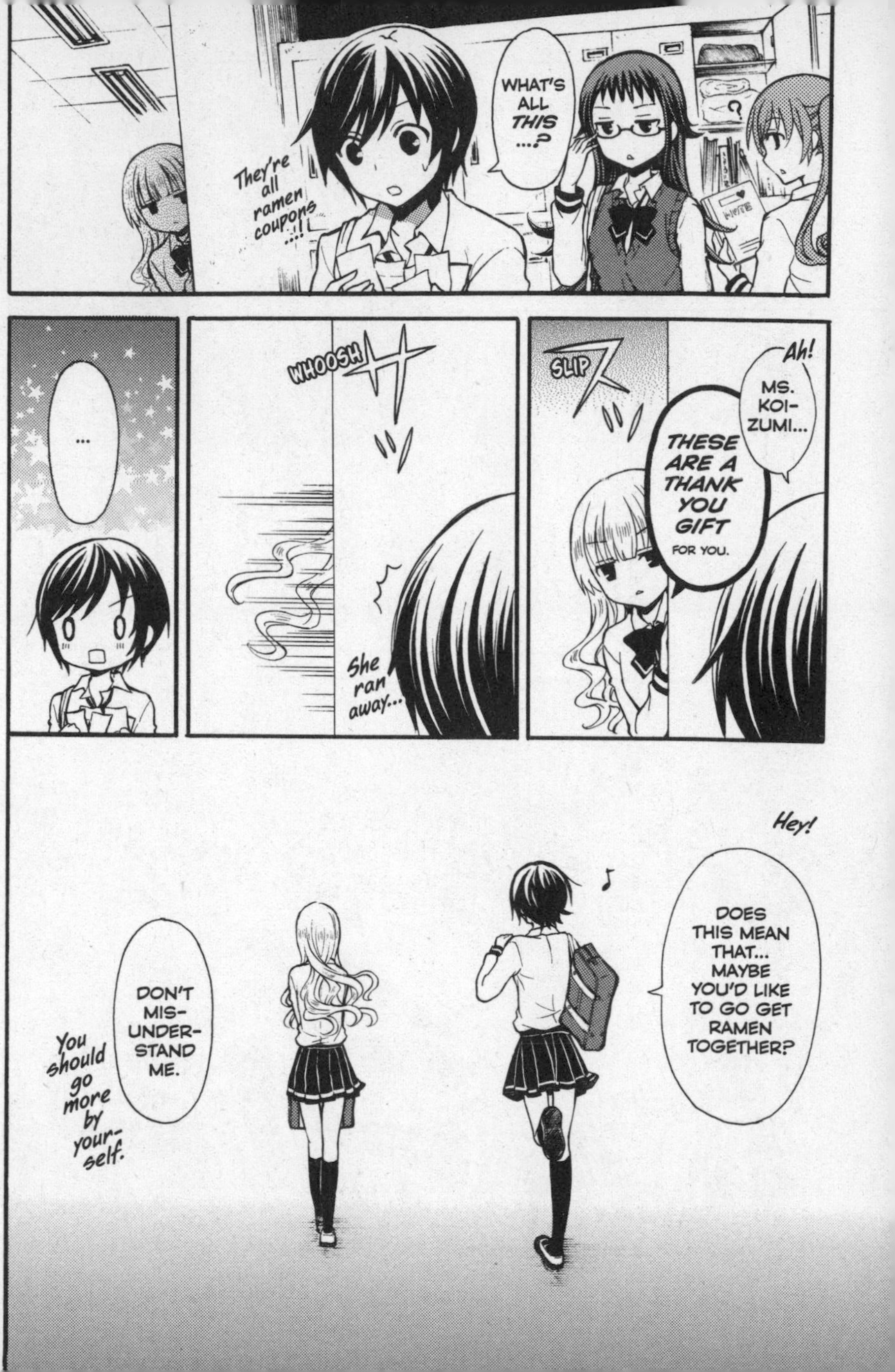
WHAT'S ALL THIS ...?
They're all ramen coupons ...!!
Ah!
MS. KOI-ZUMI...
THESE ARE A THANK YOU GIFT FOR YOU.
SLIP
WHOOSH
She ran away...
...
Hey!
DOES THIS MEAN THAT... MAYBE YOU'D LIKE TO GO GET RAMEN TOGETHER?
DON'T MIS-UNDER-STAND ME.
You should go more by your-self.

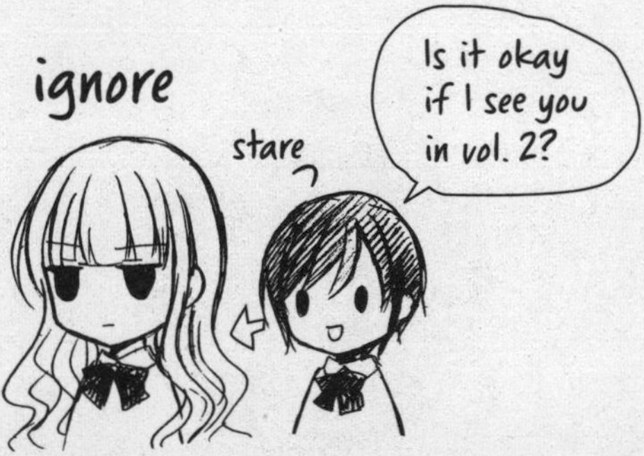
Is it okay if I see you in vol. 2?
stare
ignore

What I could really go for *right now* is a very rich ramen with a lot of backfat. I typically prefer thicker noodles, too. Also, there was this one time I got into the seasonal "sea urchin" noodles; I'll also probably get into it again this winter too.

Other women often tell me that they don't feel comfortable going to most ramen shops by themselves. I can understand how they feel. I guess I'm lucky that, for whatever reason, I started going to ramen shops by myself pretty early, as far back as high school. When you have a chance and you're up to it, push yourself to go into one of these shops, while telling yourself it's really just a cafe. You'll probably do fine.

Wait a minute—other women read this manga?! I guess I was just surprised to hear it! Thank you so much to *everyone* for reading *Ms. Koizumi Loves Ramen Noodles*!

—naru narumi

P.S. The translator notes that Narumi-sensei is joking about the fact that the magazine *Ms. Koizumi* runs in, *Storia*, is a *seinen* publication, meaning it is technically aimed at male rather than female readers. Manga magazines in Japan are typically directed at either men or women, but in reality many of them have crossover readership (a famous example is Japan's most successful manga magazine, *Shonen Jump*—*shonen* may mean "boy," but the magazine is equally popular among women and men).

twitter:
@naruminaru3

I'll tweet about
Ms. Koizumi there!

postscript

After such a long time of telling everyone how much I love ramen, finally I lucked out and was presented with this amazing opportunity to create my very own ramen manga! Thank you to everyone who worked on publishing this manga, and everyone who supported me by reading my work!

I usually write manga series that have chapters containing 40-60 pages, so it was new and really quite refreshing for me to write around 20 pages per chapter for *Ms. Koizumi* instead. I want to continue writing about the ramen I love a little longer. Also just so ya know, this manga is currently an ongoing serial in Japan in *Storia* magazine, so please read the future volumes as well!

Oh, there's more space to fill...so let's talk about ramen more!

After I started writing *Ms. Koizumi*, people would often ask me what *my* favorite ramen is, but that's a difficult question for me. Back when I was in elementary school, the first ramen I had that really made me appreciate ramen was *Hakata tonkotsu* (a style with noodles hard in the center associated with the city of Fukuoka). I also like spicy food a lot, so I tend to put a lot of *karashi takana* (mustard greens, pickled and stir-fried with hot pepper and sesame) on my ramen.

Over the past couple of years, I've probably been having miso ramen the most. When I was working on a different manga series set in Nagano prefecture, I needed to visit there often in order to do research for it. Every time I went there, I got to have Shinshu (a traditional name for Nagano) miso ramen and I got really into it.

Extra 1 About Ms. Koizumi's hairstyle

Before starting this manga series, I was experimenting with the design of Ms. Koizumi's hair in order to try to convey the image of the ramen noodle. I began first with wavy hair, because it reminded me of the distinct medium level thickness of the curly noodle so often seen in typical ramen dishes. Many people asked me if her hair is blonde, but actually it's yellow, as ramen noodles are (this is because of *kansui*, an alkaline solution which is the key ingredient in ramen making; it causes the noodles to have that distinctive yellow color and also their special springy texture you can taste). That's why sometimes when I'm sleepy and drawing her hair, it starts to make me hungry, because it looks like ramen noodles! Even just talking about it right now while writing this, I've started to crave ramen in the middle of the night. It's not easy!

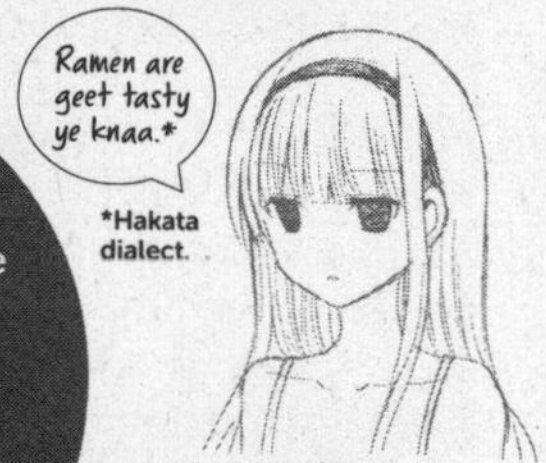
Ramen are geet tasty ye knaa.*
*Hakata dialect.

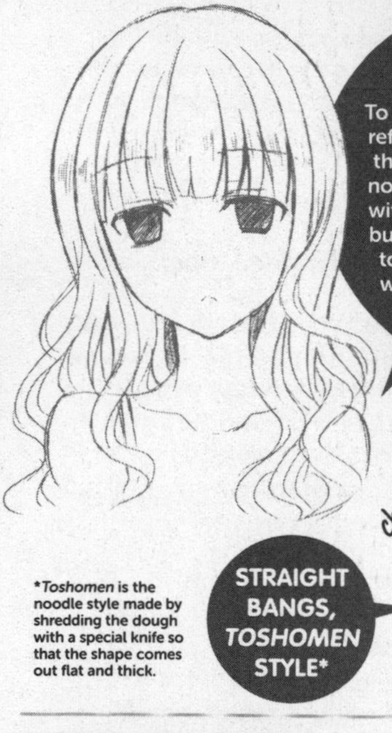

GETTING THE RATIO RIGHT

To have Koizumi-san's hairstyle reflect the water-to-flour ratio that goes into making ramen noodles, at first I drew her hair with this really wavy look to it, but I thought it made her look too mature, so I made it less wavy and more fluffy by the time I showed my editor.

HER HAIR IMAGINED AS HAKATA *TONKOTSU* STYLE STRAIGHT THIN NOODLES

Then I tried it this way, but with more hair lines like this, I thought it became too unfriendly looking for her.

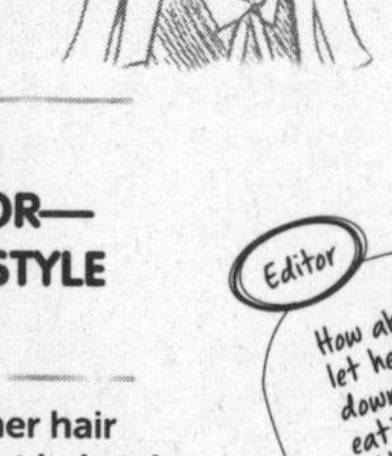
chop!
chop!

STRAIGHT BANGS, *TOSHOMEN* STYLE*

**Toshomen* is the noodle style made by shredding the dough with a special knife so that the shape comes out flat and thick.

EXCERPT FROM PHONE CONFERENCE WITH MY EDITOR—TOPIC: MS. KOIZUMI'S HAIRSTYLE WHILE EATING RAMEN

It was important to me that she tie her hair while focusing on eating her meal, but hairstyle is really crucial when it comes to defining a manga character's identity, so I could totally understand where my editor was coming from too. In the end though, we agreed that a more realistic depiction was the way to go.

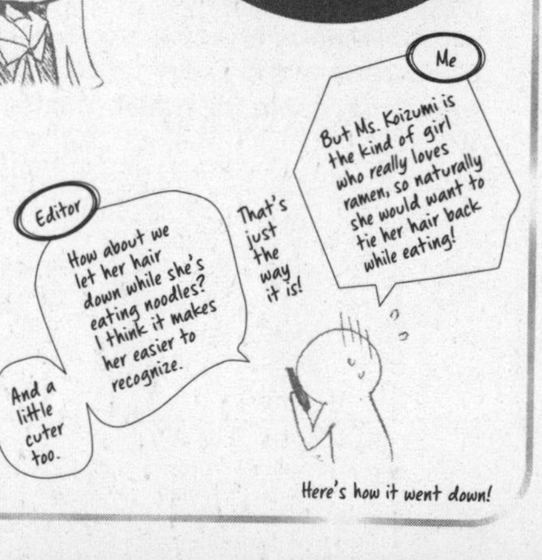
Me
But Ms. Koizumi is the kind of girl who really loves ramen, so naturally she would want to tie her hair back while eating!
That's just the way it is!
Editor
How about we let her hair down while she's eating noodles? I think it makes her easier to recognize.
And a little cuter too.
Here's how it went down!

Extra 2 A look inside Ms. Koizumi's bag!

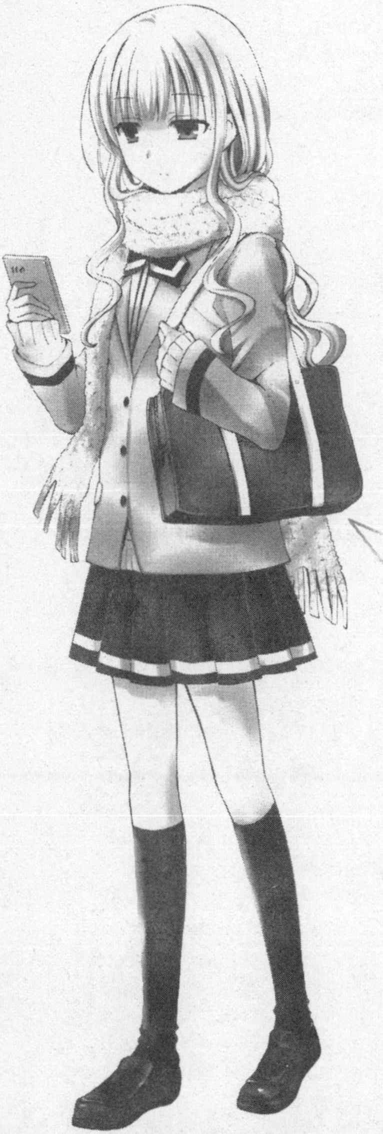

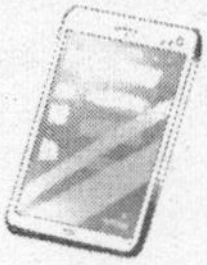

SMARTPHONE

This device can be used to research ramen. It's able to access information about wait times, special events, seasonal menus, and much more.

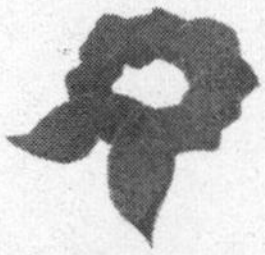

SCRUNCHIE

This is a necessary item for fastening up long hair.

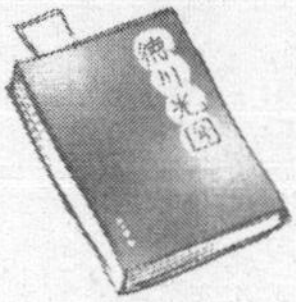

BOOK

For killing time while waiting in a long line.

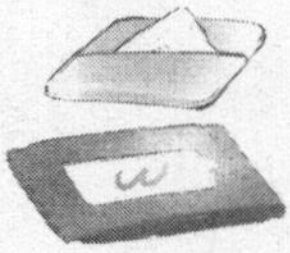

TISSUES AND WET WIPES

Very useful for any occasion.

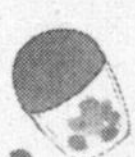

ORAL CARE ITEM

For freshening up your breath after having extra garlic and extra scallions.

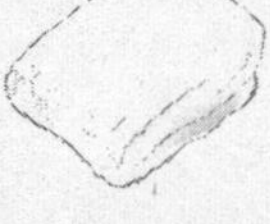

HAND TOWELS

For sweat! It's good to have a couple of them in the summertime.

Message to readers from the translator:

I've really enjoyed translating *Koizumi-san* and learning more about ramen in the process. While I moved from Japan to the US almost 10 years ago, I have to say what I miss more than anything has to be the food (and of course friends and family, haha)!

Currently I'm working in the kitchen most of the time, covered in flour and sugar while whipping up pastries, so it was a fun change of pace for me to mix it up some by sitting at my computer, translating ramen manga on my days off :) I really hope you find yourself enjoying this manga in its English version as much as one might in its native Japanese.

Sincerely,

Ayumi Kato Blystone

Ayumi Kato Blystone
Pastry Chef / Owner of Huggle Sweets LLC in Hillsboro, OR
Instagram @hugglesweets Website www.hugglesweets.com

P.S. from the editor:
I want to thank not only Ayumi, but also the person who suggested that she translate, my old friend Abby Denson. People sometimes ask if you can make manga if you're not Japanese. Well, the Japanese Ministry of Foreign Affairs thinks so—they awarded Abby their 2011 International Manga Award in bronze for her *Dolltopia*. Tuttle (since 1948 one of the most respected English-language publishers of books on Japan) has released two manga-style travel guides by Abby—the *Cool Japan Guide* and *Cool Tokyo Guide*. I've learned things from them myself! ^_^

チャーシューのこだわり

Perfection to The Finest Detail

RAMEN RYOMA

特製チャーシュー
Pork Belly Chashu

Ramen Ryoma pick only the finest quality pork belly. Our pork chashu is boiled in our soup stock for 5 hours, and then soaked in our specially formulated Tare which has been blended in with our new batch of sauce respectively through the days.

厳選した上質な豚バラのみを使用。スープで5時間トロトロになるまで煮込み、これを店舗で毎日継ぎ足し継ぎ足しで作っている秘伝の特製タレに漬け込み完成です。

Visit Ramen Ryoma in Beaverton, OR!

Getting into the spirit of the manga, we'd like in this English edition to feature some local ramen places in Dark Horse's own neighborhood (the Portland area!).

We can't think of a better point to start than a ramen place that's right next to where you can buy your manga both in English and Japanese! Of course, we're talking about Kinokuniya, Japan's great international bookstore chain that's been so important in the lives of generations of manga fans (including the editor). Kinokuniya's first store in Oregon is in Beaverton, inside the building that also houses our local Uwajimaya, the Pacific Northwest's own Asian grocery and gift retail chain.

And in the same building, just a few steps from Kinokuniya, is the perfect place to pair up your manga purchase with a bowl of ramen—Ramen Ryoma! Their specialty is pork belly *chashu* ramen, of which the proprietor says, "We very carefully boil premium black pork bones, pork *chashu* meat, and vegetables such as green and white onions, ginger, and seaweed for six hours to prepare our special soup." You'll probably finish your pork belly *chashu* ramen as fast as Ms. Koizumi—but you'll taste those six hours that went into it!

president and publisher **Mike Richardson**

editor **Carl Gustav Horn**

designer **Anita Magaña**

digital art technician **Ann Gray**

english-language version produced by dark horse comics

Ms. Koizumi Loves Ramen Noodles Vol. 1

Published by
Dark Horse Manga
A division of Dark Horse Comics LLC
10956 SE Main Street
Milwaukie, OR 97222

DarkHorse.com
To find a comics shop in your area visit comicshoplocator.com

First edition: September 2019
ISBN 978-1-50671-327-4

1 2 3 4 5 6 7 8 9 10

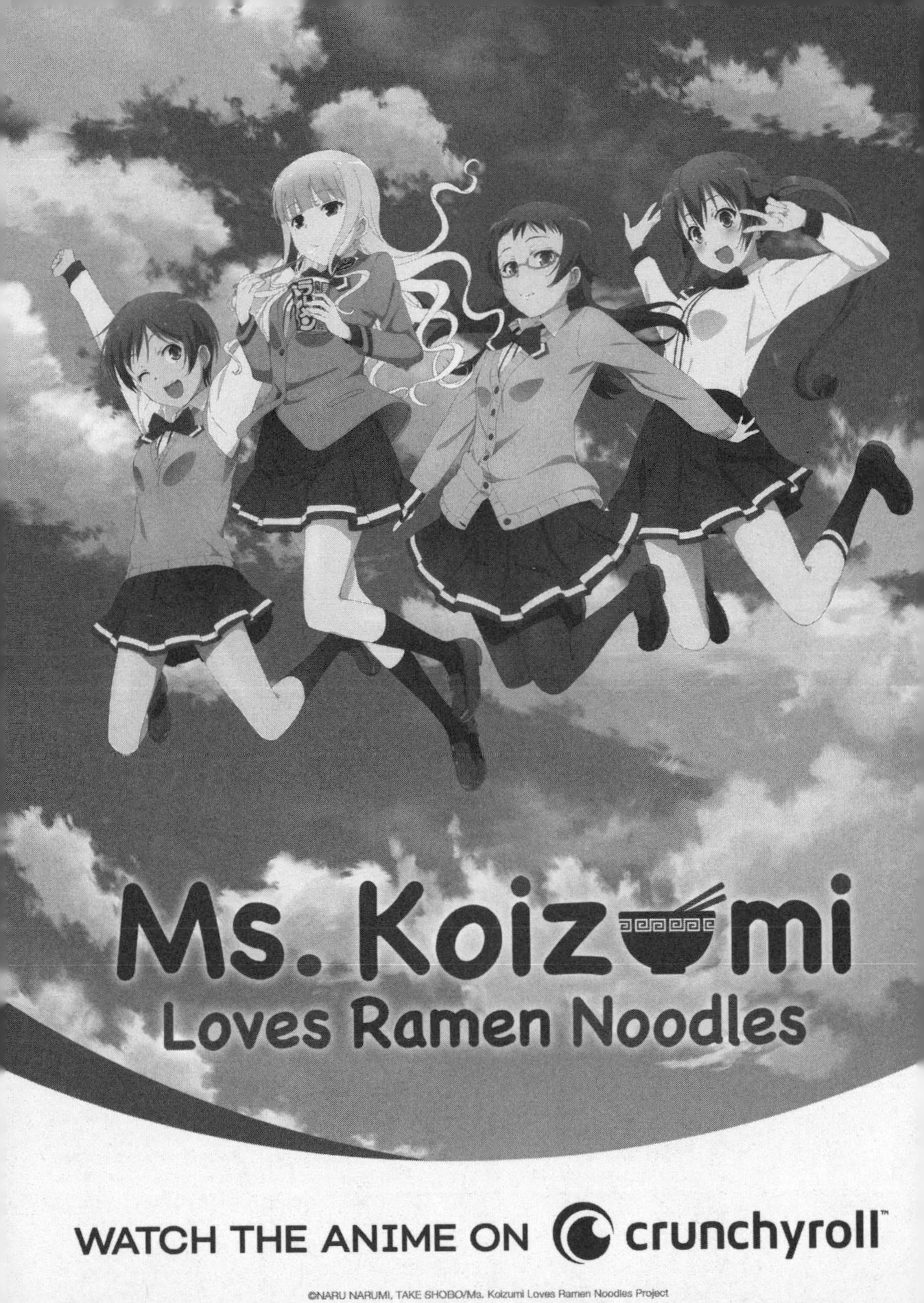
Ms. Koizumi
Loves Ramen Noodles
WATCH THE ANIME ON crunchyroll™

REPENT, SINNERS! THEY'RE BACK!

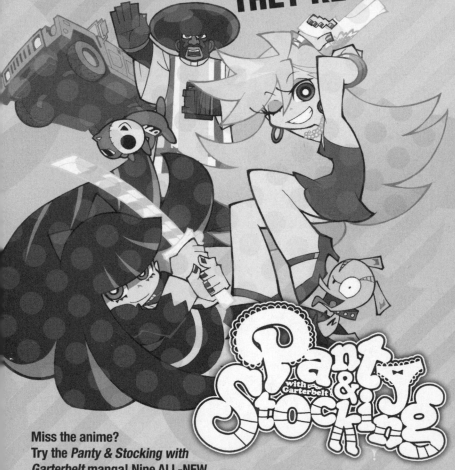

Miss the anime?
Try the *Panty & Stocking with Garterbelt* manga! Nine ALL-NEW stories of your favorite filthy fallen angels, written and drawn by TAGRO, with a special afterword by *Kill La Kill* director Hiroyuki Imaishi!
978-1-61655-735-5 | $9.99

Here's how you do it!

Ms. Koizumi Loves Ramen Noodles, like most manga, is read in the traditional Japanese style, right-to-left, so turn the book around to begin. Please do not attempt to slurp this manga.

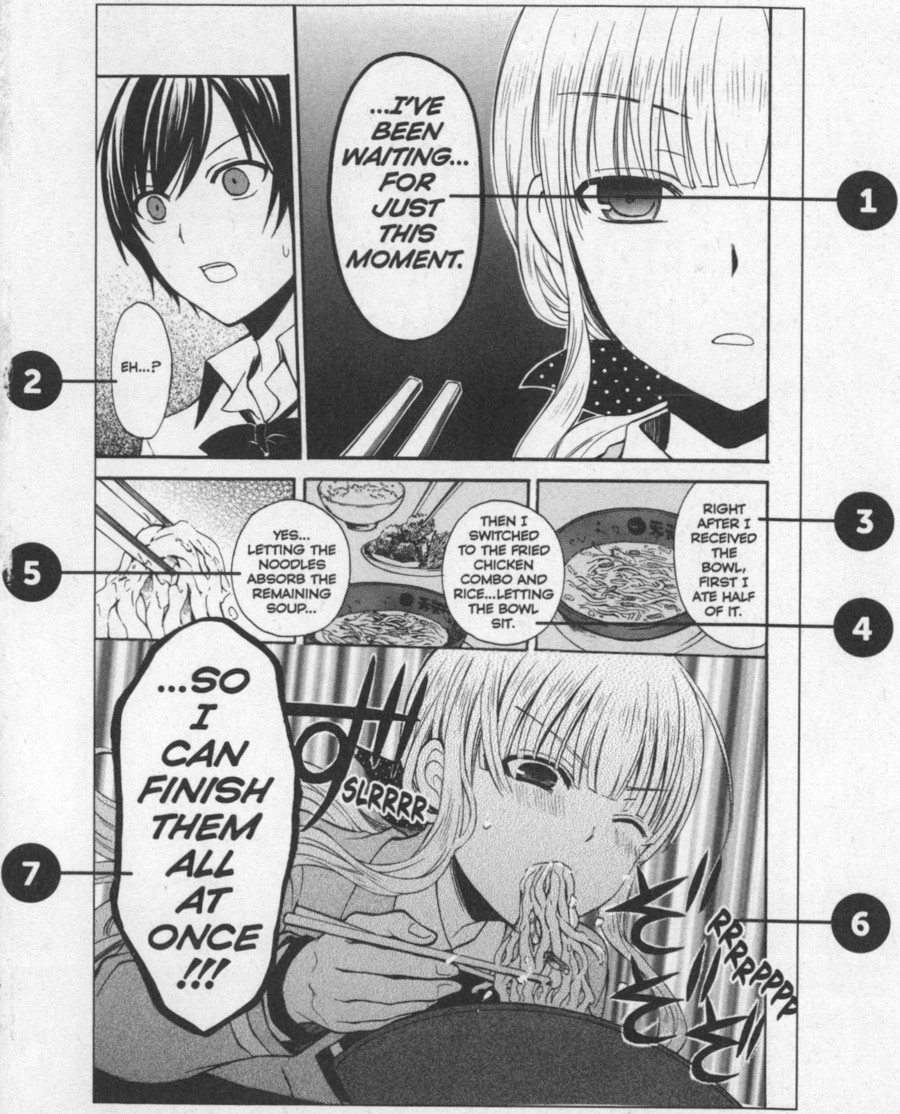
...I'VE BEEN WAITING... FOR JUST THIS MOMENT.
1
EH...?
2
RIGHT AFTER I RECEIVED THE BOWL, FIRST I ATE HALF OF IT.
3
THEN I SWITCHED TO THE FRIED CHICKEN COMBO AND RICE...LETTING THE BOWL SIT.
4
YES... LETTING THE NOODLES ABSORB THE REMAINING SOUP...
5
RRRRRPPPP
6
SLRRRR-
...SO I CAN FINISH THEM ALL AT ONCE!!!
7